AVERY
An imprint of Penguin Random House
New York

The Four Seasons of Pasta

Nancy Harmon Jenkins
and Sara Jenkins

Photography by Michael Harlan Turkell

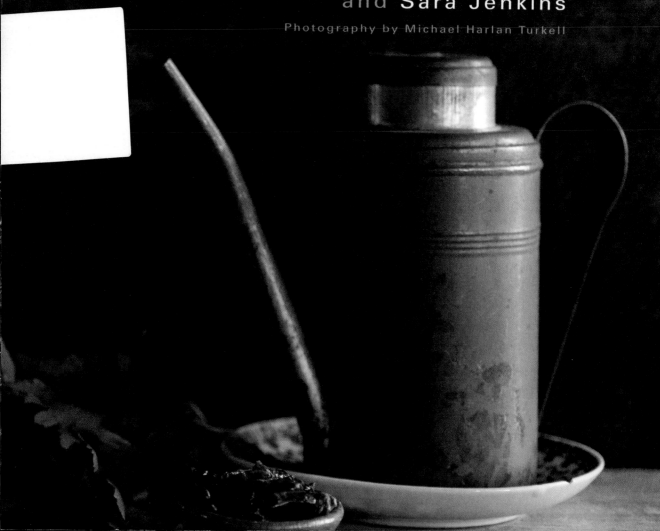

AVERY

an imprint of Penguin Random House LLC
375 Hudson Street
New York, New York 10014

Most Avery books are available at special quantity discounts for bulk purchase for sales promotions, premiums, fund-raising, and educational needs. Special books or book excerpts also can be created to fit specific needs. For details, write SpecialMarkets@penguinrandomhouse.com.

Library of Congress Cataloging-in-Publication Data
Jenkins, Nancy Harmon.
  The four seasons of pasta / Nancy Harmon Jenkins and Sara Jenkins.
     p.   cm.
ISBN 978-0-525-42748-3
1. Cooking (Pasta) 2. Seasonal cooking. I. Jenkins, Sara, 1965– II. Title.
TX809.M17J46 2015   2015015253
641.82'2—dc23

Printed in the United States of America
1 3 5 7 9 10 8 6 4 2

Book design by Renato Stanisic

IN MEMORY OF
MITA ANTOLINI, BELOVED FRIEND
AND ADOPTED GRANDMOTHER

Contents

Acknowledgments

Sara says:

A book does not get written without a lot of background support and help. First and foremost, I'd like to thank my family for all the help and love: my husband, Toufiq, our son, Nadir, and of course Cousin Matt. I couldn't do it without you. Second, I'd like to acknowledge and thank the hard work and demanding force that our agent, David Black, provides. David has always helped me clarify what it is that I really have to say. In addition, photographer Michael Harlan Turkell was, as always, a joy and a delight to work with, shooting the stunning photos in Maine and New York. Thank you, Erin Merhar, for all the skill and enthusiasm you brought to styling the food and making it look drop-dead stunning. I'd like to thank Rolando Ruiz Beramendi of Manicaretti, Kim Sayid of Academia Barilla, and Beatrice Ughi of gustiamo.com for the incredible support in fabulous pasta, cheeses, canned tomatoes, capers, and olive oil—not to mention the gourmet nutella from Cioccolato La Molina that kept us going in difficult moments.

Our fearless recipe testers who deciphered our often muddled instructions, confirmed that things worked, and helped make them work when they didn't: Judy Stein, Ladleah Dunn, Jerry Clare, and Gale Watts, many thanks to you all.

As always, the people who work with me at Porsena and Porchetta give me the freedom to pursue projects like this one by being so excellent at what they do. I couldn't do what I do without them all, past and present, in no particular order: Sal, Lauren, Ian, Hassan, James, Sammi, Placido, Alfredo, Luis Eric, Javier, Patricia, Adolfo, Stephen, Riley, Christina, Dominique, Cynthia, and Shari.

Nancy says:

All of the above, plus—special thanks to Fante's Kitchen Shop on Ninth Street in South Philly (www.fantes.com) for the beautiful hand-carved corzetti stamps and to Jon Rowley and Taylor Shellfish Farms in Shelton, Washington (www.taylorshellfishfarms.com), for a bounteous supply of mussels just when we needed them most. Thank you, too, for the warm welcome and intensive education provided by the families of pasta makers Benedetto Cavalieri in Puglia and Gianluigi Peduzzi in the Abruzzo, and by dozens of other producers of the finest pasta, olive oil, San Marzano and piennolo tomatoes, cheeses, bottarga, and all the other good things that represent the unstinting bounty of *la bell'Italia,* our second home.

Finally, from both of us, our most heartfelt thanks to Lucia Watson and her team at Avery. Lucia, your enthusiasm is what every writer dreams of encountering in the ideal editor—and your good humor tops it all.

Introduction

To three hungry diners on a chilly early-spring evening, the dish of pasta was a welcome sight when it came to the table— steaming hot fusilli, fragrant with bits of bacon, caramelized onion, and the aromatic Tuscan olive oil that garnished it all. The plump curls of pasta were tinted a gentle pink from tiny beet greens that had been chopped and added at the last minute to retain their freshness. It had taken all of fifteen minutes to prepare, including the pasta cooking time, but, topped with a grating of pecorino cheese, it was deeply satisfying after a long day of travel and a late arrival back in the home kitchen. It required no special skills, no special techniques, and certainly no special ingredients, since it was created from scratch out of what was at hand—chopped bacon and onions toasted in a skillet with plenty of extra-virgin olive oil, pasta cooked until al dente, then tossed in the skillet along with raw greens so young and tender they simply wilted in the heat of the pasta.

of Alba, a dish to set before a king—or someone else you wish to impress.

Call it macaroni. Call it spaghetti, linguine, fusilli, or conchiglie. Call it any one of a thousand or so names by which pasta shapes and sizes are known. This beloved Italian native has become a worldwide staple, and with good reason: It's easy, it's cheap, it's fun, it's infinitely adaptable, and it's utterly irresistible to young and old, rich and poor alike.

We love pasta because we can pull together a satisfying family meal in minutes, but we also love it because pasta lets us construct elaborate presentations to please the most demanding gourmands. Sara's restaurant Porsena in New York's East Village has been called "a pasta restaurant" because she focuses on a number of tasty pasta dishes, all made with Italy's finest artisanal brands (and sometimes with her own handmade *pasta sfoglia*) to gratify her customers. (She also has a full menu, by the way, if you're thinking of stopping by.) Nancy has a couple of pantry shelves devoted to pasta, on which at any one time you'll find at least five different boxes—from long and skinny to short and stubby to in between—out of which she can quickly craft a substantial meal for two or for twenty. Together, we cook pasta in our Tuscan farmhouse kitchen as often as we do in our American homes, which is to say at least three or four times a week. Truly, pasta goes with almost everything, even with the leftovers in the back of the refrigerator—so long as they haven't been left over too long. In fact, there are few ingredients in a good cook's pantry

What could be simpler, we all agreed as we grated cheese liberally over the top of our fusilli; what could be better, what could be more homely and comfortable than a bowl of hot pasta on such a night?

Pasta is like that. With good reason. It's been called the little black dress of the food world. Dress it up, dress it down, serve it topped with anchovies and bread crumbs from *la cucina povera* or make it into a dazzling luxury plate: thin, egg-rich tagliolini tossed with that most opulent and rarified ingredient, the prized white truffle

We love pasta because we can pull together a satisfying family meal in minutes, but we also love it because pasta lets us construct elaborate presentations to please the most demanding gourmands.

that beat out pasta—for healthfulness, for tastiness, for ease of preparation, for versatility, for sheer spectacle and delight. And it's as much in demand by picky eaters (our family has one who wants nothing on his pasta but plain tomato sauce) as it is by gourmets and gourmands who relish pasta with caviar, porcini mushrooms, or chunks of lobster in the mix.

In the 1970s, when we went to live in Italy, the pasta we discovered there was very different from the mac and cheese and spaghetti–tuna fish casseroles Nancy had grown up with, or the copious Italian American classics she had encountered (and enjoyed) in her student years in New York and Boston. At our neighbors' tables in Tuscany and in the modest Roman trattorie where we frequently dined, we learned that pasta is not just the starting point of a meal, but the key element around which all else revolves, taken by itself before the main course and eaten as much for the sheer pleasure of the taste of the noodles as for the flavor of the sauce. That sauce is often a mere slick of a condiment, but it is endlessly variable depending on the season, the region, the shape of the pasta, and what's available in the pantry. For most Italians a meal without pasta is simply not a real meal at all. And as the quintessential opening, the *primo*, it is an expression of everything Italians think about food—that it should be fresh, light

but filling, and above all else tasty with the direct and unmistakable flavors of its ingredients, whether as simple as *aglio-olio-peperoncino* (garlic, oil, and chili pepper) or as complex as an old-fashioned, rich, and meaty ragù bolognese.

We quickly embraced this Italian icon in our family meals, not only for its deliciousness but also for its endless variety and its ease in preparation, once a few simple, basic techniques are mastered.

As Sara grew up and began to cook in Rome, Tuscany, and later in the United States, she adopted pasta as one of her best-loved and most functional dishes, a love that she carried with her to New York, where she worked as executive chef in several acclaimed Italian restaurants before finally opening her own restaurant in 2010.

Meanwhile, Nancy was honing her craft as a food writer. One of the first stories she published, back in the late 1970s, was in what was then the *International Herald Tribune* in Paris. "Do you ever make pasta?" the features editor asked, and promptly assigned Nancy the job of writing about it. Truth to tell, she had never actually made pasta from scratch—there was no need to do so in Rome—but thanks to Marcella Hazan's *Classic Italian Cook Book*, she was able to complete the assignment with honors. The result? We learned how long to cook freshly made pasta. *"Basta dire un Ave Maria,"*

And that's why we keep going back to Italy for inspiration, returning to our Tuscan roots as well as to newer friends in the Abruzzi, Puglia, the Napoli region, and the great island of Sicily, not to mention northern Italy as well.

counseled Giulia d'Amurri, our Sardinian housekeeper, "Just say a Hail Mary."

Back in New York, we found that with few exceptions, pasta was still considered an ethnic Italian dish. You had to go to a place called da Alfredo or Piccolo Napoli or something similar to sample a recipe based on what the chef's mother or grandmother had brought over from the old country a generation or so earlier and adapted to American tastes. No one talked about the virtues of various brands or how the pasta itself was made, though it was generally conceded that imported-from-Italy pasta was far better than the homegrown product. But we also went to Raffetto's in Little Italy or the Supreme Macaroni Company on Ninth Avenue to buy loose pasta that was kept in deep drawers stacked one on top of the other. Ask for conchiglie or spaghettoni or ziti and a clerk would confidently pull out the right drawer and load up a paper sack with your requirements. (And then, at Supreme Macaroni Company on Ninth Avenue, if it was lunchtime, you could push aside the curtain, step into the back room, and be seated under the stained-glass dome for a fine plate of spaghetti and meatballs, the house specialty.)

How times have changed! Nowadays, Americans debate the virtues of artisanal over industrial production and talk as knowledgeably about Italian producers as if they were just next door. Home cooks play

with making fresh pasta, even struggling with tricky shapes like tortellini or capelletti, and there is probably not a kitchen in the entire country—a kitchen, that is, in which food is still produced and not just microwaved—where pasta in some form or other is not part of the cook's repertoire. And yet—and yet, we still labor with some mighty odd ideas about what pasta is, how to cook it, and most important of all, how to sauce it, what to put with it to make it both delicious and good for us, how to get beyond the inevitable marinara sauce and into something delightful and even a little bit different.

And that's why we keep going back to Italy for inspiration, returning to our Tuscan roots as well as to newer friends in the Abruzzi, Puglia, the Napoli region, and the great island of Sicily, not to mention northern Italy as well. Pasta remains at the very center of the Italian table. One fact confirms that: Italians consume 57 pounds (26 kilos) of pasta annually. That's 260 servings (figuring on 100 grams per serving), but in fact many Italians eat pasta at least once, and sometimes twice, a day every single day of the year. Americans are bush leaguers—consuming just 20 pounds annually per person. This, to us, suggests more strongly than anything else the total centrality of pasta in Italian life. When pasta is served, nothing is allowed to interfere. In fact, there is no lack of politeness in tucking

into a plate of pasta the minute it's set in front of you; letting it sit until everyone else is served is a gross insult to the cook. Silence reigns around the table while the pasta is consumed, and chatter resumes only with the second course, the *secondo*. But pasta, the primo, requires concentration and appreciation. "*Zita, sto mangiando la pasta*," an Italian friend says when we try to engage him in conversation over a plate of linguine: "Quiet! I'm eating my pasta." Italians call pasta *la regina della tavola*, the queen of the table. With good reason.

We offer this book in confidence that, while pasta may never become *la regina della tavola americana*, it has an important and growing role to play in our modern kitchens and on our tables. As a healthy alternative to fast food, pasta is a quick way to get more tasty vegetables and legumes into your diet—something every health researcher encourages. Pasta with vegetables, pasta with beans, pasta with very small quantities of meat—it all fits the profile that organizations from the American Heart Association to Oldways to the Harvard School of Public Health (now called Harvard T. H. Chan School) are urging us to follow.

It's for this reason that we've chosen to consider pasta in its seasonal aspects. Not that pasta, in and of itself, has a season. But what we put with it, whether we dress it with a sauce of fresh green peas or dark orange squash or earthy mushrooms, whether we serve a hearty, fragrant pork ragù or a toss of sweet ripe-red tomatoes and spicy fresh arugula, these are all ways of connecting that steaming plate of pasta

What we'd like to suggest, what we hope you'll take away from our ideas and our recipes, is the sense of pasta as a way to celebrate the seasons.

to the place and the ambiance we find ourselves inhabiting, both as cooks and as diners.

"Seasonal" doesn't mean the same thing to all people everywhere: Fava beans are in Los Angeles produce markets in February; we find them in Rome in April, but not until late June, if we're lucky, do they start to show up at our favorite Maine produce stand. Artichokes are similar: They're rigorously a late-autumn–winter–early-spring vegetable in Italy, while here in America they're in season from May through the summer. Our Italian experience leads us to think of pasta with artichokes as a decidedly wintertime dish, but if you want it to grace your table in July—well, there's honestly no reason why it should not do so. It's all in the translation.

On the other hand, there are certain styles of dishes that are linked to the seasons no matter what the ingredients. We can't imagine anything more welcoming on a winter day than a robust pork ragù, but set it in front of us on a hot night in August and, well . . . let's just forget about it!

What we'd like to suggest, what we hope you'll take away from our ideas and our recipes, is the sense of pasta as a way to celebrate the seasons. Let the recipes inspire you, then take yourself off to a farmers' market or a local produce stand

and see what you can find. If you have to make an adjustment or two, it doesn't matter—the inspiration is what counts.

And having said that, we offer one last bit of advice: Like most recipes from the Mediterranean, ours are not cast in bronze. If you find that you're out of something and it's too late to shop, or the shops you frequent don't have what you're looking for, just leave it out, substitute, work around it. Cooking should be a joyful enterprise, especially if you're cooking for friends and family—and it should be an enterprise in which all can share the joy. It won't work if you stress out about the ingredients or fret about the time. Relax, enjoy.

The Four
Seasons
of Pasta

Pasta: The Basics

Let's get one thing clear, right at the start: Marco Polo did not bring pasta back to Italy from China. That's a myth—you could even call it a fib—that's been around since 1929 when it was published in *Macaroni Journal,* an American trade magazine. When Marco returned to Italy from China in the year 1296, pasta had already been around the Italian peninsula and elsewhere in the Mediterranean for several centuries.

So what exactly is this product?

By definition, pasta is a supple, malleable dough of flour and water that can be either extruded through a press, or rolled out and cut; it is cooked by boiling in or steaming over water—that is, it's not baked and it's not fried. Theoretically, pasta can be made with almost any flour, but wheat flours are far and away the most typical. That's because when wheat flour and water are mixed together, gluten develops, and it's gluten that gives dough elasticity and extensibility, two characteristics that are fundamental for both bread and pasta.

Like its sister product bread, pasta would seem to be almost inevitable whenever and wherever people are working with flour and water to make dough. In fact, we would hazard a guess that pasta may well have developed when some enterprising baker had the bright idea of dropping pieces of bread dough into boiling water to see what would happen. And what happened, after a few tries, was pasta, similar to bread dough but without the yeast leavening that makes bread dough expand.

There are many different kinds of pasta in Italy, but basically it boils down to two subcategories, northern and southern. The northern tradition is fresh pasta, *pasta fresca*, made by hand, from soft wheat flour, the Italian equivalent of all-purpose, and water, with eggs added (often indeed a great quantity of eggs) to strengthen the dough, and intended to be cooked and eaten soon after it is made. The southern tradition is for dry pasta, *pasta secca*, the dough made of hard durum wheat flour (*semola* or *semolina*) and water, usually with no addition of egg, extruded mechanically and boxed or bagged, stored, and sold as dried pasta. That southern tradition is what has become the nearly universal Italian dish.

That being said, we have to add that, as with most things Italian, this is not an absolute. In Italy there is an exception to every rule. In Tuscany, a traditional stringlike pasta called *pici* is made with soft flour and water, no eggs, and rolled out by hand. And traditional cooks make fresh pasta with durum flour and water, like Puglia's orecchiette. One summer morning we watched Stefania Peduzzi as she made pasta alla chitarra for her extended family. Stefania, with her brother Gianluigi, owns the Rustichella d'Abruzzo pasta factory in the Abruzzese town of Pianella. But she often makes pasta by hand, mixing durum flour (*farina di grano duro*) with eggs and water to make a soft, tender, easily worked dough. Rolled out on a board, the sheet of dough is then set on top of a *chitarra*, a wooden box with wires strung from one end to the other, like a primitive guitar (for which it is named). Stefania deftly spins a rolling pin across to push the dough down between the wires, making long shapes that look like spaghetti but are square in section. (See the recipe for pasta alla chitarra, page 49.)

You could argue for days about where or when pasta was invented—and people do just that—but one fact stands out: Italians unquestionably have adopted it and embraced it with passionate conviction, to the extent that pasta today is the single most defining element in the Italian diet. Ask about Italian food almost anywhere in the world and back will come the response: "Spaghetti." (Or "pizza"—but that is a different story.) Not only that, but Italians took the pasta concept and ran with it, teased it out, played it for all it was worth, creating not dozens, not hundreds, but possibly thousands of the most sustaining, intriguing, and delightful dishes imaginable.

Such was not always the case, however. Neapolitans early on became known as *mangia maccheroni*, but it took time for the epithet "macaroni eaters" to spread throughout the entire country. Today Italy happily consumes annually something like

There are many different kinds of pasta in Italy, but basically it boils down to two subcategories, northern and southern.

57 pounds of industrially produced* pasta secca per capita, but up until well after the middle of the last century, the consumption of factorymade pasta in the north was almost exclusively an urban, working class phenomenon. In the countryside, and even in northern cities like Florence, bread was the basic carbohydrate. Housewives prided themselves on handmade, homemade, egg-rich pasta, but for special occasions only, not as an everyday treat. Our own village, deep in the mountains between Tuscany and Umbria, is typical and illustrates the reasons behind this. Even in the early 1970s when we stumbled on the place, there were few cars; motor scooters and the little three-wheeled farm-to-market vehicles called Ape were the only mechanized means of transport. Going to town was a major expedition, and returning home again, on mule back or in the bus that wound its way twice a day across the mountains to our village, one would be laden with the kinds of goods that were simply unavailable in Teverina—salt, sugar, black pepper, and other spices for curing

pork, tools, seeds, grain, coffee, and other vitals. There was no room in the market basket for boxes of commercial pasta secca, not when there was good bread at home baked in the farmhouse oven. Bread was the staple and pasta was a luxury—and it was that way for many Italian families.

Gianluigi Peduzzi confirmed that for us when we visited him at the *pastificio* in Pianella, near Pescara, where he and his sister are the third generation of their family to make Rustichella d'Abruzzo, one of a number of artisanal pasta producers—a number that seems to grow each year. "It was an elite product until very recently," he said of his own family's production. This surprised us until we thought of our neighbors for whom it would indeed have been an elite and expensive addition to the family table.

What changed all that? First, of course, industrialization, which brought down the price of pasta and, not coincidentally, drove many of the small pasta producers out of business, superseded by the likes of Barilla and Buitoni (the latter now part of Nestlé).

But another contributor to the market surge was actual physical access to the market. With the development of a strong national system of highways and railways, and with the growth of the economy to the point that every Italian family could own a car for driving to town, pasta secca became a mainstay in every kitchen in Italy. So: a stronger economy, a cheaper and more

---

We realize that the term industrially produced *can be taken pejoratively in English and we hasten to correct that impression. So-called artisanal pasta in Italy, made with bronze as opposed to Teflon dies and dried slowly at low temperatures, is a far cry from more high-industry, speedy drying at high temperatures. Nonetheless, both are in fact industrial production. To be truly artisanal, the word that is conventionally used, pasta would have to be produced by hand and dried in the sun.*

widely available product, expedited access to markets for both the producer and the consumer, all of this led to pasta finally becoming a truly national product. And, of course, pasta is a great way to feed a lot of people: If you have only a kilo of meat, and you've got ten people sitting around the table, what better way to extend that kilo than by turning it into a meaty ragù with vegetables and serving it over a bowl of spaghetti?

Today pasta secca is not just common but fundamental on the Italian table. Where once it was for the elite, and later for the working class, now pasta secca is for everyone. Except in a few regions of the north, Italians don't bother much with pasta fresca at all. For everyday meals— and most Italians eat pasta at least once a day—whether in high-priced Milanese restaurants or humble Tuscan farmhouses, Italian cooks rely on the stuff in the box. And they don't apologize for it, either.

There's a myth in America that the best pasta is always made with eggs and soft flour, hand-rolled into a broad and delicate sheet so thin you can read a newspaper through it. That's wonderful *pasta sfoglia*, pasta fresca as made in Bologna by experts, almost all of them women, called *sfogline*. It is one of the glories of the Italian table. We love it too, and we've included recipes for making fresh pasta, from simple sheets for oven-baked lasagna to more complex filled pastas such as ravioli and agnolotti.

But most Italians rarely eat pasta sfoglia, and southern Italians almost never. Indeed, if you sit down with an Italian at one (or more) of the 260 pasta meals that, according to statistics, he or she will consume in a year, you will most likely sit down to a plate of pasta secca, store-bought pasta made in a factory and sold in a box or a bag. Pasta secca is the backbone of the Italian table and it's the kind of pasta we cook, day in and day out, for ourselves and our families. Almost all the recipes in this book are about that kind of pasta. It's what we reach for when we're tired, or when we have unexpected guests to feed, or when we're challenged by an unfamiliar ingredient, or just when we want something really good and easy and substantial. *"Butta la pasta!"* we say, along with millions of Italians at mealtime, "Throw the pasta into the water and let's eat!"

Italian law requires that commercial pasta be made from hard wheat (durum) semola or semolina,* which is generally richer in gluten and protein than softer bread wheat or all-purpose flour. Since other countries are more lenient in their requirements, for the best pasta we invariably buy Italian made. It could be one of the big industrial Italian pasta makers, such as De Cecco, Delverde, or Barilla. These are all commercial pastas. But in recent years, like discerning cooks and pasta lovers in Italy, we have turned away from big industrial pasta makers, instead seeking out smaller firms, usually family owned and multigenerational, that have been tagged as artisanal.

---

* *The Italian terminology is different from terminology used in America, and it's the source of confusion. Semola in Italian is what we call* semolina *in the United States, a gritty grind of durum wheat;* semolina *in Italian, also known as* rimacinata, *is semola reground to make a finer flour. In North America,* rimacinata *is sold as durum flour.*

So just what does artisanal mean? There are two major differences that distinguish artisanal pasta makers from major conventional producers such as Barilla and Buitoni. They are:

> Pasta is extruded through bronze dies that have a rougher surface than conventional Teflon-coated dies; this microscopic roughness transfers to the surface of the pasta and allows it to bond and meld more closely with the sauce.
> Pasta is dried at low temperatures for a longer period of time; conventional pasta is produced and dried quickly. You can see this in the sleek, polished, amber-colored surface of the pasta itself, while artisanal pasta has a visibly rougher surface and paler color, as well as more of the nutty flavor and aroma of durum wheat.

There's no danger that Barilla will go out of business, however. Wherever the subject of pasta comes up, Barilla, the largest-selling pasta brand in the world, is the elephant in the room, responsible for more than 40 percent of the Italian market—and about 25 percent of the U.S. market. That amazing company, still tightly controlled by the Barilla family from its headquarters in Parma, continues to dominate the market, processing an incredible 1.4 million tons of durum wheat semolina in a year—almost all of which goes into pasta production. Nonetheless, increasing interest in the Mediterranean diet has given new life to artisanal producers such as those we list next.

There are many fine artisanal pasta makers in Italy; among our favorites, all available in North America, are:

> Bionaturae, organic whole wheat from Tuscany
> Benedetto Cavalieri, from Maglie in Puglia
> Cav. Giuseppe Cocco, from Fara San Martino in the Abruzzo
> Pastificio Faella, from Gragnano, southeast of Naples
> Martelli, from western Tuscany near Pisa
> Pastificio G. Di Martino, also from Gragnano
> Pastificio Masciarelli, from the Abruzzo
> Rustichella d'Abruzzo, from Pescara in the Abruzzo
> Pasta Setaro, from Torre Annunziata, southeast of Naples

What should you look for if you can't find one of these brands? Note that all of these listed are actually sold online at www .amazon.com, as well as in many fine retail outlets, including Whole Foods. But if you happen not to find any of the above, look for a label stating the pasta is "artisanally made," or "made with bronze dyes," or some equivalent language. The biggest clue is in the texture and color of the pasta: Pasta made this way will have a slightly rough exterior texture from the bronze dies, and a pale, creamy color, the result of being dried at low temperatures that do not cook the wheat to a rich, toasted gold. Golden pasta with a slightly shiny surface might be very good—but it is not artisanally made.

Increasingly, we have had opportunities to sample artisanal pastas made in the United States. Two brands have been standouts—Della Terra from Oklahoma City (www.dellaterrapasta.com) and Baia (www .baiapasta.com) from Oakland, California— and we hope there will be others to add to this list in the future. Just as American-made wine, bread, and olive oil have taken tremendous strides toward excellence in recent years, so we expect to see more and more high-quality production of artisanal pasta, produced with American-grown durum wheat, in the years to come.

As for whole wheat pasta, traditionally, it has not been significant on Italian tables, although that may be changing as producers of fine artisanal pasta turn their attention to whole wheat products, and as nutritionists continue to signal the benefits of whole grains in a healthy diet. We're all for healthy diets, but we confess that we tread a bit gingerly when it comes to whole wheat pasta, primarily because much of what we've tried is quite strong in flavor, which interferes with the marriage of pasta and sauce. Another drawback we've also found is that, even with attention paid, it's difficult to cook most whole wheat pasta to the supple, tender-with-a-bite, al dente stage that a good pasta cook demands. Too much of it ends up as a gluey, sticky mess.

That said, we have found certain brands to be more than acceptable. Among them are Rustichella d'Abruzzo, Di Martino, and Benedetto Cavalieri, venerable companies with their whole wheat brands available in U.S. retail stores. Barilla also makes good whole wheat pasta, as does another Italian,

Bionaturae, also widely available in North American markets. Whole wheat pasta in Italian is called *pasta integrale*—look for those words on the package.

And what about gluten-free? Gluten-free is every bit as modish in Italy as it is in America, and it is just as difficult in Italy as it is in America to understand how a product that has nourished people around the globe for about ten thousand years has suddenly become toxic. That said, if you are one of the hundreds of thousands who feel better when not consuming gluten, you perhaps had better swear off pasta. We don't believe that pasta made from lentils, corn, or quinoa can actually be pasta. But we do know that many of the sauces and ragùs in our recipes will taste just as good served over gluten-free polenta (made from corn, polenta is naturally free of gluten) instead.

A more serious question for nutritionists is the glycemic index of pasta, and there we are on more solid ground. (Glycemic index [GI] is a way of measuring the effects of carbohydrates on glucose levels; high glucose levels provoke an insulin response.) Foods that take longer to digest generally have a lower GI than those that are quickly digested, thus pasta cooked al dente has a lower GI than pasta cooked until it is very soft. Durum wheat is digested more slowly than regular wheat. And the GI can change depending on what you put on the pasta when you serve it—pasta and beans, pasta with tomato sauce, pasta with ragù, pasta with olive oil, chili peppers, and anchovies— all react differently, but all will have a lower GI, in other words, a more healthful profile, than plain, unadorned pasta.

Before You Begin

Equipment, Ingredients, Some Basic Recipes, and Techniques

Useful and/or Necessary Equipment

➤ An 8-quart pot for cooking pasta—large enough to hold 6 quarts of water plus the pasta; ours are made of stainless steel with a removable insert, making it easy to drain the finished pasta without losing the pasta water.

➤ Several long-handled wooden spoons: A kitchen can never have too many wooden spoons, and long-handled ones are essential for stirring pasta into the cooking water.

➤ A big stainless steel colander for draining.

➤ A large serving bowl for dressing and serving pasta.

➤ A box grater or Microplane for cheese— actually both are useful, since the box grater gives you a choice between fine and coarse grating.

➤ An immersion blender for mixing sauces: We prefer this to either a food processor or a regular blender because it's easier to control the texture of the sauce. Most immersion blenders will not produce a perfectly smooth sauce, but most pasta sauces should not be perfectly smooth anyway.

For making fresh pasta

➤ A pasta rolling board, called a *spianatoia* in Italian: This is not as easy to find as it ought to be; in fact you may have to ask a local craftsperson to make it for you. It should be large, at least 28 inches in one direction—although 36 inches is better— less so in the other (but make sure it will fit your countertop); it should be reversible, with a lip at either end that hangs over the edge of the counter and keeps the board from sliding away as you work; and it should be smooth so that, even if it's made of two pieces of wood, the division between them is almost undetectable.

➤ A rolling pin (*matterello*): A proper rolling pin for pasta is thinner than a normal pastry rolling pin, no more than 1½ inches in diameter, and the same dimension continuously throughout. About two feet long is ideal.

➤ Hand-cranked pasta machine—we prefer the Atlas for its sturdiness. Imperia is another brand that is also widely used. We do not recommend the kind of electric machine that both mixes the dough and extrudes the pasta. It makes a very industrial-feeling product.

Some things that aren't necessary but will make your life a little easier

➤ A wheeled pasta cutter for ease in cutting and trimming.

➤ A salt box next to the stove: So much easier to reach into the salt box for that handful of *sale grosso*, coarse salt, you need for the pasta water.

➤ A Japanese mandoline, about a third of the price of a stainless steel French mandoline and the perfect tool for thinly slicing onions, carrots, indeed just about anything to go into a pasta sauce.

➤ A large, heavy-duty mortar with accompanying pestle: This is really hard to find and costs a small fortune if you do find it, but you will never regret having it. We were fortunate to be able to buy a heavy marble mortar in a Ligurian hardware store some years ago, and even though it was a chore and a half to get it back home, we are grateful that we did so every time we use it. It crushes everything from basil leaves to fennel seeds to black peppercorns. We cannot live without it.

SOME BASIC RECIPES

STOCKS AND BROTHS

What's the difference between stock and broth? Not much, it turns out, and most people use the terms interchangeably. If you want to get pedantic, the Culinary Institute of America defines stock as made with bones, which give it a gelatinous content, while broth is made with meat, which makes it richer. (Which leads to the question of what is bone broth? We will leave that to future historians of twenty-first-century American food fads to figure out.) Most of the time we make stock with meat *and* bones so, we hope, our stock is rich and our broth is gelatinous and it's all very good.

Italian cooks, especially in the north, often serve deeply flavorful broths with pasta, especially little filled pastas such as tortellini, but they don't use a lot of elaborate stocks, *fonds de cuisine* in French terminology, as the basis for sauces. In Italian kitchens, most sauces are built in the pan, the flavor generated from what cooks in the pot. Many Italian recipes call for the addition of *un dado*, meaning a bouillon cube, but this is one area where we turn our backs and reject out of hand modern Italian traditions. To us, canned stocks and stocks made from bouillon cubes all too often taste of yeast extracts, hydrolyzed soy proteins, and the tin of the can that contains them. In most Italian recipes, if you don't have stock, we recommend using plain water rather than a commercial product, no matter how organic it claims to be.

That said, it is often important to have a good chicken stock available—and chicken stock is a great rainy Sunday project. Once the stock is done, it can be frozen in pint containers, giving you a ready source whenever needed. Vegetable stocks are another useful substitute for preparing vegetarian pastas and risottos, while fish stocks or broths are important in many seafood dishes.

Rich Chicken Stock

This tasty chicken stock is perfect for any kind of pasta in brodo, such as the springtime Pasta and Parmesan Broth with Peas and Pea Shoots on page 112. You could use the same concept all year long, simply using whatever greens are in season. It's a great basic stock to have on hand for the many times when a well-flavored stock is called for. The recipe makes a lot of stock, so we freeze leftovers, in 1-cup and 1-pint containers, to have a supply ready whenever it's called for.

The technique described, adding cold water periodically, is intended to keep the stock cooking at a low simmer. The stock should never come to a rolling boil, as that simply redistributes impurities.

MAKES 4½ QUARTS CHICKEN STOCK

¼ cup extra-virgin olive oil
5 medium carrots, roughly chopped
4 celery stalks, roughly chopped
1 large onion, with peel, cut into 8 pieces
1 head garlic, cut in half crosswise
2 large (3 to 4 pounds) chickens, cut into
    8 parts, plus neck
1 large bunch flat-leaf parsley
1 cup dry white wine

Combine the olive oil, carrots, celery, onion, and garlic in a large stockpot or soup kettle and set over high heat. Cook, stirring, until the vegetables are browned, about 8 minutes. Add the chicken, parsley, and wine and just enough water to cover the chicken and vegetables, about 12 cups.

Reduce the heat to medium-low. When the broth comes to a simmer, add 2 cups cold water and reduce the heat to low. Allow the stock to gently simmer, checking every ½ hour or so to skim the surface of fat and add water as needed. The chicken and vegetables should always be barely covered with liquid. Cook until the stock is very rich, about 4 hours. Strain the stock, discarding the vegetables and setting aside the chicken for the household cat. Refrigerate the stock for 2 to 3 days or freeze for up to 6 months until ready to use.

COOK'S TIP: *Skimming constantly and cooking very gently at a low temperature is the only way to get a very clear stock, but not everyone has the patience to do this. Another useful method to get the fat off is to refrigerate the strained stock for several hours or overnight. The fat will rise to the surface and congeal, making the fat easy to remove with a slotted spoon. But the stock will not necessarily be clear—if that's your goal, you* must *skim. And skim.*

Fish Stock

The carcasses (head and bones) of any white-fleshed fish may be used to make a flavorful fish stock—monkfish, snapper, cod, haddock, weakfish, whatever is available. Do not use oily fish such as bluefish, mackerel, or salmon, however, because the flavor is too strong. Fish or seafood stock should never be cooked for as long as a meat stock, as overcooking will make it bitter.

MAKES 6 TO 7 CUPS FISH STOCK

Head and bones of one 4- to 6-pound fish,
  preferably haddock, cod, or snapper
2 or 3 bay leaves
1 medium onion, halved
1 teaspoon whole black peppercorns
About 15 flat-leaf parsley sprigs (⅓ to
  ½ bunch parsley)
1 cup dry white wine
6 cups water
Sea salt and freshly ground white pepper

Combine the fish, bay leaves, onion, peppercorns, parsley, wine, and water in a heavy stockpot or soup kettle and bring slowly to a boil over medium-low heat. Cover, turn the heat down to a bare simmer, and continue cooking for 45 minutes. Strain the stock through a double layer of cheesecloth in a colander and discard the solids. Taste and adjust the seasoning, adding salt and white pepper to taste, keeping in mind that the salt will be concentrated if the stock must later be reduced.

Vegetable Broth

You will never get the same flavor impact with vegetable broth as you do with broth made from meat, chicken, or fish; in fact, vegetable broths as such are rarely used in Mediterranean kitchens—this one is for the benefit of strict vegetarians.

MAKES 8 CUPS VEGETABLE BROTH

2 fat leeks, rinsed carefully, cut in 2-inch pieces
1 head garlic, unpeeled, cut in half horizontally
1 shallot, unpeeled, cut in quarters

Half a bunch of chives
3 scallions, sliced in 3-inch pieces
2 medium yellow onions, unpeeled, cut in
  quarters
2 dark green outer celery stalks, cut in chunks

6 small or 3 medium carrots (about ½ pound), peeled and cut in chunks
1 piece star anise
1 tablespoon whole black peppercorns
1 tablespoon whole coriander seeds
1 teaspoon whole mustard seeds
3 to 4 sprigs fresh thyme
½ bunch flat-leaf parsley
2 bay leaves
½ cup dried porcini mushrooms
8 cups water
1 tablespoon mild white vinegar

6 plump brown fresh mushrooms (wild, if available, otherwise shiitake or cremini), cleaned and cut in quarters

Combine all the ingredients and set over medium heat. Bring to a boil, then turn down to a gentle simmer. Cook slowly for 20 minutes, stirring several times. At the end of the cooking time, remove from the heat and let steep for another 15 minutes. Strain through a narrow-mesh sieve, discarding the vegetables.

Béchamel

Béchamel, or *besciamella* in Italian, is a fundamental white sauce, familiar for its many uses in European cuisines. Basically, it's just hot milk or cream added to a roux of butter and flour and stirred together over heat until it thickens. It's easy enough to make, but it does require attention and it's not something that can be made ahead and held for more than a couple of hours. We use béchamel as a sauce layer in most lasagnas and also in baked pasta dishes such as pasta al forno or mac and cheese, but we steep the milk with aromatics to add more flavor to the final sauce.

To make the béchamel, simply combine whole milk in a saucepan with aromatics and bring to a simmer, then remove from the heat and let steep for an hour while the milk absorbs the flavors. When the milk is ready, strain out the added flavorings and measure the milk. You will find that the milk has reduced in quantity since the seasoning vegetables will have absorbed a certain amount.

The following recipe, calling for 6 cups of milk, will make 4 to 5 cups of béchamel (some of the liquid inevitably evaporates during the cooking process). If the recipe calls for a lesser quantity, simply decrease the amount of milk proportionately. That is, if the recipe requires 3 to 4 cups of béchamel, make it with 4½ cups of milk, adding a little less butter and flour to the roux. In the end, the sauce should be the consistency of thick, heavy cream but not of sour cream and certainly not of library paste. If it is too thick, add more milk, a little at a time, until it is the right consistency; if it's too thin, keep cooking it down until it has thickened properly.

MAKES 4 TO 5 CUPS BÉCHAMEL

6 cups (1½ quarts) whole milk
1 medium onion, cut in half
1 leek, split, cleaned, and cut into 2-inch
  chunks
2 or 3 bay leaves
1 teaspoon whole black peppercorns
2 garlic cloves, peeled but left whole
3 or 4 fresh thyme sprigs
2 medium celery stalks, cut into 4-inch pieces
Several flat-leaf parsley sprigs
4 tablespoons (½ stick) unsalted butter
¼ cup unbleached all-purpose flour
¾ cup freshly grated parmigiano-reggiano
Sea salt
Freshly grated nutmeg

Combine the milk, onion, leek, bay leaves, peppercorns, garlic, thyme, celery, and parsley in a saucepan. Set over medium heat and bring just to the simmering point, then remove from the heat and set aside, covered, for at least 1 hour while the milk absorbs the aromatic flavors. When the milk is ready, strain out the added flavorings and measure 5 cups milk. Return the 5 cups to the saucepan and heat just to the simmering point. Turn off the heat but keep the milk warm while you make the béchamel.

In a separate saucepan large enough to hold all the milk, melt the butter and stir in the flour with a wooden spoon, stirring constantly and smoothing out any lumps. Cook for about 3 minutes, or until you no longer smell the odor of raw flour. Now start adding the hot flavored milk, about ½ cup at a time, stirring after each addition to amalgamate the milk with the flour-butter paste thoroughly before adding more. At a certain point, you will find it easier to switch to a wire whisk instead of the spoon. Keep adding the milk and stirring until all 5 cups of milk have been added. Stir in the parmigiano with a pinch of salt and several gratings of nutmeg and continue cooking and stirring for about 5 minutes, or until the sauce has thickened to the desired consistency. The sauce should be smooth and velvety in texture.

If you cannot use the sauce immediately, remove it from the heat but keep it warm and settle a sheet of plastic wrap right on the top of the sauce to keep a skin from forming.

BREAD AND BREAD CRUMBS

We use traditional crusty, country-style bread, preferably made all or in part with whole meal flour. We save softly stale ends and tuck them in a plastic bag in the freezer. Then, when we have enough, we let the bread thaw, cut it into chunks, and pulse it in the food processor until it's reduced to coarse crumbs. These can be kept in the freezer and browned in a skillet with a little oil whenever called for to top pastas or thicken sauces. Or they can be turned into the following spicy bread crumbs.

Seasoned Fresh Bread Crumbs

These keep well in the freezer for quite some time, so make a batch every so often to have on hand. If you want to tame the heat of the peppers, shake the seeds out of dried chilies before you crumble them. Or use milder ground red peppers such as piment d'Espelette or Spanish pimentón.

MAKES 2¼ CUPS BREAD CRUMBS

¼ cup extra-virgin olive oil
2 garlic cloves, finely chopped
⅓ cup chopped flat-leaf parsley
2 dried serrano, de árbol, or other not-too-hot chilies, crumbled
2 cups coarse fresh bread crumbs

Heat the olive oil in a large, heavy skillet over medium-high heat. Add the garlic and cook until just lightly browned, about 2 minutes. Remove from the heat and combine in a bowl with the parsley and chilies. Stir in the bread crumbs. Return the bread-crumb mix to the skillet and set over high heat. Cook, stirring constantly, until the bread crumbs are crisp, 5 to 7 minutes, being careful not to let them burn. Transfer to a bowl to cool, then store in a sealed container in the refrigerator or freezer until ready to use.

HELPFUL TECHNIQUES

PEELING FRESH TOMATOES

Bring a pot of water to a rolling boil and drop in each tomato for about 15 seconds, then remove to a colander in the sink. When all the tomatoes are done, peel them with a small, sharp paring knife, just lifting the skins off and discarding them. To seed or not to seed? Sara thinks seeds add unwelcome bitterness to the sauce, while Nancy likes their slightly acerbic touch, especially since she learned that the antioxidant lycopene is concentrated in the gel surrounding the seeds, and is in fact made more bio-available by cooking. Seed the tomatoes, if you wish, cutting them in half horizontally and gently squeezing to extract the seeds, but keep in mind that you will be losing some valuable nutrients.

PREPARING FRESH ARTICHOKES

In Italy there's a limited autumn harvest of artichokes, but most of the crop bridges the gap between winter and spring. In Castroville, California, the source of most of the artichokes consumed in the United States, it's a little different and the season runs from March through May. Millions of the fat, spiky globe artichokes are shipped out from the town that calls itself, with happy disregard for truth, the Artichoke Capital of the World. Still, one of our favorite Maine farmers has small, sweet artichokes on sale at her farm stand in July, and there's no reason why more market gardeners around the country could not grow them as well.

Preparing artichokes looks daunting until you've done it once or twice, after which it's just a "normal" kitchen chore—and worth it for the delightful tastes that emerge.

Often, as with most fruits and vegetables, the local supply has a fresher, more intense flavor than anything shipped in from distant places. We're told that artichokes grow best close to the sea, so farmers in New Jersey, Maryland, and farther south, down along the Carolina coast, should be growing artichokes for the national market just as those around Monterey Bay are.

Preparing artichokes looks daunting until you've done it once or twice, after which it's just a "normal" kitchen chore—and worth it for the delightful tastes that emerge. Try to buy artichokes with a couple of inches of stem attached—they're usually better quality and the stems are full of good flavor. Buy ones that are fairly compact and feel dense and heavy for their size. You'll find lots of information about preparing whole artichokes in recipe books and online. Here we're talking about getting them ready to use in a pasta sauce.

Most important: Have ready a bowl of acidulated water, cool water to which you've added the juice of half a lemon. Use the other lemon half to rub over the cut surfaces of the artichokes as you work in order to prevent them from oxidizing and turning black. If the artichoke has a stem, cut it back to the tender part, about 1 inch of stem. Cut the stem off at the base and peel it as if it were an apple. Slice into 2 or 3 pieces and toss in the lemon water. Remove the tough outer leaves, or bracts, by simply bending them back until they

snap off. If necessary, use a paring knife to clear away any dark green bitter bits that remain. As you work, remember to rub the cut surfaces with the reserved lemon half. When you get down to the pale, tender inside of the choke, slice off the top inch or two. Then cut the artichoke in half and, if necessary, using a serrated spoon, scrape away every bit of prickly spines or choke, just above the heart. (Note that very fresh, young artichokes may not have spines, but most of the commercial ones available in U.S. markets do, and getting rid of them is crucial to enjoying artichokes.) Toss the halves in the lemon water and continue with the rest. If they're very large, you might cut them in 2, 3, or more pieces before proceeding with the recipe.

What about using frozen artichoke hearts? We've done this with excellent results in almost any pasta sauce. Since they are usually parboiled before freezing, you can just toss them into a sauce and let them heat up. Larger ones, of course, will benefit from being cut in half or quarters. As for canned artichoke hearts, we have never found anything we like at all.

ROASTING PEPPERS

This is best done over a charcoal or gas outside grill (charcoal contributes wonderfully smoky flavors). Second best is over a gas flame on your stovetop. Least satisfactory is to roast peppers under the oven broiler.

With an outside grill, simply lay the peppers on the grill and, using tongs, keep turning them as their surfaces blacken and blister. With a gas flame, use a long-handled kitchen fork and hold each pepper over the flame to blacken and blister it all over. With the oven broiler, turn the broiler on high and set the peppers on a grid over a roasting pan, turning them as they blacken. But with the last method, they will never get as satisfactorily blackened as they do with the other two. Don't try to get every single speck of pepper surface blackened. Do the best you can, then remove the peppers from the heat, drop them into a paper bag, and roll the bag up. Set them aside for 30 minutes or so. The heat in the peppers will continue to work its magic and loosen that thin pellicle of skin on the outside of the peppers.

Now, using a small paring knife, split each pepper in half over a bowl to capture the flavorful juices. Cut away and discard the seed cluster inside each pepper, along with the whitish membranes. Then scrape away the blackened, blistered surface. Don't be tempted to do this under running water, as you will wash away a lot of flavor. A quick rinse at the very end, to get rid of any excess blackened surface, is fine, but nothing more than that.

PREPARING MUSSELS AND CLAMS

Unless you harvest them yourself or buy them directly from a forager, most of the mussels and clams available in markets are farmed. Shellfish aquaculture is one of the most sustainable methods of fish farming and it has added benefits for the cook because the bivalves have been purged of the sand and grit that are often pervasive in wild specimens. A quick rinse in cold running water should be sufficient to get rid of any surface detritus.

Mussels and clams *must be alive before cooking*. Any that are not should be discarded.

Mussels don't need soaking, but you should go over them carefully, discarding any with broken shells or that feel suspiciously heavy (an indication they may be full of mud). Most cooks pull away the "beard" that clings between the shells, but we have never found that to be necessary unless it's particularly heavy—it's basically a cosmetic question. Tap any open mussels against the side of the sink and discard any that don't close up in a minute or two. Also discard any that have not opened at the end of the cooking time.

Most clams do need soaking, and even if they appear to be pristine, it's a good idea to soak—nothing ruins a cook's mood faster than discovering that the sauce for spaghetti con vongole is too gritty to eat. As with mussels, examine them carefully, discarding any with broken shells or that feel suspiciously heavy. Then set the clams to soak for an hour in cold water in which you've dissolved plenty of salt (a cup or more of salt to a gallon of water). Lift the shellfish out at the end of that time, swishing them through the water as you do so. (If a lot of sand is left in the bottom of the bowl, you might want to repeat this process.) Again, as with mussels, any that don't open by the end of the cooking time should also be discarded.

A FEW SPECIAL INGREDIENTS

TOMATOES

In the Summer selection of recipes, we offer plenty of ideas for sauces using the fresh, ripe products of your own or neighbor farmer's garden. But our pasta kitchen also depends to a large degree on tomatoes in their preserved phases, the result of techniques that maintain the fresh, bright taste of summer tomatoes throughout the year. Following are some of the ways you'll find tomatoes in Italy and imported to North America.

Pelati: The Italian term for any kind of canned whole tomatoes, the word simply means "peeled," presumably because most tomatoes are peeled before canning. We happily use canned tomatoes when fresh ones are not in season. But what kind of canned tomatoes? San Marzano is the instinctive answer, the famous pear-shaped preserving tomatoes from the area around Naples, now safeguarded by its very own DOP (Denominazione di Origine Protetta, or protected denomination of origin).

Alas, despite the DOP, the name alone can be deceptive. Not all San Marzanos are true to the breed. In fact, one notorious American brand is actually called San Marzano, its label painted the red, white, and green of the Italian flag, but the spherical little tomatoes inside are grown and canned in California. If it's truly San Marzanos you want, then you must look for DOP Pomodori San Marzano dell'Agro Sarnese-Nocerino on the label. (Incidentally, these are the only tomatoes allowed for La Vera Pizza Napoletana,

which also has its own DOP.) The very best San Marzanos, in our opinion, are those produced by the Gustarossa cooperative and available through www.gustiamo.com. If the label simply reads "certified San Marzanos," without the prestigious DOP, it means nothing.

But that's not the end of the story. There are other tomatoes besides San Marzanos, and other, less expensive brands that offer a good, full-flavored tomato experience, if you will. Among our favorites are Academia Barilla's pomodorini pelati, sweet-tart peeled cherry tomatoes; Muir Glen from California (certified organic); and even, perhaps surprisingly, good old Hunt's, a favorite of our mother and grandmother. If you get serious about the quality of your pelati, it's a good idea to organize a taste test with some friends and see what you conclude. Be sure to taste the raw, straight-from-the-tin tomato and then the same tomato heated up—the taste can change remarkably.

Keep in mind that when we refer to a 14-ounce (or 28-ounce) can of tomatoes, we mean whole tomatoes, not crushed or diced, with nothing added but a little salt and citric acid. Any other flavors should be added by the cook.

Passata di Pomodoro: Often called for in Italian recipes, this is simply a puree of tomatoes, nothing more. It can be raw (*cruda*), made with ripe tomatoes fresh from the garden, or cooked (*cotta*). Passata is easy to produce on your own, by simply draining a can of best-quality tomatoes (reserving the juice from the can) and either putting them through a food mill or using a handheld blender to reduce to a puree. If necessary, stir in some of the reserved juice from the can to reach the right consistency. A 28-ounce can of pelati, drained, yields about 2 cups passata. Passata is also available as a commercial product. The best known is Pomi, imported from Italy and called "strained tomatoes"—a useful product for the pantry shelf.

Pomarola: This is the term used in Tuscany and central Italy for tomato sauce, made at home and preserved for the winter in the farmhouse *dispensa*, or pantry (see the recipe and directions for making your own on page 177). It could be just plain tomatoes, but it is more often tomatoes to which various aromatics have been added— garlic, onion, carrot, basil, rosemary, parsley, any or all in combination.

Doppio Concentrato, aka Estratto: Tomato paste ideally is a thick concentration of all the summertime goodness and sweetness of tomatoes. Some cooks think of it as a crutch, but we follow generations of Italian home cooks and restaurant chefs alike in finding it an invaluable flavor booster, to be used with caution and in small quantities. (The idea of mixing a can of tomato paste with boiling water to make a pasta sauce, recommended in earlier American cookbooks, is anathema.) The finest kind, we think, comes from Sicily, where sweet, ripe tomatoes are crushed, then the pulp spread out to dry in the late-summer sun over many days while flavors concentrate into a thick, dark paste called *'strattu* or *estratto di pomodoro*, tomato extract. This Sicilian product can be found online from several sources, among them www.markethallfoods.com, where the paste is made by Maria Grammatico, the legendary pastry chef in Erice, and www .gustiamo.com, whose 'strattu is made by olive oil producer Lorenzo Piccione from his mother's recipe. These are worth seeking out. They are expensive, but they will last a long time. After using a small amount, smooth over the surface in the little jar and spoon a thin layer of olive oil over the top, then refrigerate to store. Mutti is a very good, more commercial brand of tomato concentrate, with the advantage that it comes in a tube so you use what you need and keep the rest sealed in the fridge.

ANCHOVIES

So many people rush to say, "Oh, I really hate anchovies," and then it turns out that they're eating them all the time without even being aware of it. Good restaurant chefs know that a hit of anchovies in the very beginning of a sauce will give that sauce great depth of flavor, especially with pasta. And yet, people go on saying, "Oh, I really hate anchovies."

If you're one of those people, we recommend you try a sauce like, for instance, Roman-Style Artichokes with Mint and Garlic (page 116)—add anchovies to half the sauce, leave them out of the other half. Taste both and we think you'll agree— anchovies are important and must be in your pantry.

Nancy believes in buying salted anchovies and boning and rinsing them yourself. This is traditional in Italy, where a big can of salted anchovies sits in the deli case and shoppers buy one or two as needed. Sara has come around to buying oil-packed fillets, which are potentially just as good and remove one step from the cooking process. She buys Italian or Spanish anchovies in olive oil, either in small glass jars or in flat cans. Two brands we like are Ortiz and Roland, both widely available. (Don't confuse oil-packed anchovies with the white, lightly pickled kind; the latter are fantastic as an appetizer but not suitable for cooking.)

If you want to use salt-packed anchovies, rinse the salt off under running water, then soak in cold water for 30 minutes to get rid of the salt. Pull the fillets off the bone and rinse briefly in a bit of Italian white wine vinegar. Use immediately or store for a week covered in extra-virgin olive oil in the fridge.

AROMATICS

Italians call them *odori*, and they are the backbone of flavor in Italian sauces, soups, braises, and so on, even providing a bed on which meat is roasted, or chopped together to stuff into the cavity of a fish for grilling. *"Odori, signora?"* says our Signora Benigni when we finish our Saturday market shopping, and she extends a little bundle of carrot, celery, parsley, maybe a sprig of rosemary or sage—her offering for the gift of our business. We always accept, of course, and take the bundle home to use in different combinations, maybe just a simple chop of garlic and parsley, or perhaps a more complex mix including sage, bay leaf, and maybe a little prosciutto fat as the basis for a ragù, cooked out and simmered slowly with water and tomato paste before the meat is even added. The odori that go into soffritto are never precise, and if you find you're missing one or two of the aromatics called for in a recipe, don't despair, just go ahead without it. The important factor is the flavor base and not any scientifically specific ingredients.

Celery: North American cooks tend to think of celery as a salad vegetable, not an aromatic, but in the Mediterranean, dark green, unblanched celery adds a deep flavor to many preparations.

Chili peppers: Outside of Calabria, which actually sports a chili fest in the town of Diamante every year, Italians swear they don't really like the heat of hot chili peppers. To a large extent it's true; chili is tolerated as a faint note, not a dominant one, in the overall flavor of a recipe. Italian cooks buy small dried red chili peppers called peperoncini and crumble them into whatever they're cooking. That said, the Calabrese are very proud of their spicy food (and personality!), and whenever we find their little dried red chilies, or their chili-hot 'nduja sausage, we pick them up; they're spicy enough to use with caution, but they have a lot of flavor. In North America we also look for not-too-hot, medium dried chilies—de árbol and New Mexico are two preferred varieties. Piment d'Espelette and some Middle Eastern peppers (Aleppo pepper, for instance) can also be used.

Fresh and dried herbs: Basil, rosemary, parsley, sage, thyme, chives, savory: All these should be used fresh. The best way to have them on hand is in an herb garden, even just a single row in front of your house or on a window ledge. Failing that, buy these fresh, whether at a farmers' market or from a supermarket produce section. Oregano and bay leaves, on the other hand, are better dry than fresh. The best oregano comes from Sicily or Greece, where it's called *rigani*. If you can buy oregano on the branch, it's best of all. Most ground, dried oregano sold in North America is Mexican, with a stronger, more pronounced flavor than sweet Mediterranean oregano. If you buy dried herbs or spices, write the date of purchase on the bottle, keep the herbs or spices in a cool, dark pantry cupboard, and toss them after a year.

Fennel pollen: Wild fennel pollen is a bit of a misnomer as it is not really pollen but the flowers of the wild fennel that grows all over the Mediterranean. It's a very common ingredient in our Tuscan territory, considered critical for seasoning pork, and we always assumed it was a pan-Tuscan aromatic, but in fact it is very specific to our Arezzo region and into neighboring Umbria. The rest of Italy uses the feathery fresh greens of wild fennel, most memorably in the Sicilian classic pasta con le sarde (see the recipe on page 155), but also to stuff the belly of a fish grilled over charcoal or roasted in the oven. Wild fennel also grows all over California, but unless you know what it looks like, don't pick it; apparently it's very similar to poison hemlock.

Parsley: We want to stress the importance of parsley. The kind used throughout the Mediterranean is flat-leaf or Italian parsley. With its sweet, almost licorice flavor, it goes into just about everything. If you don't have room for

The important factor is the flavor base and not any scientifically specific ingredients.

anything else, you really should have a big pot of parsley growing on a sunny kitchen windowsill. Some time ago, a chef friend pointed out that the tender stems of parsley should never be discarded—that's where the sweetest flavors lie, he said, and he is right.

Sea salt: We are convinced that Sicilian sea salt from the ancient salt flats on the west coast of Sicily around Trapani is the only sea salt worth bothering with. Dried by the hot Mediterranean sun, often using technology that goes back to the Phoenicians who first settled there, it has a purity of flavor that nothing else comes close to. We have coarse Sicilian sea salt for seasoning the pasta water, and fine Sicilian sea salt for everything else.

BEANS, DRIED AND FRESH

With dried beans, the problem is, curiously, freshness. Too often we've bought dried beans only to find that no amount of soaking and simmering will soften them up. That's because the big bean counters, the Goyas and their ilk, buy up as many beans as they can when the price is right, storing them for three years or more to avoid the vagaries of nature. Because they are rarely date-stamped, it's impossible to know how old those beans are, and by the end of that time, they are inevitably hard, stale, and impossible to cook to an ideal creamy tenderness. For that reason,

all things being equal, we buy from local co-ops and health food stores since these are places with fairly rapid turnover. In Maine we get current-season dried beans at our local food co-op and elsewhere we rely on Rancho Gordo (www.ranchogordo.com) in Napa, California, and their amazing range of freshly dried beans, which they will ship anywhere. Those Maine and Rancho Gordo beans cook up easily in 30 minutes or so with a delightfully soft, almost creamy texture that will make you swear off old stale supermarket beans forever.

Without knowing how fresh dried legumes are, it's difficult to give precise cooking times for them. This is one area where "cook until done" is the only thing that applies. That said, keep in mind that chickpeas (aka garbanzos or ceci) take longest to reach a tender stage, while some lentils can be done in as little as 20 minutes.

Apart from lentils, most legumes benefit from an overnight soak in water to cover to give them a sort of pre-softening. Sara soaks them right in the pot in which she plans to cook them, adding a couple of unpeeled garlic cloves and a sprig of fresh herbs. Nancy drains them after their overnight soak, then covers them with fresh water to cover to a depth of 1 inch, adding garlic and other flavorings (a small dried red chili pepper, a sprig of rosemary or sage, a bay leaf or two, perhaps some freshly ground black pepper) at that point. Whichever you decide to do, bring the beans to a simmer over medium heat, then turn the heat way down once the water is simmering, cover the pot, and cook very

slowly until the beans are soft, adding a little boiling water from time to time if necessary. No salt, however, until the beans are almost done—this can take from 40 minutes to 2 hours, depending on the size and age of the beans.

When the beans are done, remove the garlic cloves and squeeze the soft pulp into the bean liquid. Discard the other seasonings. Strain out the beans but don't discard the bean liquid. If not required for the recipe you're making, keep it, frozen if necessary, until you're making any kind of hearty, country-style bean soup to which it will add lots of flavor.

One pound of dried beans makes about 2 cups; when simmered in water until tender, they will yield 4 to 5 cups cooked beans.

We are not big fans of canned beans of any kind. Most of the time they seem to have an unpleasantly metallic taste. Only for emergencies do we keep canned garbanzos, cannellini, or other beans in the pantry. If you must use them, we recommend buying reduced- or no-sodium beans and then draining, rinsing, and reheating in plain water with garlic, bay leaf, and a hit of olive oil.

Another treat that is delicious in any bean pasta recipe is freshly picked shell beans. In Tuscany in the fall, the markets fill with *sgranati*, beans for shucking, which are still in their pods. The pods are often rather unappetizingly withered and dry looking, not like young fresh green beans, but the beans inside will still be delicious. Look for fresh shell beans in late summer or fall in your local farmers' market and shuck them yourself. They will be a fine substitute for dried beans in any of our recipes, though remember that they will cook up in a shorter period of time.

FRESH FAVA BEANS

We confess to being impatient with the widespread American idea of peeling individual fava beans after they have been shucked from their pods. It was never done traditionally in the Mediterranean, where the beans are harvested when they are no bigger than a thumbnail. In Italy, where fava beans (aka broad beans) are one of the great spring vegetables, home cooks and restaurant chefs alike would refuse the fat, overly mature beans that are presented in most North American markets. What they look for instead are small, tender beans, no bigger around than an index finger or at most a slender thumb. Inside the pod, the beans are equally small and very sweet. The idea of peeling each individual bean is unheard of. Restaurant chefs and food writers in the United States probably adopted the idea of peeling each individual bean because all they can get are late-season, overripe beans. We insist that our suppliers bring us only small, tender beans, but if the fat ones are all you can find, you will have to peel them individually. Here's how:

First shuck the beans from their pods while bringing a pot of water to a rolling boil. Plunge the shucked beans in the boiling water for just 5 minutes, no longer; drain and shock the beans with cold water, after which the outside peel or skin will easily slide off.

And if for any recipe you can't find fava beans, just add peas.

BOTTARGA

Bottarga is the salted, pressed, and air-dried roe of either tuna (*bottarga di tonno* from Sicily) or gray mullet (*bottarga di muggine* from Sardinia). We have also recently had a delicious bottarga, called *poutargue*, from the South of France. You can buy it as a whole piece, either vacuum packed or sealed in wax, or as crumbled bottarga in a jar. We prefer the whole piece—you just peel back the wax or the plastic packaging and, using a Microplane, grate as much as you need over the pasta, then seal the package back up again or wrap it in fresh plastic wrap, and it will keep for several months in the refrigerator. It should be a bright orange color and have some pliancy—but not too much.

Much like anchovies, bottarga adds a briny, salty, fishy flavor that we love—but it is definitely not to everyone's taste. Sara's first experience with it was a huge lobe of bottarga di tonno that Nancy brought back from Sicily to the Tuscan winery where Sara was teaching cooking. Sara had no idea what to do with it, but a Sicilian who worked at the winery quickly stepped up and showed her how to grate it and mix it with lemon zest and toasted bread crumbs to dress a spicy pasta with garlic and olive oil. In Sicily we've also eaten it on dark Castelvetrano bread, sometimes toasted, with just lemon and butter. These days we don't use bottarga di tonno since the dwindling bluefin tuna population that congregated off Sicily's west coast is poised for extinction thanks to predatory commercial fishing practices. Instead we use Sardinian bottarga di muggine and enjoy it in the same ways.

CAPERS

We use salt-cured capers from the Mediterranean, usually the Sicilian islands of Pantelleria or Salina, although there are also good-quality salted capers from Greece. Small to medium capers are best. They must have the salt rinsed off before adding to any dish or sauce or salad. A quick rinse under running water, followed by a long soak in cold water for a couple of hours, changing the water every half hour or so, is how they should be prepared. Leftovers can be kept in a jar in the fridge with fresh water to cover and should be good for at least a week, though we've occasionally let them go much longer without any ill effects.

CHEESES

Ricotta: The word means "re-cooked." Traditional ricotta is made from the whey left over from cheese making. It is re-cooked (in Italian, *ri-cotta*), heated to a higher temperature, which causes residual proteins in the whey to come together in little clumps. All too often what is offered to us in North America is simply milk that has been coagulated by the addition of vinegar or lemon juice. It may taste good, but it is not really ricotta.

If you cannot find a local cheese maker who produces real whey-based ricotta, you can purchase it online from Paula Lambert's Mozzarella Company in Dallas, Texas (www.mozzarellaco.com). If you are in Northern California, Bellwether Farms in Sonoma County also makes ricotta from whole Jersey cow's milk that has been naturally acidified, as well as another ricotta made from whey. Failing all that, a good

commercial brand of ricotta is Calabro, which is widely available, at least on the East Coast, and quite preferable to the soured milk product.

Ricotta salata: When ricotta is salted, pressed, and aged for about three months, it becomes ricotta salata, a very useful firm, white cheese from Sicily and southern Italy. It's a curious cheese in that it is nothing on its own but really adds a great deal when grated or shaved over pasta. It takes the place of parmigiano-reggiano or grana padano in many southern pasta dishes—and it's usually much cheaper than the two more prestigious cheeses too. It is de rigueur for Sicilian pasta alla Norma.

Parmigiano-reggiano: The greatest cheese in Italy and one of the greatest in the world. Nancy calls it the Marcello Mastroianni of cheese, but unfortunately a lot of people don't even know who he was anymore. But most people do know and recognize the greatness of parmigiano-reggiano, the controlled denomination cheese from the area around Parma, Reggio, and Modena in the Po valley region of Emilia-Romagna. To qualify for its DOP, parmigiano-reggiano must be made from raw, partially skimmed milk of cows raised on grass and hay in the region. It is made in huge forms that start off at close to one hundred pounds and, after two years of aging, weigh about eighty-four. A hard cheese that fractures easily with the help of a special blade, parmigiano-reggiano is recognizable first of all by the distinctive brown lettering branded into the rind of the cheese, then by its clean, nutty fragrance and flavor, and finally by its crystalline structure—the nuggets of cheese almost crackle between the teeth. It is superb for grating on pasta but should by no means be dismissed as just a grating cheese—it is terrific at the end of a meal, accompanied by apples or pears or walnuts, all of which complement it beautifully, as does a drop or two of *aceto balsamico tradizionale*, the real stuff.

Grana padano: But parmigiano-reggiano is expensive, and an exceptional wheel, perhaps one made from the milk of the heritage breed of *vacche rosse* (red cows), should no more be grated into mac and cheese than a fine estate-bottled extra-virgin olive oil should be used to fry onions. Enjoy that rare cheese on its own with a glass of amontillado sherry and instead try grana padano to grate over your pasta. Grana padano is also a DOP cheese, similar to parmigiano-reggiano, and follows similar strict protocols. But it is made in a much larger geographical area, using the milk of Holstein Friesian cows, and not usually aged for the same length of time. And it generally costs less.

Pecorino: The name tells it all. Pecorino is made from the milk of sheep (*pecore*). But that's only the beginning of the story. Sara says there are as many different pecorinos as there are churches in Italy, and she may be right. South of the Po valley, cows start to disappear and sheep take over; thus pecorino is made all over peninsular Italy, in Tuscany and Umbria, in Lazio and the Abruzzi, in Puglia, Campania, Calabria, Sicily, and Sardinia. Each region's pecorino has a slightly different flavor profile. One of our favorites is an aged pecorino from the island of Sardinia, made for and imported by Academia Barilla, called Gran Cru.

Pecorino toscano is another favorite that we love because it comes in several different iterations, from a young fresh creamy cheese, to a medium-aged wheel that's full of flavor, to a very aged cheese that can be used for grating; look for pecorino toscano wrapped in walnut leaves for a special treat.

Pecorino romano (curiously, despite its name, mostly made in Sardinia) is another one we mention because it is often confused with a North American cheese called romano that has nothing to do with good cheese.[*] Avoid sour-tasting romano, but do seek out pecorino romano, a salty, pungent cheese that is delicious on its own or grated over pasta and brings a taste of authenticity to typical Roman pastas.

Pecorino cheeses in general range from small three-pound forms in various stages of maturity, the oldest being what's used to grate, to large cheeses like Gran Cru, aged to the exacting specifications of a parmigiano-reggiano. The flavors can vary from jaw-achingly sharp to mild and buttery to practically rancid tasting. We don't have easy access to all this variety here in America, but we encourage you to learn about and taste the differences among, say, pecorino romano, toscano, siciliano, and sardo. Then make a decision on what you like best and use that.

As much as possible, we use specific regional cheeses to match a sauce: Abruzzese cheese with a chitarra pasta, for

---

[*] *Here's what Wikipedia has to say about "romano": The "[m]ilk can be bleached with benzoyl peroxide or a mixture of benzoyl peroxide with potassium alum, calcium sulfate, and magnesium carbonate."*

example, or an aged Tuscan pecorino with a Tuscan wild boar sauce, and of course Sicilian ricotta salata with pasta alla Norma. Before the 1960s, when some of the regional divisions that have always existed in Italy began to dissolve, most people grated on their pasta whatever local cheese was available, and parmigiano-reggiano or grana padano were reserved for city folk who were buying cheese in a shop or city market rather than just eating what was produced locally.

Mozzarella: Properly speaking, the name refers only to a fresh stretched curd cheese made from the milk of water buffalo, mostly in the Campania region north and south of Naples. A similar fresh, stretched curd cheese made from cow's milk is called fior di latte. However, nowadays, even in Italy *mozzarella* is a catchall term for any stretched curd cheese intended to be eaten when no more than a couple of days old. So you have to distinguish between mozzarella di bufala and mozzarella di anything else. Unfortunately, we don't have much buffalo milk in this country, so most of our mozzarella is made from anything else. For a price, it is possible to get imported buffalo milk mozzarella when it's still just twenty-four to forty-eight hours old. In many cheese shops, especially in old Italian neighborhoods, it is also quite easy to find the anything-else variety, freshly made and sitting in its own brine. Just don't confuse it with the rubbery product tightly wrapped in plastic that is sold in many supermarkets—it bears no relationship to the real thing.

CURED PORK PRODUCTS

The Italian tradition of salting and air-drying pork in various guises goes back at least to the Romans about two thousand years ago and possibly to the Etruscans, a thousand years earlier. It was and is a way of preserving meat throughout the year. Prosciutto is the most famous example, but over the centuries, each different region of Italy has developed diverse methods and individual names for the various parts of the pig and the various combinations of salami, from spicy 'nduja, a soft, spreadable sausage from Calabria that is popular in the United States, to lightly cold-smoked hams from the Alps called speck. In Tuscany pancetta is the salted, spiced flat belly of the pig, and in Rome guanciale are similarly treated pig's jowls, both products that are cured along with prosciutto and salame. In Puglia, Locorotondo's famous capocollo is made from the pig's neck and upper shoulder, cured in wine must. In Umbria, mazzafegati are sausages made with pork liver, and in the marble mountains of Carrara, it's slabs of fatback that are aged in herbs to make the regional specialty lardo.

All these pork products have critical roles to play in Italian cooking, adding richness and complexity, even in small quantities, to a diet that is, on the whole, quite sparse in terms of meat consumption. For this reason alone, it's important to get the different varieties straight—even though, in many cases, they can be switched around with

In Tuscany pancetta is the salted, spiced flat belly of the pig, and in Rome guanciale are similarly treated pig's jowls.

equanimity. Unfortunately, many of them cannot be found here, but the list of cured pork in the Italian style that is available in North America, whether imported or made on site, grows longer each year.

Prosciutto, of course, is well known as the salted, air-dried hind leg of a mature pig. The best is prosciutto di Parma or prosciutto San Daniele, both of which are imported from Italy, usually boned—which is too bad, as the bone, once the meat has been sliced off, can be a great addition to any sort of bean dish. More and more prosciutto is being made in North America to Italian specifications, but it varies enormously in quality. The best way to tell whether it's any good or not is to ask for, or to buy, a small sample to taste.

Much of the time, when you order prosciutto in an American shop, it is sliced paper-thin. That's fine if you're planning to serve it draped over a fresh wedge of melon (a wonderful summertime antipasto), but for use in sauce recipes, ask to have the prosciutto sliced in one piece so that you can more easily dice it to add to the rest of your ingredients.

Don't throw the prosciutto fat away. In the Italian tradition nothing goes to waste, so the scraps, the fatty bits that might be cut off when prosciutto is served as part of an antipasto, are used in the same way as pancetta or guanciale, bits of seasoned fat in which to cook out the vegetables that form the base of a ragù. Sara jealously guards all those scraps at her restaurants, reserving them until she has enough to sweat out in the pan when she begins a ragù. She also saves salami scraps and grinds them up in a meat grinder for a ragù

base. And if you are lucky enough to come upon a prosciutto bone, it makes a great addition to the soup pot.

There is a great deal of argument over whether guanciale or pancetta should be used in any given dish, but if you think of the two as meaty flavoring agents, it doesn't really matter which you use. Guanciale is generally fattier and probably more adapted to tomato-based sauces where the acidity will balance it out, but on occasion in desperation we have substituted bacon, a different flavor for sure, but one that still fills the role of porky supporting character. Even ten years ago, the prospect of finding Italian-style cured meat in America was dismal at best, but that situation has changed as more and more Italian and other chefs have discovered larder basics as the foundation of good cooking. Not only do we have great American-made, Italian-style salume and cured pork products from Fra' Mani (www.framani.com) in California and La Quercia (www.laquercia.us) in Iowa, there is also a renewed interest in our American heritage with delicious dry-cured hams from Benton's in Tennessee (www .bentonscountryhams2.com) and Edwards (www.edwardsvaham.com) in Virginia. These won't be exactly the same as what we taste in Italy, but again they will work the same, adding more flavor and richness to whatever you are making. Seek out real Italian-style pancetta, guanciale, and prosciutto for sure, but also check out local farmers' markets and traditional shops in your own region.

EXTRA-VIRGIN OLIVE OIL

This is the only kind of oil that we use, and we use it profusely. Yes, it is expensive,

especially the fine estate-bottled oils that we use for garnishing. Most of these are Italian, but there are some superior Spanish and Greek oils as well, and at least one French oil that is in this category, not to mention a couple of excellent California oils. Nancy's book *Virgin Territory* is a great resource for information about all these different oils.

Olive oil, even the finest kind, degrades naturally with exposure to light and heat, so in general, what you want to look for is oil packaged in dark, light-proof bottles or tins with a recent harvest date. Not all oils carry a harvest date, but more and more quality producers, recognizing the market value of this information, are including it on their labels. (Note that the use-by date may be very different and is not always a reliable indicator of quality.)

Spanish, Greek, French, and Italian oils may carry a DOP (protected denomination of origin) or IGP (protected geographical indication) stamp from the European Union, a further indication of quality, although if the olive oil is very old, it doesn't really matter if it has a DOP. The best advice we can give you is to buy from reliable purveyors. Some of the best are online: www.gustiamo.com, www.olio2go.com, and www.dipaloselects.com, for Italian oils; www.markethallfoods.com for Californian and Mediterranean oils; and www.zingermans.com for oils from most of the olive oil–producing areas of the world, including Chile, Tunisia, and South Africa.

But don't ignore the cheaper, somewhat more mass-market extra-virgin oils. Many of these are great to use for cooking—not Bertolli and Carapelli, which are industrial

packagers of oil from all over everywhere— but solid, well-produced oils, often from specific regions. Academia Barilla has four or five different oils from different parts of Italy (Liguria, Sicily, and so forth) as well as "100% Italiano," all of which are quite widely available. In her restaurants, Sara uses Iliada, a very good Greek oil. We also like California Olive Ranch for an all-purpose extra-virgin, as well as Olisur from Chile.

Do not believe those who claim you cannot cook with extra-virgin olive oil. It is not true that it has a low flash point or smoke point or burn point. The smoke point for extra-virgin olive oil is around 410°F, which is way higher than you would want for any sort of frying. Most of the time you will be cooking at around 310° to 350°F. Moreover, because of its high concentration of polyphenols, extra-virgin olive oil is actually more stable at high temperatures than many other oils.

We do not recommend using plain olive oil (that is, not marked extra-virgin) because it is highly refined and, apart from the fact that it's a monounsaturated fat, has little going for it. You might as well use canola.

FLOURS

Italian flour is rather different from the types of flour available in North America. The first distinction is between bread wheat (*Triticum aestivum*), called *grano tenero*, and durum wheat (*T. durum*, or *T. turgidum* ssp. *durum* in some taxonomies), *grano duro*. The kernels of bread wheat (despite its name, bread wheat is widely used for pastries and fresh pasta) crush to a soft, talcumlike flour; durum wheat has vitreous kernels that crack when milled and make a gritty flour—think cornmeal grits.

Here's a quick rundown on what you might find in an Italian supermarket:

00 flour (called *doppio zero*—"double zero"—in Italian): Made from soft wheat (*T. aestivum*); roughly equivalent to North American unbleached all-purpose flour.

0 flour (zero): The same as 00 but with a somewhat coarser grind.

Semola: Made from hard durum wheat (*T. durum*), semola is required by Italian law for commercial pasta secca; it is also used in the Italian south to make many breads and fresh pasta by hand. Confusingly, this is called semolina in North America.

Semolina or semola rimacinata: Also from hard durum wheat but milled a second time to make a finer flour that is easier to work with by hand. We have found that many southern Italian cooks make their pasta fresca (for example, orecchiette) with semola rimacinata—the name tells it all, "re-machined semola." Durum flour, such as that available from King Arthur Flour, is the American equivalent.

Farina integrale: As in North America, this can mean either what is conventionally called whole wheat flour, meaning it is processed in roller mills and some (but not all) of the bran and germ are added back after milling; or (and this is far and away the best) the whole grains are milled in a stone gristmill. This will never be as fine in texture as more commercial flours, but it makes up for that in its nutty, wheaten flavor.

Northern Italian cooks generally use their soft wheat 00 flour for making fresh egg pasta, while southern cooks swear by hard durum wheat flour, as semola and as rimacinata. Most American cooks, we've found, use regular unbleached all-purpose flour for both, but over the years we've found that it makes more sense to use durum flour, either entirely or mixed roughly fifty-fifty with all-purpose flour to get the best results. Whatever you decide to do (see pages 33–49 for more pasta information, including recipes for making your own), we highly recommend King Arthur Flour, not only for the quality of their flours and other bakers' and pasta makers' implements but also for the copious amount of information about all of these, made available on their website (www.kingarthurflour.com). Incidentally, they're located in Norwich, Vermont, with a great shop plus ongoing classes in baking and pasta making.

MUSHROOMS, DRIED AND FRESH

Farmers' markets are a great resource for fresh wild mushrooms in season, from morels in the spring to chanterelles and black trumpets in summer, to dark, earthy porcini (aka cèpes or boletes) in autumn. If you want to go foraging for mushrooms, look for a local mycological society and sign up for an expedition. (Your local Cooperative Extension Service should be able to help with this.) There are many, many delicious edible wild mushrooms, but there are also some that are toxic, even fatal; be sure of what you harvest.

Fresh mushrooms should be brushed free of all dust, earth, bits of straw, and so forth, using a damp kitchen towel. It is best not to wash them since most mushrooms absorb water like a sponge. However, if necessary, give them a very quick rinse and shake them dry—but only just before you are to use them. Examine the mushrooms and cut out any wormy bits, then slice or chop depending on the recipe.

Fresh wild mushrooms make great pasta sauces. And if no wild mushrooms are available, use the cultivated mushrooms in your supermarket produce section. You should easily find shiitake and oyster mushrooms, but even button mushrooms or cremini will be tasty if you add to them a few reconstituted dried porcini to boost the flavor of the sauce.

Here's how to reconstitute dried mushrooms: Put the dried mushrooms in a bowl and cover with very hot water. Set aside to steep for about 30 minutes, or until the mushrooms are softened. Remove the mushroom slices but *do not discard the soaking water,* as it is full of flavor. Pat the slices dry with paper towels, then chop or leave whole, depending on the recipe. Strain the soaking water through a fine-mesh sieve and add the water to the recipe whenever it calls for liquid. (If you don't use the soaking liquid in the recipe, save it and add it the next time you make a stock or broth.)

OLIVES

They come as black, green, or mixed; large or small, plump or wrinkled; Niçoise, Gaeta, Moroccan, Kalamata, and so on. Each one fits a different flavor profile from strong and bitter to sweet and mild. Sara's favorites are Gaeta from the Tyrrhenian coast of Italy south of Rome, small, black, soft-fleshed, and very flavorful olives that are easy to pit, and the large green Sicilian olives called Castelvetrano. If possible, always ask for a taste before you make up your mind which olives to buy. We tend to steer away from olives flavored with herbs or spices as the additional aromatics interfere with the flavor of the sauce we're focused on, and all too often the added flavors are there to mask the fact that these are inferior olives. Similarly, prepitted olives are probably never of the best quality. The salt-cured dried olives from the south of France and North Africa are often overpoweringly strong in taste, and the lye-cured bella di Cerignola olives from Puglia are much too mild to bother with. Both of these are fine to offer with a glass of wine, but we avoid adding them to our pasta sauces, believing they have either too much or too little to contribute. One other olive we avoid: so-called California-style olives, the kind of soft, flabby olives your mother (or my mother at least) put out for cocktails.

In the Pasta Kitchen
A Cook's Companion

HOW TO COOK PASTA

Pasta needs a *lot* of water to cook properly and the water must be boiling vigorously so that each strand, each shape, is surrounded, totally enveloped in its cooking medium. That is why our pasta cooking instructions almost always begin with: "Bring a large pot of water to a rolling boil." We figure 6 quarts of water for 500 grams (about 1 pound, usually one package of imported Italian pasta) of any type of long, spaghettilike pasta; for smaller shapes, you could use 4 quarts, but go with 6 quarts as a rule and you won't ever go wrong.

Salting is also a critical point. All the talk about lowering salt in the diet is directed at people who consume a lot of packaged food, fast food, and the like. If you're eating a normal diet of freshly prepared food and you're not suffering from extreme hypertension, there is no need to restrict salt. In any case, 2 to 3 tablespoons of salt (a small handful) in 6 quarts of water is not going to be harmful. Anything less than that and the pasta will lack flavor. We favor coarse sea salt, preferably from Sicily, for this.

Add the salt after the water has come to the boil. And then, when the water boils again, which it will do almost immediately, add the pasta.

Which pasta goes with which sauce? Which sauce goes with which pasta? Don't get hung up on this. There are said to be five hundred to six hundred different pasta shapes in Italy alone. And, along with penne, spaghetti, fusilli, linguine, and so forth, many pasta manufacturers give their own names to shapes—Benedetto Cavalieri's ruote pazze (crazy wheels), or Pastificio Faella's Vesuvio, which looks like small turtles. In general, smooth sauces, like many tomato- or cream-based sauces, go best with long, skinny, spaghetti-type pasta, while roughly cut vegetable and meat sauces are better with short, chunky shapes such as penne rigate or tortiglione. Lasagna has its own shape, the flat rectangles that are layered in the dish, but pasta al forno is best made with short, twisted shapes, with lots of quirks in which to nestle the sauce.

Back to the pasta: If you're using long pasta, work it into the water with a long-handled wooden spoon or fork to get all of it immersed in boiling water as quickly as possible. If it's short pasta, simply stir it—not once but several times during the cooking process.

Cover the pot until the water returns to the boil, then remove the lid and let the pasta cook vigorously until done. Start timing from the moment the pasta water returns to a boil. Follow package directions for the cooking time, but start checking a couple of minutes before the projected finish. Extract a piece of pasta and either bite into it or cut it apart. Al dente pasta has a slight, pleasant resistance to the bite, and a thin white vein, a tiny dot, at the center, when it is ready.

Fresh pasta will be done in a matter of minutes. Our old housekeeper in Rome, who taught Nancy how to make pasta fresca by hand, used to say, *"Basta dire un Ave Maria"*—just long enough to say a Hail Mary. In truth it takes a little longer, but not more than a couple of minutes. (Most fresh pasta is done when it floats—the Italian word is *galleggiante*.)

Do not overcook the pasta. Have a colander ready in the sink. Remove the pasta and drain it the moment it is done, keeping in mind that it will continue to cook in the residual heat even after it has been drained. (In 1937, Americans were advised to cook spaghetti for twenty minutes, according to a recipe book published by the North Bennet Street settlement house in Boston's Italian North End. How times have changed!)

If pasta is overcooked to a mushy stage, it is not only unpleasant to eat but the glycemic index actually goes up. If you are trying to keep a low glycemic profile, by all means have your pasta very much on the underdone side.

A useful tip: Italian cooks, when draining the pasta, sometimes set aside a cup or more of the pasta water to add to the sauce. The starches in the water help to thicken and amalgamate a sauce that isn't quite coming together.

Several rules or reminders

➤ Do not add a spoonful of oil to the water. It is unnecessary, it makes the pasta greasy, it will not keep the pasta strands from clumping together, and it makes the pot just that much more difficult to clean out.

➤ Do not rinse the drained pasta under cold water. There is no need for a procedure that only chills the pasta to no good purpose. With just a few exceptions, hot pasta and hot sauce are prerequisites for a satisfying meal.

➤ Do not oversauce the pasta. Less is more in the Italian lexicon. The point is to taste the noodles as much as the sauce, a balance between the two. Thus, there should not be more than a spoonful of sauce left in the bottom of the bowl when all the pasta has been consumed.

Almost all pasta must be served immediately, so in most cases plan to have

Here's a Quick Rundown on Pasta Cooking

For about 1 pound (500 grams) of pasta, bring 6 quarts of water to a rolling boil. Add a big spoonful of salt and then the pasta. Use a long-handled wooden spoon to push the pasta down into the boiling water—this is especially important for long, skinny pasta. It must be entirely immersed in the boiling water. Cover the pot until the water returns to a boil, then uncover and start timing the pasta according to the package directions. Start testing at least 2 minutes before the recommended time. Have ready a warm serving bowl. When the pasta is al dente, drain and turn it into the bowl with whatever sauce you intend to use. Toss and serve immediately.

the sauce ready before you add the pasta to the water and dress the pasta as soon as it's drained. Have ready a warm serving bowl to receive the hot pasta. (One quick way to warm the bowl: Transfer a couple of ladles of boiling water from the pot to the bowl and let it rest and warm while the pasta is cooking.)

One other tip from Italian experts: When it's appropriate, cook the pasta until it's slightly underdone, drain it, and then finish it off in the sauce you've made. The pasta will absorb some of the flavors from the sauce and the result will be a beautifully integrated dish. This technique is called *saltare in padella*, or tossing the pasta right in the pan with the sauce.

Serve the pasta immediately and encourage all the hungry eaters gathered around the table to tuck right in as soon as the pasta is in their plates. Don't wait for everyone to be served. Italians take pasta seriously: It's an insult to the cook, they say, not to eat it while it's hot.

Buon appetito! everyone says as they dig in their forks.

And *buon appetito!* we say to you too, wishing you the happiest of adventures cooking and eating this loveliest of all the products of *la cucina Italiana*.

A note about portion sizes: Italians count on 80 to 100 grams of dry pasta per person. We reckon a pound (roughly 500 grams) of pasta will serve 6 people comfortably, especially if pasta is served, as it is in Italy, as a first course. If you serve it as a main

Almost all pasta must be served immediately, so in most cases plan to have the sauce ready before you add the pasta to the water and dress the pasta as soon as it's drained.

course, a pound will probably serve 4 or 5. Most of our recipes are written for "4 to 6 servings"—6 if pasta is served in the Italian fashion, as a *primo*, or "first course," to be followed by a *secondo* that is often focused on protein, whether meat, fish, or beans. If pasta is served as it is often done in North America as a *piatto unico*, a "single course" ("*pasta e basta*" is what Italians say, "pasta and that's it"), then count on 4 servings.

Italians tend to eat pasta with less sauce than many North Americans are used to. In Italy the point is the pasta, and the sauce is there to garnish it and make it more interesting. In North America, we sometimes unhappily feel, the sauce is the point: It fills the plate and the pasta simply serves as a carbohydrate extension, like a piece of bread. We, being natural-born Italophiles, prefer to eat our pasta the Italian way.

We are adamant, however, in following the Italian tradition of not ever, or hardly ever, serving pasta as an accompaniment to a main course, as if pasta were something like potatoes or boiled rice. Pasta is the queen of the table and as such deserves an honored place, all by itself, at the start of the meal. Pasta may not be followed by anything at all, but it should never need accompaniment beyond a most delicious sauce.

Dressing the pasta can be as simple as the aglio-olio-peperoncino on page 55. Or even simpler, just a spritz of good olive oil and a sprinkle of cheese, or as in Sicily, olive oil and crisply fried homemade bread crumbs, or a handful of chopped fresh herbs and a spoonful of good butter. In Roman trattorie it's guanciale, diced and fried in lard or olive oil, with a bit of chili pepper and a little onion, and the spaghetti finished right in the *padella*, the frying pan, to absorb the flavors. In Piemonte, fresh pasta might be dressed with just the juices from the Sunday roast—a good bet for Sunday night supper. And in Liguria they layer the pasta in a baking dish with the roast meat juices and a lot of grated cheese between the layers, making sure the topmost layer is meat juices and cheese, then pop the dish into a preheated oven until the top is nicely glazed. With pasta, nothing gets wasted. Ever.

PASTA FRESCA: MAKING YOUR OWN

So much has been written about the glories of the Bolognese *sfogline*, the white-capped ladies who briskly and competently turn out kilos and kilos of egg-rich pasta each morning for the lunch tables of that city's bourgeoisie, that it's a wonder anyone else would dare take up a *matterello* (rolling pin) and approach the *spianatoia* (pastry board) to roll out a paper-thin sheet of sunny golden pasta. In Bologna those gorgeous rounds, or *sfoglie*, are sliced into broad sheets for lasagna, thin noodles for tagliatelle and the like, or filled with dabs of delicious forced-meat or ricotta stuffings to make cappelletti, tortellini, agnolotti, and so on.

This means average home cooks in Bologna don't have to know how to make fresh egg pasta at all, not if they can just pick up exquisite tagliatelle or tortellini down at the local pasta shop whenever they want. In North America, if you want really amazing fresh pasta, you mostly have to make it yourself. In a pinch, store-bought fresh lasagna sheets or cut noodles are okay, as long as you trust the pasta maker, but we would never buy any type of filled pasta, as the quality is so often just not there.

Making fresh pasta at home is a skill that does require practice. If you've never made it before, don't expect to be a master right out of the gate. Start by making lasagna sheets, which are easiest of all, and learn to work with and understand the dough before you move on to ravioli. Home pasta makers in Italy grow up learning to make pasta from their mothers, their grandmothers, and their mothers-in-law, and have spent years practicing and mastering it. It won't take you years if you've never done it, but it might take a few tries to get it right.

In addition to the egg-rich pastas of northern Italy, made with soft white flour, there are other Italian pasta traditions that are just as venerable and just as delicious. On the streets of Old Bari, down in Puglia, the pasta makers line up each morning, working right in the open air, rapidly and deftly turning out orecchiette, the little ear-shaped pasta typical of the region. Their flour-and-water dough (no eggs) is made from locally grown hard durum wheat. In the hills around Siena housewives roll out long, thin strings of pici, again flour-and-water (no eggs), but made this time with refined 00 flour, each string laboriously rolled by hand. In the Tuscan Mugello on the border with Emilia-Romagna, cooks turn out the local specialty, tortelli di patate, fat dumplings of pasta dough filled, surprisingly, with tasty mashed

Italians tend to eat pasta with less sauce than many North Americans are used to.

potatoes. Over in Liguria each pasta maker has a wooden stamp, called a *corzetto* or *croxetto*, carved with initials or symbols to stamp an identification mark on her very own pasta. And in the western part of Sicily cooks make busiate from locally grown tumminia wheat, a heritage grain, and wind the strands of pasta around knitting needles to give them their characteristic twist.

Wherever you go in Italy there are pasta stories to be heard and pasta dishes to be tried. This is Sara's story:

I learned to make fresh pasta from our late, beloved Tuscan neighbor Mita Antolini, farmwife, gardener, chicken and pig raiser, and cook. When I first met Mita, I was just ten years old and she was maybe forty. She ran her farm and her family efficiently and frugally with a smile on her face but with a will that brooked no contradiction. She made two kinds of pasta: thin, flat tagliatelle or broad sheets of lasagna, both using the same recipe— fresh eggs laid by the hens in her *cortile* (farmyard), a little water, a splash of olive oil, and refined white flour.

I loved to linger in Mita's kitchen. In the beginning it was for the fascinating smells that came out as well as for the attention she expressed long before I had begun to master the language. There was a lot of cheek pinching and a lot of hard candies doled out from a jar on the counter. It was a typical Tuscan

farmhouse kitchen with a large fireplace in the center where everyone sheltered in cold weather, a long communal table capable of seating up to twenty, and an alcove with a two-burner gas ring and a *cucina economica*, a small wood-fired cookstove that everyone hated to use in the summer heat but that helped to warm up the drafty farmhouse in cold weather. Mita cooked on the fireplace, on the gas burner, on the woodstove, in the bake oven that was situated outside beneath the stairs that led to the front door, and in what had once been the family chapel but was now a sort of summer kitchen in which all mass meals, such as for the annual harvest dinner, were produced. But she made her pasta right there at the long table in the main room while people came and went, cats mewed for offerings, and her religious sister-in-law Beppa went down on her knees Sunday mornings to say mass with the pope, broadcast on television live from the Vatican.

To make her pasta, Mita piled flour onto a wooden board laid across the big table, made a well in the center into which she cracked her orange-yolked eggs, added a half cup or so of water, and then kneaded it all quickly into a soft mass that she finished off with a tablespoon or two of extra-virgin olive oil pressed into the outside. She wrapped the dough tightly and let it rest for at least fifteen minutes, then rolled it out. When I was first watching, in awe, she used a long, thin wooden rolling pin, but later she acquired a small home pasta

I loved to linger in Mita's kitchen. In the beginning it was for the fascinating smells that came out as well as for the attention she expressed long before I had begun to master the language.

machine, the kind most Italian home cooks still use today. She made a fine, supple, and delicate dough suitable for ravioli as well as for cut shapes like tagliatelle.

Once I had mastered Mita's recipe and her technique, I used it exclusively for many years in every restaurant and home kitchen I worked in. Along with most cooks, whether Italian or American, I believed that fresh egg pasta was a northern Italian technique, made exclusively with soft white flour. And I also believed that the durum wheat used in the Italian south was suitable only for eggless, water-based doughs that made tougher, harder, thicker shapes such as orecchiette and handmade fusilli. They were more rustic, I thought, than the refined egg pastas of central and northern Italy.

But in the summer of 2014, while traipsing through a hot, dusty flour mill in Puglia, where hard durum wheat was milled for many of the finest artisanal pasta producers in the country, the fragrant nutty aroma of the wheat awakened memories of the wheat harvests of my Tuscan childhood, and I remembered a Tuscan chef who had told me she always mixed durum wheat into her egg pasta to add flavor and strength to the typical 00 flour.

That summer, Stefania Peduzzi of the Rustichella d'Abruzzo pasta-making family showed me how to make classic Abruzzese pasta alla chitarra, mixing eggs and just a splash of water into durum flour (called in Italian *semolina* or *semola rimacinato*) before pressing the dough on the guitar-shaped chitarra to be cut into long strings. If Stefania used durum flour with eggs, I decided, so could I.

It's true that refined white 00 flour makes a soft, delicate pasta dough, suitable for the most tender ravioli, tagliatelle, and delicate sheets for Tuscan lasagna. But as I experimented with the durum wheat flour I discovered that it added not just flavor but structure and strength as well, bringing a pleasing texture to fresh pasta as well as a good deal of flavor. When you make a wet filling like that for the eggplant and ricotta ravioli on page 224, you want that added strength.

I was also amazed at what a difference a lot of eggs can make to the structure of the dough, especially when I made *tajarin* (Piemontese dialect for *tagliolini*) to go with white truffles (see page 284). What I had thought of as excessive began to make sense. For a frugal Tuscan housewife, pasta dough evolved to use a minimum number of eggs, which, even with chickens in the courtyard, were a precious commodity. But in Piemonte, if you're already eating expensive and rare white truffles, who cares about being reticent with the eggs?

The fat and protein in egg yolks give a springy, tensile strength to pasta dough, making it actually much easier to work with. Mita's dough always has to be dusted with lots of semolina and it does not really last. Ravioli made with Mita's dough must be eaten right away, whereas the tajarin, with all its eggs, is still good three or four days later. And the egg-rich dough of the north needs only a light dusting of flour; in fact, with its springy texture, it is a much more successful dough for tricky filled pastas such as agnolotti del plin from Piemonte and the famous tortellini of Bologna. The recipe for agnolotti that we've included is fairly simple (see page 265), but traditional tortellini are much more complex. This is, however, intended to be a collection of recipes that are for the most part simple and easily executed. Even I, who pride myself on my pasta-making skills, am daunted by the idea of constructing intricately filled pastas without the help of my professional kitchen to back me up.

SARA'S NOTES ON MAKING AND ROLLING OUT PASTA

One of the cornerstones of successful pasta making is to use as little added flour as necessary. Too much flour toughens the dough. With that in mind, I like to use a large board or wooden countertop for making the dough and for rolling it out.

I mound the flour on the board and form a deep well in the center, cracking eggs and adding water to the well. Using a fork, I break the yolks and beat the eggs right in

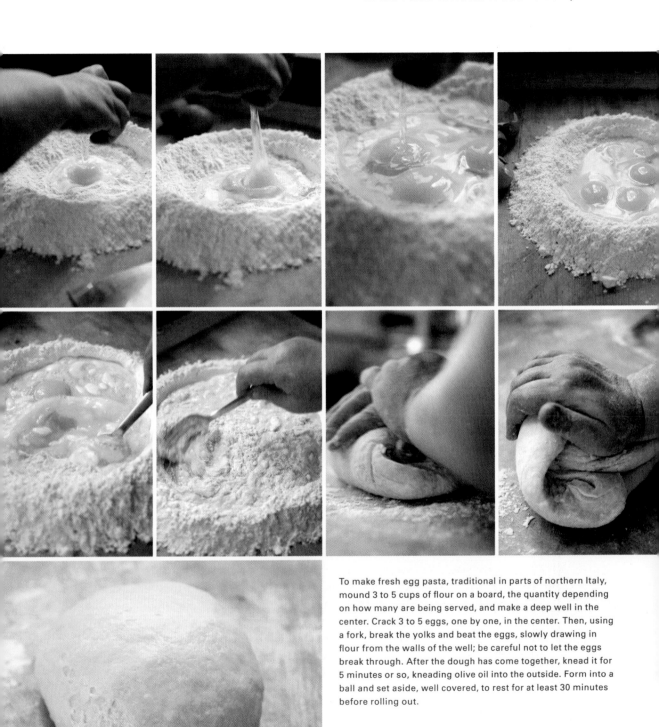

To make fresh egg pasta, traditional in parts of northern Italy, mound 3 to 5 cups of flour on a board, the quantity depending on how many are being served, and make a deep well in the center. Crack 3 to 5 eggs, one by one, in the center. Then, using a fork, break the yolks and beat the eggs, slowly drawing in flour from the walls of the well; be careful not to let the eggs break through. After the dough has come together, knead it for 5 minutes or so, kneading olive oil into the outside. Form into a ball and set aside, well covered, to rest for at least 30 minutes before rolling out.

When I'm ready to roll out the dough, I dust the board down with flour and cut off a portion of dough about the size of a lemon, leaving the rest wrapped until I'm ready to use it.

the well, slowly drawing in flour from the inner walls of the well to mix with the liquid in the center, being careful not to let the eggy liquid break through the flour wall and deluge the board. (Note that many cooks prefer to mound the flour and start mixing the eggs in a large mixing bowl to prevent the eggs from leaking out and making a mess.) When the dough is formed and it's no longer possible to mix with a fork, but it's still too sticky and wet to use my hands, I use a baker's bench scraper, scraping and turning over, constantly adding a bit more of the flour on the board. At the end I use my hands to knead the dough smooth for five minutes or so, depending on the recipe. Finally, I knead a couple of tablespoons of extra-virgin olive oil into the outside of the mass of dough, then wrap the dough tightly with plastic wrap and set it aside to rest for at least thirty minutes, overnight if refrigerated.

When I'm ready to roll out the dough, I dust the board down with flour and cut off a portion of dough about the size of a lemon, leaving the rest wrapped until I'm ready to use it. I dust the working portion heavily with flour and begin rolling it out on the widest opening of the pasta machine. I roll the whole thing through, dust it with flour again, and fold it lengthwise into thirds, working to form an even shape. Then I roll it through on the widest setting once more.

I do this at least three times in order to get a very even, supple shape, but also to work in more flour. If the dough is very wet or relaxed, I continue to fold and flour a few more turns. Then, when I'm satisfied with the texture, I begin rolling the dough out for real, rolling and dusting lightly with flour after each roll-through, reducing the size of the opening every couple of times. How thin I make it depends on what I'm going to make. If I plan to cut tagliatelle or tagliolini or make pasta alla chitarra, I take it down to two or three notches on the pasta machine before the end. But if I'm making ravioli or another filled pasta, I want it to be as thin as possible, so I take it down to the narrowest opening, being careful to dust lightly with flour and handle the dough carefully and gently with my hands.

When I'm cutting ravioli or another filled pasta, I scatter a bed of semolina or fine cornmeal on a sheet pan or tray for the finished shapes to rest on; it prevents the filled pastas from sticking and, unlike all-purpose flour, will fall off in the pasta cooking water. If I'm cutting noodles, I toss them frequently in flour, durum or regular flour, depending on what I used to make the pasta. I curl them into nests and let them dry a little on a cookie rack or grid, tossing them occasionally so they don't slump and clump together.

Basic Pasta Fresca Dough (Mita Antolini's Pasta)

Note that we prefer to use unbleached all-purpose flour because the Italian 00 available in North America is often stale and old.

MAKES 1¼ TO 1½ POUNDS PASTA DOUGH

3 cups unbleached all-purpose flour
3 large eggs
½ cup water
2 tablespoons olive oil
Pinch sea salt (optional)

Mound the flour on a board, make a well in the center, and drop the eggs into the well. Using a fork, gently break up the eggs a little, then add about three-quarters of the water and start to incorporate the flour from around the inside of the well. When the dough begins to thicken, switch to a bench scraper and lift and fold over the dough, incorporating more and more of the flour, a little at a time, until you have a dough that is easy to knead. By the time you've incorporated about half the flour, you'll be able to change your technique and to knead the dough with your hands until it all comes together in a mass. If the dough seems too dry, sprinkle a few tablespoons of the remaining water over the dough.

On the other hand, if the dough seems too wet, add a sprinkle of flour and knead it in. Knead until you have a smooth, compact dough, rubbing the outside with the olive oil and kneading it in.

Set the dough aside, covered in plastic wrap, for at least 15 minutes. It will be quite a wet, soft dough, but it makes exceptionally tender and delicate pasta. You may also refrigerate the wrapped dough for up to 6 hours, but bring it back to room temperature before rolling it again.

If you are making lasagna, roll out the pasta sheets on a board using a long wooden rolling pin. The texture is amazing and it's not difficult to do. But this dough dries out quickly, and, once rolled out, it should be used quickly. So if you're planning to make filled pastas, a hand-cranked pasta machine will definitely speed everything up. When we make ravioli, we have at hand a spray bottle of water. After rolling out the dough but just before filling it, if the dough seems too dry, it gets misted from the spray bottle.

Roll out the dough to the thinnest possible sheet. For lasagna, cut it into rectangles 4 to 5 inches wide and 10 or more inches long. Most lasagna pans are 9 x 13 inches, but when it comes to it, you can cut the lasagna sheets to fit the pan.

For other pasta shapes, follow the directions in the various recipes.

Pasta Verde

Green Pasta

Fresh pasta is often flavored with blanched, finely chopped, and squeezed-dry greens of some sort. Spinach is most common, but in the spring when nettles rear up their ugly stinging leaves, they make a delicious green pasta; borage is used for pasta verde in Liguria, and in her restaurant, Sara finds that green pasta is a great way to use up miscellaneous greens that she finds in her walk-in—turnip tops, radish tops, Swiss chard, and the like.

Follow the directions for Mita Antolini's pasta fresca (page 43), but add greens prepared as in the following, substituting them for the ½ cup water.

Rinse ½ pound greens (such as spinach, nettles, chard) well, destem if necessary and set in a saucepan over medium-low heat. Bring to a simmer and cook briefly, about 3 minutes or so, just long enough to soften the greens. (Some greens will take more time, some less; they should be soft enough to chop when done.) Drain the greens in a colander and chop, then drain again, squeezing to rid them of as much liquid as possible, and chop again. They should be as fine and dry as possible before mixing with the flour and eggs.

Mound the flour on the board, make a well in the center, crack the eggs into the well, and add the squeezed-dry, finely chopped greens. With a fork, break up the eggs, mixing them with the greens, and start slowly to draw in flour from the edges of the well to form the dough. Proceed as directed.

Durum Flour Pasta Dough

This is basically exactly the same as Mita Antolini's pasta fresca (page 43), but substitute 3 cups durum flour (semola rimacinata) for the 3 cups unbleached all-purpose flour. This is the recipe to use for pasta alla chitarra or for any sort of ravioli that needs a particularly strong envelope around the filling (Ravioli con Ricotta Melanzane Bruciacchiate, page 224, for example).

Once you gain confidence in your pasta-making skills, you can start to play around with different flours as well. In Tuscany and in Liguria, two places where chestnuts are an important resource, cooks commonly add a little sweet chestnut flour to the dough, and many fresh pasta makers swear by a small amount of semola rimacinata added to egg pasta dough for both flavor and structure. Farro and buckwheat flour are also sometimes mixed in (not together), and if you have access to local flours, we encourage you to experiment. A ratio of one part alternative flour to two parts regular flour would be a good place to start, remembering that if there is no gluten in the flour (as in chestnut or buckwheat), you probably cannot add more than a third. If you add too much, the resulting dough will lack elasticity.

MAKING A BASIC LASAGNA

There are three critical elements to lasagna that, once mastered, will assure you of a deliciously savory, rich, and yet light-textured meal every time. The first, of course, is the pasta, and we urge you to make your own in order to have the gorgeously silken texture that Italian cooks strive for. We've had lasagna in Italy that has had as many as ten different layers of pasta, yet the dish as a whole was light in texture and delightful, each delicately thin layer simply embracing the other ingredients. Of course, not everyone has the time to roll out the pasta, so we understand if occasionally you turn to packaged lasagna. But we urge you to use one of the fine, artisanal pastas with which Italy abounds. Di Martino, Faella, and Rustichella d'Abruzzo are among several firms that make boxed lasagna. We also encourage you to make lasagna from scratch every now and then—just so you'll know the difference.

The second-most important element is the béchamel (*besciamella*), the white sauce that provides lasagna with a comfortable bed, cushioning the more assertive flavors of the sauce. We make our béchamel with milk that has been steeped with aromatic vegetables and herbs to give extra flavor and structure to the dish, then beat the hot strained milk into a roux of butter and flour and cook until it is thick enough for the task. (See page 11 for directions.)

And finally, of course, is the meat sauce or ragù—which is not always meat, by any means, although it is always the structural foundation of the lasagna. Sometimes indeed a vegetarian lasagna may be what's called for, and it's a sumptuous way to present a vegetarian dish. But seafood can also provide that critical link.

If you think of lasagna as an architectural construct, then the pasta provides the bricks, the béchamel the mortar, and the ragù is the foundation that defines the structure—and that tells you what style and period the building represents. Many of our recipes for ragù can be used in lasagna, indeed are intended for that very purpose. The ragù should be made ahead, but each of the other elements—the béchamel and the pasta—should be prepared shortly before you're ready to put the lasagna together. Once ready, they cannot be held, so be sure you have everything else set to go.

The second-most important element is the béchamel (besciamella), *the white sauce that provides lasagna with a comfortable bed, cushioning the more assertive flavors of the sauce.*

For the pasta: Use the recipe and directions on page 43 for Mita Antolini's pasta fresca, using 3 cups unbleached all-purpose flour and 3 eggs for a lasagna to serve 6. When it is time to roll out the dough, you may do so with a rolling pin and board or you may use a pasta machine. In either case, pull off about one-sixth of the pasta dough that you've made and keep the rest covered with loose plastic wrap or a clean dish towel while you work. Lightly dust the piece of dough with flour and roll it out on a board as thin as possible. Cut it into rectangles 4 to 5 inches by 10 inches. Or put the dough through a pasta machine, gradually reducing the size of the opening until you have reached the smallest and thinnest one. Lay the lasagna sheets out on a clean kitchen towel and proceed with the next batch of dough. As you proceed, cover each layer of lasagna sheets with a clean, dry kitchen towel.

When all the dough has been rolled, bring a large pot of water to a boil. Add salt to the water. Have ready a bowl of ice water near the stove to receive the lasagna sheets as they finish cooking. Drop a sheet into the pan of boiling water (you can do several at once) and cook for just 1 minute. Use a wide slotted spoon or spatula to remove the sheets and drop them into the bowl of ice water. Leave them for 30 seconds, then lay them out flat, once more on clean, dry kitchen towels. Repeat until all the sheets are done.

At this point in the process you will have your ragù (you will need about 3 cups), your béchamel (4 to 5 cups), and your pasta. What more do you need?

1 to 2 cups freshly grated parmigiano-reggiano
Freshly ground black pepper
1 to 2 tablespoons unsalted butter
A little extra-virgin olive oil

Set the oven on 375°F.

Combine about ⅓ cup béchamel with ¼ cup ragù and spread it over the bottom of a 9 x 13-inch ceramic or glass baking dish. Cover it with several overlapping layers of pasta sheets. Combine ⅔ cup béchamel and ½ cup ragù and spread over the pasta, then sprinkle with about ¼ cup grated parmigiano and a good sprinkle of pepper. Continue in this fashion until all the pasta has been used up. Your topmost layer should consist of about 1⅓ cups béchamel mixed with ¼ cup ragù and topped with ½ cup grated cheese. Dot the top with the butter, dribble olive oil over the top, and transfer to the preheated oven. Bake for about 45 minutes, or until the top is golden and the sauce is bubbly. Remove from the oven and let stand for 10 to 15 minutes before cutting. Serve immediately.

MAKING CORZETTI FOR PESTO

Corzetti (singular, corzetto) are round stamped pasta shapes typical of the Riviera di Levante, the Ligurian coast east of Genova. They are said to resemble a medieval coin called a corzetto. To make corzetti you need a two-piece wooden tool, typically cut from pear wood, made up of a round cutter and a round engraved stamp carved in a design that embosses itself on the pasta. (These tools, hand-

To make corzetti you need a two-piece wooden tool, typically cut from pear wood, made up of a round cutter and a round engraved stamp carved in a design that embosses itself on the pasta.

made in Liguria, are available by mail order from Fante's Kitchen Shop in South Philadelphia, www.fantes.com, or, if your travels take you to the delightful town of Chiavari in Liguria, you can buy them from master corzetti carver Franco Casoni.) Use the cutter to cut out the corzetti from a freshly rolled pasta sheet, then press each corzetto between the two sides of the stamp, pressing a logo or your initials or a fanciful design onto the pasta disk. Lightly dusted with a little semolina or fine cornmeal, they should be laid out on a sheet pan in a single layer until ready to cook. They look really cool on the plate, even if we aren't convinced they taste different from trofie, tiny matchsticks of hand-rolled pasta, also typically served with Genovese pesto.

MAKING PASTA ALLA CHITARRA

You must have a chitarra for this, a large open box, strung with wires sort of like a guitar, traditionally used in the Abruzzi to make a long, thin spaghetti pasta that is square in section. The dough is rolled out (easily enough with a rolling pin, but you can also use a hand-cranked pasta machine) to a thickness equal to the width of the gap between the chitarra wires, that is, about ⅛ inch. The sheet, which should be roughly the length and width of the chitarra, is then draped over the wires. The sheet is gently pressed through the wires, using a rolling pin, and the cut pasta falls to a tray below. Then the strings are gathered up, turned into a little nest, and dusted gently with semolina or finely ground cornmeal.

Chitarra pasta is traditionally made with durum wheat flour and eggs, making a strong and flavorful mix. Use the recipe for Mita Antolini's pasta fresca (see page 43), but substitute durum flour for the all-purpose in the recipe.

Another nice touch: Because the Abruzzi is famous for its saffron, steep a pinch of saffron in the water to be used in the pasta dough, doing this several hours ahead of time. It gives both color and a subtle flavor.

The pasta may be cooked and sauced just like any of the other pastas in the book. A simple tomato sauce is traditional, but so is a more complicated lamb ragù, as in the recipe on page 298.

Winter

Of all the seasons, winter is the hardest to love. Yet for devoted cooks and food lovers, the pleasures of this coldest, darkest time of the year are abundant, beginning with the fragrance of wood fires. The one in the big kitchen stove in our Tuscan farmhouse must be lit afresh each morning, a chore that is always designated for the first person awake. (And isn't it amazing how long folks can lie abed, waiting for the aromas of wood smoke and coffee to rise up through the cold tiles of the farmhouse floors?) That stove is the warm focal point of the entire house throughout the cold weeks of winter. Wet socks are dried there, cold hands are warmed, the teakettle is always bubbling away, and most often, to the fragrance of wood smoke and coffee is added the seductive aroma of a meaty, tomato-y, oniony ragù, just waiting for a big bowl of ziti or handmade tagliatelle to enhance with its rich and complex flavors.

Truth to tell, we have never spent a great deal of time in our Tuscan farmhouse in winter. The thick stone walls make it just a little too cold and rustic. But on the rare weeks when we can get away, when the fire in that kitchen stove is cranking and the ragù is simmering, when the air is brisk but the sky is blue and the shouts of hunters and the yips of their dogs ring across the mountain—then it is a winter wonderland.

The winter table might look meager compared with the bounty of August, but it is not without style and compelling flavors. Beans and greens are foundation features, as appetizing in combination as they are full of good sustenance. This is the time of year when we happily cook with dried fava beans, chickpeas, lentils, white cannellini beans, or speckled borlotti, and mix them in a pasta sauce with robust bitter greens standing in Tuscan winter gardens, or with brightly colored seasonal squashes and orange pumpkins, not to mention all the stored alliums—onions (red, white, and yellow), leeks, garlic, shallots—and little white turnips, big green cabbages, cauliflower, and broccoli. We cruise winter markets for radicchio with its gorgeous maroon-and-white-stippled leaves, or romanesco, the jade-green spiraled cauliflower that decorates market stalls, or artichokes in five or six different varieties, so decisively connected to the Mediterranean winter table, and we bring them all home to mix with pantry staples, the tomato pomarola that was made last summer and put up in jars, the wild mushrooms that were gathered, sliced, and dried in the sun, the chestnuts and walnuts that sit in sacks on high shelves away from

ravening field mice, and of course the olive oil that arrives fresh on our tables at the very edge of winter, bringing lush texture and richness to the sparse winter board. Just a simple bowl of pasta with that new olive oil and a sprinkle of sea salt or grated cheese can be sufficient—or call it what it is, pure abundance.

But winter is also a time for feasting on meat. This is the moment in the year when pigs are slaughtered, roughly from mid-December to mid-January, and that means a wealth of fresh meat as well as sausages and hams. Hunters, the fortunate ones, bring in boar, wild birds, and deer, all to be enjoyed at the great year-end feasts of Hanukkah and Christmas, New Year's, and the Feast of the Epiphany. In Italy it sometimes seems like a perpetual banquet from December 8 (Feast of the Immaculate Conception) right through until February 2 (Candelora, the religious equivalent of Groundhog Day). Spicy, fragrant ragùs warm chill bodies exposed to the icy winds of the *tramontana*, the north wind that blows down from the Alps; those same ragùs, not incidentally, also help stretch a meager portion of meat—pork or beef, duck or lamb—to feed many hungry mouths.

Winter, wherever you are in the world, always seems like a time of ingathering. So use the season to gather friends and family around a table, pile plates high from a big and warming bowl of pasta, fill the glasses with wine, and settle in for a comforting meal. It's winter—you need no other excuse for a feast.

Spaghetti Aglio-Olio-Peperoncino
Spagetti with Garlic, Oil, and Hot Chilies

Pasta alla Pomarola Invernale
Pasta with a Winter Tomato Sauce

Bucatini all'Amatriciana

Linguine alla Dispensa Napoletana
Linguine from a Neapolitan Pantry

Fusilli with Caramelized
Onions and Bacon, Topped with
Baby Beet Greens or Spinach

Spaghetti alle Ulive Verde
Spaghetti with Green Olive Sauce

Fusilli with Radicchio di Treviso
and Walnuts

Spaghett'anatalina
*Neapolitan Christmas Eve Spaghetti
with Walnuts*

Wintertime Almond-Hazelnut
Pesto for Tagliolini

Fusilli ai Carciofi, Uova, e Pancetta
Fusilli with Artichokes, Eggs, and Pancetta

Penne Rigate con Cavolfiore alla Siciliana
*Penne Rigate with Sicilian Cauliflower
and a Touch of Chili Pepper*

Pasta with Chickpeas, Pancetta,
Garlic, and Escarole

Anelloni with Spicy Lamb and Greens

Ragù Bolognese

Tuscan Wild Mushroom and Sausage
Ragù with Sagna Riccia

Pappardelle with Duck Ragù

Ragù del Macellaio
Butcher's Ragù, with a Mix of Meats

Ragù di Maiale
Simple Pork Ragù

Pasta al Forno con Ragù e Ricotta
Oven-Baked Pasta with Ragù and Ricotta

Spaghetti con le Vongole
Classic Pasta with Clam Sauce

Tubettini con Cozze e Fagioli
Pasta with Mussels and Beans

Nodi Marini con Scungilli alla Marinara
*Pasta with Whelks in a Nontraditional
Tomato Sauce*

Fettuccine with Scallops in a Lemony Cream

Conchiglie with Shrimp and Orange Sauce

Mezze Rigatoni con Pesce Spada e Olive
Mezze Rigatoni with Swordfish and Black Olives

Manicotti with Four Cheeses

Fresh Cannelloni with a Savory Ragù

Turkish Pasta with a Garlic-Yogurt Sauce
and Brown Butter

Spaghetti Aglio-Olio-Peperoncino

Spagetti with Garlic, Oil, and Hot Chilies

T he simplest, easiest, most basic pasta recipe imaginable, this is for when hunger strikes and there's "nothing in the house to eat"—because there's always spaghetti, garlic, extra-virgin olive oil, and a dried hot red chili pepper or two. But the real beauty is this: The "sauce," such as it is, can be whipped together in the time it takes the pasta to cook.

The technique we describe is one widely used in Italy called *saltare in padella*, meaning "sautéed in the pan." The pasta is cooked until not quite done, then drained and finished in the sauce, so it absorbs flavors from the sauce and the sauce envelops the pasta. Very often, as here, a ladleful of pasta cooking water is also added to help the flavors come together.

SERVES 4 TO 6

Sea salt and freshly ground black pepper
About 1 pound (500 grams) spaghetti,
* linguine, vermicelli, or other long, thin*
* pasta*
½ cup extra-virgin olive oil
4 plump garlic cloves, minced
1 small dried hot red chili, crumbled, or
* crushed red pepper flakes to taste*
¾ cup minced flat-leaf parsley (optional)

Bring a large pot of water to a rolling boil. Following the directions on page 33, add salt and the pasta and cook, checking the package recommendations for time.

While the pasta cooks, heat the oil over medium-low heat in a saucepan large enough to hold all the pasta once it has been drained. Add the garlic and cook very gently just until it softens and starts to turn golden—do not let it brown. Add the chili and parsley (if using), along with a ladleful of starchy pasta water. Turn the heat up a notch and let the sauce simmer vigorously for about 5 minutes.

When the pasta is almost done, drain and turn immediately into the pan, mixing the pasta together with the sauce. Let simmer for a minute or two, then serve immediately with more salt and pepper.

Pasta alla Pomarola Invernale

Pasta with a Winter Tomato Sauce

If you canned your own tomatoes at last summer's seasonal peak (see page 177), use them in this sauce. Otherwise, seek out the best-quality canned whole peeled tomatoes. As we've said, DOP San Marzanos from the Agro Sarnese are our favorites (see page 16), but they are costly, to be used for special occasions, perhaps for this delicious sauce, which relies almost entirely on tomatoes—enhanced by the usual soffritto of onion, garlic, carrot, and parsley—for its splendid flavors. We recommend using only whole tomatoes since diced or crushed canned tomatoes often have too much cheap tomato paste in the mix.

Because it's winter and good-quality fresh basil is not generally available, we use dried Greek or Sicilian oregano in the sauce.

Use spaghetti, maccheroni, vermicelli, tagliatelle, linguine, spaghettoni, or any other long, thin pasta with this sauce.

SERVES 4 TO 6

1 small onion, finely chopped
1 garlic clove, finely chopped
1 medium carrot, chopped
¼ cup minced flat-leaf parsley, plus more for garnish
¼ cup extra-virgin olive oil
One 28-ounce can whole tomatoes, preferably San Marzano, with their juice, chopped (about 2 cups chopped tomatoes plus the juice)
½ teaspoon, more or less, dried oregano, preferably Greek or Sicilian; or ¼ cup slivered fresh basil leaves, plus more for garnish, if available
Sea salt and freshly ground black pepper
About 1 pound (500 grams) long, thin pasta (see headnote)
¾ cup freshly grated parmigiano-reggiano

In a heavy saucepan over low heat, gently sauté the onion, garlic, carrot, and parsley in the oil until the vegetables are soft but not brown, 10 to 15 minutes. Add the tomatoes, raise the heat to medium, and cook rapidly, further breaking up the tomatoes with the side of a spoon, until the liquid has condensed and the tomatoes have reached a thick, jammy consistency. (If using dried oregano, add it with the tomatoes.)

Bring a large pot of water to a rolling boil. Add salt and the pasta and cook following the directions on page 33.

Taste the sauce and add salt and pepper, if necessary. Stir in the fresh basil (if using). When the pasta is done, drain and immediately turn it into a warm bowl. Top with the sauce and half the parmigiano. Turn the pasta in its sauce at the table just before serving. Pass the remaining cheese with the pasta.

VARIATION: *Make this with short, stubby penne, add dried hot red chili, and call it penne all'arrabbiata.*

Bucatini all'Amatriciana

A Roman classic and a favorite of neighborhood osterie, this is usually made with guanciale, cured pork cheeks, but pancetta or even slab bacon can be substituted. Bacon will give the sauce a smoky flavor that some cooks appreciate. But it's not part of the original, and if you don't want it and can't get unsmoked guanciale or pancetta, blanch a whole small piece of slab bacon briefly in boiling water to get rid of the smokiness before dicing it.

The name *amatriciana* is the subject of endless debate. Many Romans say it refers to the town of Amatrice, high up in a mountainous spur of land that was once in the Abruzzi and is now part of the region of Lazio. It's said that the best cooks in Roman trattorie and osterie traditionally came from Amatrice, hence the adoption by Roman sophisticates of an old-fashioned mountain farmhouse dish.

In Rome this is traditionally made with bucatini, long, hollow pasta like big spaghetti with a hole in the middle, but it's also good with just about any other pasta shape, from spaghetti to spaghettoni to penne rigate to rigatoni. Romans do not like garlic in the Amatrice sauce and some even frown on the onion, but we think it adds to the sauce, just don't call it amatriciana if serving it to an authentic Roman!

SERVES 4 TO 6

1 large garlic clove, minced

1 medium onion, finely chopped

2 ounces cured pork, preferably guanciale (or pancetta, or bacon), diced small

3 tablespoons extra-virgin olive oil

1 small dried red chili pepper, crumbled

One 28-ounce can whole tomatoes, preferably San Marzano, with their juice

Sea salt and freshly ground black pepper

About 1 pound (500 grams) bucatini or other pasta (see headnote)

Freshly grated aged pecorino

Combine the garlic, onion, and pork with the oil in a saucepan and set over medium heat. Cook gently, stirring occasionally. When the meat just begins to brown and render its fat, add the chili and stir, then add the tomatoes, breaking them up with your hands as you add them. Stir to mix and continue to break up the tomatoes in the pan, using the side of a spoon. As soon as the tomatoes start to bubble, turn the heat down and simmer gently, stirring occasionally, until the sauce is dense, 20 to 30 minutes. Taste and add salt and plenty of black pepper.

Meanwhile, bring a large pot of water to a rolling boil. Add salt and the pasta and cook following the directions on page 33. As soon as the pasta is al dente, drain and turn it into a warm serving bowl. Immediately pour the sauce over the pasta and serve, turning the pasta and sauce together at the table and passing the grated pecorino.

Linguine alla Dispensa Napoletana

Linguine from a Neapolitan Pantry

Ingredients tell the story of this recipe, which is an old Neapolitan favorite, made with what's available in every dispensa, or pantry cupboard, in that crowded town, one of the oldest continuously inhabited cities in the world. Ingredients as important as these should be carefully selected to be sure you're using only the very best. Check pages 16–31 for more information.

Black olives, for instance: Use naturally cured olives, perhaps small Gaeta olives, and be sure to take the pits out. If you can't find Gaetas, use wrinkled, salt-cured Moroccan or French olives (sometimes called oil-cured olives, though they're not actually cured in oil at all). And anchovies, for another instance: We love the elusive meaty, salty, umami flavor anchovies give to just about anything they're added to. They're a key component to this dish, so use a lot or a little, depending on your own preference, but don't leave them out.

SERVES 6

6 to 8 oil-packed anchovy fillets
2 tablespoons salt-packed capers
1 cup pitted black olives, preferably Gaeta
Sea salt, for the pasta
About 1 pound (500 grams) linguine,
vermicelli, spaghetti, or other long, thin
pasta
¼ cup extra-virgin olive oil
2 garlic cloves, chopped
½ cup minced flat-leaf parsley
Freshly ground black pepper

Chop the anchovy fillets into small pieces. Rinse the capers thoroughly to rid them of salt, then chop coarsely. Coarsely chop the pitted olives.

Bring a large pot of water to a rolling boil. Add salt and the pasta and cook following the directions on page 33, checking the package recommendations for time. Linguine will take 10 to 12 minutes, thinner pasta a little less—but follow the package directions.

While the pasta is cooking, combine the oil and garlic in a pan over low heat and cook gently until the garlic softens and just begins to turn golden. Do not let it brown. Add the capers and olives with a ladleful of boiling pasta water. Add the parsley, with a little more water if it seems necessary, along with several grinds of pepper. Let the mixture cook at a bare simmer, then, just before the pasta is done, add the anchovy bits and mix well, pressing with a fork to dissolve the anchovies into the sauce.

As soon as the pasta is done, drain and turn it into a warm bowl. Immediately add the sauce and turn to mix well. Serve immediately.

Fusilli with Caramelized Onions and Bacon, Topped with Baby Beet Greens or Spinach

Quick and easy, this is the pasta dish that started us thinking together about the seasonality of pasta and what a terrific and (mostly) stress-free way it is to put good food on the table. Use any pasta shape you wish with this, although we prefer curly fusilli or cavatappi to trap all the tasty bits of bacon and caramelized onion.

SERVES 6

½ cup diced lean bacon

2 tablespoons extra-virgin olive oil

2 medium white onions, halved and very thinly sliced

Sea salt and freshly ground black pepper

1 teaspoon sugar

1 pound baby beet greens, spinach, or another winter green, rinsed, stemmed, and coarsely chopped, if necessary

About 1 pound (500 grams) fusilli, cavatappi, or other curly pasta

Freshly grated parmigiano-reggiano, grana padano, or pecorino

Combine the bacon and oil in a wide heavy skillet large enough to hold all the onions and set over medium heat. Cook, stirring frequently, until the bacon starts to brown, then add all the sliced onions along with a little salt and plenty of pepper. Stir to combine everything well. Lower the heat and cook the onions slowly, stirring frequently, as they soften and start to caramelize. After about 10 minutes the onions will be thoroughly softened but still pale in color. Add the sugar and stir to mix well. Continue cooking for 30 to 40 minutes or longer, stirring frequently, until the onions are caramelized. The point is not to brown and crisp the onions as would happen if you were to fry them over higher heat, but rather to let them braise gently, softening and releasing their sweetness so that they actually caramelize in their own sugars, helped along by the added teaspoon of sugar.

As the onions cook down, bring a large pot of water to a rolling boil. Add salt and the pasta and cook following the directions on page 33, checking the package recommendations for time.

By the time the pasta water comes to a boil, the onions should be ready. Have the greens trimmed and ready to toss with the cooked pasta.

When the pasta is al dente, drain and turn it immediately into a warm bowl. Top with the onion-bacon mixture and add the greens. Toss together quickly so that the heat of the pasta and onions slightly wilts the greens. Add a handful of grated cheese and serve immediately, with more cheese to pass at the table.

Spaghetti alle Ulive Verde

Spaghetti with Green Olive Sauce

A traditional pasta from Puglia, this is a fine example of *la cucina povera*, or how poor cooks, using the best ingredients available to them, often make superb dishes. Here, plain green olives take the place of more expensive meat or fish, and crisp fried bread crumbs stand in for the luxury of grated cheese; the result is a meager dish that is nonetheless full of good flavors.

The best olives for this, if you can find them, are big green olives from Castelvetrano in Sicily; truth to tell, just about any good-quality green olives will do, as long as they are simply brine-cured and not mixed with other flavorings.

SERVES 6

6 tablespoons extra-virgin olive oil
¾ cup unflavored bread crumbs
6 anchovy fillets
3 plump garlic cloves, peeled and left whole
1 small dried red chili pepper, crumbled, or
  crushed red pepper flakes to taste
1½ cups coarsely chopped pitted green olives
  (1 to 2 pounds whole olives before pitting)
Sea salt
About 1 pound (500 grams) spaghetti or other
  long, thin pasta

Heat 1 tablespoon of the oil in a small saucepan. Add the bread crumbs and toast until they are golden brown and crisp. Remove from the heat and set aside. Chop the anchovy fillets coarsely.

In another saucepan, heat 3 tablespoons of the oil. Gently cook the garlic over medium heat until the cloves are brown. Add the anchovies and, using a fork, stir and crush them into the oil. Crush the garlic cloves slightly to release their flavor, then remove the whole cloves and discard. Add the chili pepper and olives and let them cook for about 3 minutes, just long enough to mix the flavors. Set aside.

Bring a large pot of water to a rolling boil. Add the salt (keeping mind that the anchovies will add saltiness) and the pasta and cook following the directions on page 33.

When the pasta is done, drain it and turn it into a warm bowl. Immediately add the remaining 2 tablespoons olive oil and the bread crumbs to the olive sauce and turn this over the pasta. Toss and serve immediately.

Fusilli with Radicchio di Treviso and Walnuts

Radicchio is a gorgeous winter vegetable, its dappled maroon-red leaves decorating gardens, farm stands, and salad bowls. There are actually several varieties of this handsome winter crop. Round balls of radicchio di Chioggia, looking like small red cabbages, are easily found in North American supermarket produce sections where they're considered salad "greens"—and delicious too with a crunch and edgy bitterness. Radicchio di Treviso (or radicchio di Verona), on the other hand, may take a little searching for. It has the same coloration, but its shape is long and slender, and, unlike its cousin, it is often cooked—painted with oil and roasted whole on the grill, or chopped and braised to serve with pasta, as in this recipe, or in a risotto. If you come across it, snap it up—its bitterness is a welcome clue to the health-giving antioxidants that lurk inside.

If you can't find Treviso, could you do this with radicchio di Chioggia, the round kind? Yes, you could, but it does not have the refreshing bitterness of Treviso and, because it contains a good deal more water, it will take more time to caramelize successfully.

Keep in mind that the best ricotta is always the freshest, and even better if it's made with whey from cheese making, either sheep or goat, but cow's-milk ricotta will also do for this dish (see page 22 for more on ricotta).

SERVES 4 TO 6

1 medium onion, diced
¼ cup extra-virgin olive oil
1 cup walnut halves
4 cups coarsely chopped or sliced radicchio
  di Treviso
1 cup real ricotta
Sea salt and freshly ground black pepper
About 1 pound (500 grams) fusilli or other
  short, complex pasta shape

Combine the onion with the oil in a deep skillet large enough to hold all the sauce ingredients and set over low heat. Give the onion an occasional stir, but otherwise just let it cook gently while you prepare the rest of the sauce—the onion should melt in the oil but not brown.

Set the oven on 300°F.

While the onion is cooking, spread the walnut halves on a cookie sheet and toast for several minutes, until the nuts begin to release their odor. It's okay if they turn a little golden, but don't let them get deep brown.

When the onion slices are done, stir in the chopped radicchio, cover the pan, and return to the heat, raising it slightly to medium-low to cook. Check from time to time—if the radicchio doesn't release enough liquid, add a couple of tablespoons of hot water to the pan. When the radicchio is thoroughly wilted, uncover the pan and

raise the heat again, this time to medium, cooking vigorously to caramelize slightly.

Chop the walnuts coarsely. Set aside a couple of tablespoons to use as a garnish and stir the rest of the walnuts into the radicchio. Add salt and plenty of pepper and keep the sauce warm while you cook the pasta.

Bring a large pot of water to a rolling boil. Add salt and the pasta and cook following the package directions, until al dente. Just before draining the pasta, add a ladleful of pasta water to the radicchio sauce and return the sauce to a very low simmer. Remove the pan from the heat and stir in the ricotta.

Drain the pasta, transfer immediately to a warm bowl, add the sauce, and toss to mix thoroughly. Garnish with the reserved walnuts and serve immediately.

VARIATION *If you wish, pass a bowl of freshly grated parmigiano-reggiano to add to the pasta at the table.*

Spaghett'anatalina

Neapolitan Christmas Eve Spaghetti with Walnuts

Even though the long Advent fast leading up to Christmas is no longer obligatory for Catholics, La Vigilia (Christmas Eve) in Italy is invariably meatless. This delightful dish, which also celebrates the early winter harvest of prized walnuts from the Sorrento peninsula south of Naples, is a Neapolitan favorite for the feast.

SERVES 4 TO 6

1¼ *cups walnuts, the fresher the better*
Sea salt
About 1 pound (500 grams) spaghetti,
   linguine, or similar-shaped pasta
½ *cup plus 1 tablespoon extra-virgin olive oil*
6 *garlic cloves, finely chopped*
10 *anchovy fillets, coarsely chopped*
½ *cup unflavored bread crumbs*
1 *cup minced flat-leaf parsley*

Set the oven on 300°F.

Spread the walnuts out on a cookie sheet and toast in the oven for several minutes, or until they begin to release their fragrance. It's okay if they turn a little golden, but don't let them get deep brown. Remove from the oven, and when the nuts are cool, chop them coarsely and set aside.

When you're ready to cook, bring a large pot of water to a rolling boil. Add salt and pasta and start to cook following the directions on page 33.

While the water is heating and the pasta is cooking, finish the sauce: Over low heat, combine ½ cup of the oil and the garlic in a saucepan large enough to hold all the cooked pasta. Cook gently, stirring occasionally, until the garlic starts to soften. Add the anchovies and continue cooking, using a fork to mash the anchovies into the oil. Stir in the chopped walnuts and cook for about 1 minute.

Meanwhile, toast the bread crumbs in the remaining 1 tablespoon oil in a small saucepan, tossing and stirring to brown and crisp them.

When the pasta is almost al dente, remove about ¾ cup pasta water and add to the walnut-anchovy sauce. Let it simmer while you drain the pasta, then add the pasta directly to the walnut sauce, turning to coat it well with the sauce as it finishes its last minute or so of cooking. Taste and add salt if necessary (there may be sufficient salt from the anchovies).

Turn onto a warm serving platter, garnish with the parsley and toasted bread crumbs, and serve immediately.

Wintertime Almond-Hazelnut Pesto for Tagliolini

Far from the fresh basil of summertime pesto, this pounded almond and hazelnut sauce is perfect for winter nights. You could use all almonds or all hazelnuts if you prefer. Don't overdo the chili pepper here—too much will kill the nutty flavors. Our preferred ground chilies are Aleppo pepper or piment d'Espelette, warmly spicy but not setting your palate on fire.

We make this with any kind of long, skinny pasta.

SERVES 6

½ cup hazelnuts
½ cup extra-virgin olive oil
½ cup blanched almonds
¼ cup freshly squeezed orange juice
1 tablespoon freshly grated orange zest
Sea salt and freshly ground black pepper
¼ teaspoon medium-hot dried red chili
  pepper, or more to taste
¼ cup freshly grated parmigiano-reggiano,
  plus more to pass
About 1 pound (500 grams) long, skinny pasta

Set the oven on 350°F.

Toss the hazelnuts in a bowl with about ½ tablespoon of the oil, then spread on one end of a cookie sheet. In the same bowl, toss the blanched almonds with another ½ tablespoon of oil and spread them on the other end of the sheet. Transfer to the oven and toast, stirring occasionally, until they are golden brown, about 10 minutes. Remove and set aside to cool slightly.

Wrap the hazelnuts in a kitchen towel and rub vigorously—this will remove a lot of the loose brown skin. Don't be concerned if you can't get it all off. When you've cleaned them as well as you can, combine with the almonds in a bowl.

Take about ¼ cup nuts and chop coarsely. Set aside to be used as a garnish for the finished pasta.

In a blender or food processor, combine the remaining nuts with the remaining oil, the orange juice, orange zest, and a pinch of salt. Puree to a smooth butter, then add black pepper and the chili pepper to taste. Blend in the grated parmigiano and taste again, adding more salt if necessary.

Bring a large pot of water to a rolling boil. Add salt and the pasta and cook following the directions on page 33.

While the pasta is cooking, transfer the nut sauce to a saucepan large enough to hold the drained pasta with its sauce. As the pasta finishes cooking, add ½ cup of the pasta water to the saucepan with the nut sauce. Bring to a simmer.

Drain the pasta and immediately stir it into the sauce. Let cook for just about 1 minute, then turn into a warm bowl. Garnish with the reserved nuts and more grated cheese, if you wish.

Fusilli ai Carciofi, Uova, e Pancetta

Fusilli with Artichokes, Eggs, and Pancetta

See page 13 for instructions on cleaning artichokes. If you use the big ones from California, you will need 4 or 5; if you have access to smaller, more tender artichokes, you might need 6 or 8, and you may not need to clean out the spiny chokes. Could you make this with frozen artichoke hearts? Yes, in a pinch. The sauce won't have the bright artichoke flavor that fresh ones bring to it, but it will still be very good. If you use frozen artichoke hearts, you will need enough to make 3 cups when they're sliced.

SERVES 4 TO 6

½ lemon, for preparing the artichokes
4 or 5 large artichokes, trimmed (enough to make 3 cups, sliced)
1 medium onion, minced
2 ounces pancetta, diced small
2 tablespoons extra-virgin olive oil
Sea salt and freshly ground black pepper
1 cup dry white wine
About 1 pound (500 grams) fusilli or other short, stubby pasta (conchiglie, small shells, and the like)
2 large eggs
1 teaspoon freshly squeezed lemon juice
2 tablespoons freshly grated pecorino or parmigiano-reggiano, plus more to pass

Prepare the artichokes as described on page 13. Slice the trimmed artichokes quite thin, top to bottom, dropping the slices into a bowl of acidulated water. (If you're using frozen artichoke hearts, simply slice them, top to bottom, and set aside.)

In a heavy saucepan set over medium-low heat, gently braise the onion and pancetta in the oil until the onion is soft but not brown. Drain the artichokes and add to the pan, stirring to mix well. Cover and leave to stew gently for 10 minutes.

Meanwhile, bring a teakettle of water to a boil. Add a pinch of salt to the artichokes and then the wine, a little at a time, mixing after each addition and adding more as the wine evaporates. When all the wine has evaporated, add boiling water just to cover the vegetables, cover again, and cook for 30 minutes, or until the water has been absorbed and the vegetables are tender. (If using frozen artichokes, 15 minutes will be plenty.) Remove from the heat and set aside.

Bring a large pot of water to a rolling boil. Add salt and the pasta and cook following the directions on page 33, checking the package recommendations for time—10 to 11 minutes for fusilli.

While the pasta is cooking, return the artichokes to low heat to warm up. Beat the eggs in a small bowl and beat in the grated pecorino. Add the lemon juice and lots of pepper. As soon as artichokes are hot, remove from the heat and slowly add the egg mixture, stirring constantly with a wooden spoon. The heat from the artichokes will thicken the eggs to a sauce; do not put the pan back on the heat—you don't want to scramble the eggs.

Have ready a warm bowl. Drain the pasta when done, turn it into the artichoke sauce, and stir to mix well. Transfer to the warm bowl. The hot pasta will further thicken the eggs. Serve immediately, passing more grated cheese, if you wish.

Penne Rigate con Cavolfiore alla Siciliana

Penne Rigate with Sicilian Cauliflower and a Touch of Chili Pepper

Creamy white cauliflower is a Brassica, like broccoli and Brussels sprouts, and like them it is astonishingly good for us—eat Brassicas at least two or three times a week, nutritionists advise. It's also delicious, which means it's easy to add to your menu—especially when prepared Sicilian fashion, like this recipe with its touches of chili pepper, golden raisins, and pine nuts. Romanesco, the lime-green version of cauliflower, works just as well in this recipe. Or try mixing the two together, for a green-and-white presentation. This way of combining pasta and cauliflower is a favorite of our friend Salvatore Denaro, a Sicilian chef who cooks and gardens in Umbria.

SERVES 6

⅓ cup extra-virgin olive oil

*2 leeks, white and light green parts, thinly
  sliced to make 2 cups*

2 garlic cloves, thinly sliced

*About 1 pound cauliflower, separated into
  1-inch florets*

*1 fresh red or green chili pepper, seeded and
  thinly sliced*

½ cup dry white wine

*½ cup golden sultana raisins, plumped in hot
  water and drained*

Sea salt and freshly ground black pepper

About 1 pound (500 grams) penne rigate

½ cup freshly grated sharp pecorino

½ cup pine nuts, toasted

Combine the olive oil with the sliced leeks and garlic in a large, deep skillet and set over low heat. Cook, shaking the pan and stirring, until the leeks are softened but not browned. This will take about 10 minutes.

Add the cauliflower and the sliced chili. Cover the pan and cook over low heat, stirring occasionally, until the cauliflower is tender, 10 to 15 minutes. Check from time to time to be sure the vegetables are not sticking to the pan. If they do, add a tablespoon or two of water or some of the wine. When the cauliflower is tender, add the wine along with ¼ cup water and raise the heat slightly. Simmer over medium-low heat until the liquid has reduced to about ½ cup, about 10 minutes. Toss in the plumped and drained raisins and simmer just long enough to mix all the flavors together.

While the vegetables are cooking, bring a large pot of water to a rolling boil. Add salt and the pasta and cook following the directions on page 33, until al dente. Drain the pasta, then toss with the vegetables in the skillet. Turn into a warm serving bowl, toss again with the pecorino and pine nuts, season with salt and black pepper, and serve.

Pasta with Chickpeas, Pancetta, Garlic, and Escarole

Hearty bean and pasta dishes are welcome fare on cold winter nights. This one uses chickpeas (aka garbanzos or ceci). If you have a lot of small, mixed pasta shapes in your larder, it's a great way to use them up. Otherwise, use cavatappi or a similar small, twisted shape.

If you don't have pancetta, bacon is fine to substitute. If you can't find escarole, use spicy broccoli rabe (rapini), first trimming it of tough stems and slicing the leaves. In fact, almost any wintertime green does well in this dish.

This is easily converted into a vegetarian dish simply by omitting the pancetta and adding another tablespoon of extra-virgin olive oil.

Pasta and legume dishes are often served like a soup, in a deep bowl, and are generally quite a bit saucier than, for instance, a pasta with tomato sauce. Serve it with forks and spoons so that those who deem it a soup can spoon it up, and others can use their forks to mash the beans in the thick and tasty liquid.

SERVES 6

2 ounces diced pancetta, guanciale, or bacon (about ⅓ cup)

1 tablespoon extra-virgin olive oil, plus more for garnish

½ cup dried chickpeas, soaked overnight in plenty of water

1 small yellow onion, very coarsely chopped

1 garlic clove, crushed with the flat blade of a knife

1 bay leaf

1 fresh rosemary sprig

Sea salt and freshly ground black pepper

½ pound pasta (see headnote)

¾ to 1 pound escarole or spicy greens, rinsed and sliced into 1-inch ribbons

Freshly grated parmigiano-reggiano

Bring a teakettle of water to a boil. Combine the pancetta and olive oil in a saucepan large enough to hold the legumes. Set over medium heat and cook, stirring, until the pancetta has given up a lot of fat and started to brown.

Drain the chickpeas and add to the pancetta, along with the onion, garlic, bay leaf, and rosemary. Cover with boiling water to a depth of 1 inch. Set on the stove over medium heat. When the liquid is simmering once more, turn the heat down to low, cover the pan, and cook until tender, 1 to 2 hours, depending on the age of the legumes. Check the pan from time to time, adding more water if necessary; otherwise, just let the chickpeas cook and soften.

When the chickpeas are done and most of the cooking water has been absorbed, add salt to taste and plenty of pepper.

Remove and discard the bay leaf and rosemary.

Bring a large pot of water to a rolling boil. Add a big spoonful of salt, then the pasta and escarole together. Cook until the pasta is al dente, 8 to 12 minutes, or even a bit longer. Using a slotted spoon, scoop out the pasta and escarole and transfer directly to the chickpeas. Now it's time for you to judge—if you want a soup, add more of the pasta-escarole cooking water to the pan. If you want a dish to eat with a fork, let the spoonsful of pasta and escarole drip thoroughly before adding them to the chickpeas. Whatever you do, however, there should be a lot of moisture in the mixture at the end.

Serve in warmed deep soup plates. Garnish each plate with a good dribble of olive oil and pass parmigiano to top the dish.

COOK'S TIP *In old-fashioned country kitchens where this dish is a favorite, cooks often put in the bottom of each plate a slice of toasted country-style bread, rubbed with a cut garlic clove and with olive oil dribbled on top, before spooning the beans and pasta over it.*

Some cooks like to add a tablespoon of tomato paste dissolved in ¼ cup boiling water, stirring it into the chickpeas before the pasta and escarole are added.

Anelloni with Spicy Lamb and Greens

Sara makes this popular dish at her restaurant, using a pasta shape called anelloni, tubular rings made by Pastificio Masciarelli. The rings are smooth on the outside and ridged inside, about an inch in diameter and a little more than an inch long. Although typical of the Abruzzi, these anelloni are not always easy to find here, but the sauce is so delicious it will go with almost any hearty pasta shape. Try, for example, calamari, paccheri, or large ridged shells.

Spicing the ground lamb with North African flavors, including cumin and harissa, makes something similar to North African merguez sausage. If you have access to good-quality merguez, use that instead, discarding the skin and crumbling the sausage meat.

Mustard greens are easily available, but if you prefer, you may use broccoli rabe, in which case blanch the greens in boiling water for 2 minutes before adding them to the pan with the lamb.

SERVES 6

¾ pound lean ground lamb

1 to 2 tablespoons dried Greek or Sicilian oregano

1 tablespoon Aleppo pepper, more or less to taste

1 teaspoon Moroccan harissa, or more to taste

1 teaspoon ground cumin

1 teaspoon ground coriander

4 garlic cloves, finely minced

¼ cup finely chopped flat-leaf parsley

Sea salt and freshly ground black pepper

2 tablespoons extra-virgin olive oil

¼ cup heavy cream

1 bunch mustard greens, trimmed and sliced about 1 inch thick (6 to 8 cups)

About 1 pound (500 grams) anelloni or any other ribbed tubular shape

¼ cup toasted unflavored bread crumbs

3 tablespoons freshly grated parmigiano-reggiano, or to taste

Mix the lamb in a bowl with the oregano, Aleppo pepper, harissa, cumin, coriander, garlic, and parsley, kneading to mix well. Add salt and black pepper to taste.

Add the olive oil to a saucepan large enough to hold all the ingredients, including the pasta, and set over medium heat. Add the spicy lamb mixture and cook, sautéing and crumbling the lamb, until it has changed color. Do *not* let the lamb dry out until crisp and brown. Add the cream and, if necessary, a tablespoon or two of hot water; lower the heat to medium-low and let the liquid simmer for 15 to 20 minutes. Add the sliced mustard greens and let them just wilt in the liquid in the pan.

Meanwhile, bring a large pot of water to a rolling boil. Add salt and the pasta and cook, following directions on page 33, for 8 minutes, or until it is almost but not quite done.

If the meat gets too dry in the meantime, add a ladleful of pasta water to the saucepan.

When the pasta is almost done, drain (but not too thoroughly) and add to the meat and greens in the pan. Toss to combine and finish cooking, 3 to 4 minutes over medium heat.

Transfer the pasta to a warm serving bowl. Sprinkle the top with toasted bread crumbs and parmigiano and serve immediately, passing more cheese at the table, if desired.

Ragù

Though the terms *bolognese* and *ragù* are often used interchangeably, bolognese is in fact just one type of ragù, geographically specific to Bologna and justifiably famous, but only one version of a technique that, like so much else in the Italian kitchen, exists in countless slightly different versions, depending on where we find ourselves on the boot. In a sense ragù is like a dialect of the Italian kitchen. Spoken dialects are still strongly regional in Italy: Sicilian is very different from Venetian, which is different from what's spoken deep in Puglia's Salento, but they are all recognizably Italian nonetheless. Just so, all ragùs share a basic structure that tells you they're Italian even when what you're eating in Napoli is so different from what you might be served in Genova or Padova or Verona—but it's all ragù. Indeed, ragù is found all over Italy, in every province, in every village and town, and if the technique is basic, the flavors, aromas, and ingredients change from one region to another, often from one household to another, to yield an astonishing variety. A book could be written, and perhaps it has been, simply on ragùs.

We love spending lazy winter Sundays at home with a pot of ragù simmering on the stove, warming the house and scenting the air. It might take a couple of hours to cook a true ragù, with the depth of flavor that comes from long, slow cooking, but the effort itself, once started, is minimal—just keep an eye on the pot, don't let the ragù dry out or burn, and the slow cooking will work its magic to transform tough fibrous dark meats into tender fragments melded with aromatic vegetables and a glaze of tomato. We often make big pots of the sauce and freeze it in smaller portions, providing easy dinner solutions in the months ahead.

So what exactly is ragù?

One authoritative Italian-English dictionary translates it as "stew"—which it most definitely is not, unless you define stew as a meat-based mixture cooked very, very slowly for a very long period of time. But a true ragù, meaty and dense with many layers of flavors and aromas, is one of the most glorious productions of *la cucina Italiana*, and you certainly can't say that about stew in the Anglo-Saxon kitchen. Call ragù sauce instead, because in almost every instance that we've experienced, ragù is made to be a sauce or condiment for pasta—often, because of its richness, a sauce for the Sunday pasta that is the cornerstone of the Italian week and the crown of the Italian family table.

At its most basic, ragù is meat (pork, beef, veal, rabbit, wild game, duck), ground or chopped or, especially in the south, a whole piece rolled and tied, cooked very slowly with some kind of liquid (tomatoes most often, occasionally wine, sometimes stock, sometimes just plain water) and some kind of vegetables (onions, garlic, carrots, parsley, celery, herbs) until the meat is so tender that it falls apart and the chopped vegetables dissolve into the liquid. At that stage the ragù is thick and unctuous, suitable to coat pasta, in whatever shape. (And ragù isn't always made with meat—there are a couple of vegetarian recipes in our collection as well, and they are fully as rich and complex as the more typical meat ragù.)

Once you've understood the basic concept of ragù, deciding what to cook, what to combine, what flavors to use, becomes easy, based on the amount of time you have and the availability of ingredients. It's a great way to extend small pieces of meat to provide for a number of people, and it's also a terrific technique for tenderizing cheaper, tougher cuts such as oxtail or chicken livers. At Sara's restaurant Porsena, she makes a tasty ragù with the rib meat trimmings from pork racks used just down the street at her pork-sandwich bar Porchetta. At Porsena too prosciutto trimmings and scraps are used as a base for ragù in place of more usual pancetta or guanciale. Toasted in the pan with aromatic vegetables at the beginning of the whole process, these pork bits add richness to the overall sauce.

Ragù varies in texture, depending on whether it is made with ground meat, with small pieces of meat that fall apart as they slowly braise, or with meat on the bone—the bones adding richness and gelatinous consistency to the overall sauce, then being removed before the sauce is finished. It also varies in flavor, depending not just on what kind of meat goes into it but also on whether you use a simple soffritto of onion-garlic-carrot-parsley or add different vegetables, leeks or shallots, for instance, or wild mushrooms, whether fresh or dried. As for aromatics—bay leaves are almost required in northern Italy, a pinch of sun-dried oregano in the south, rosemary and fennel pollen in Tuscany, sage in Umbria, juniper with wild boar, aromatic flat-leaf parsley universally.

Here's how Sara describes making ragù in her restaurant:

I like to play around with the texture of ragù and because I have a big kitchen, an industrial meat grinder, and a full-time prep cook, I might make a duck or rabbit ragù with ground raw meat. (If I'm cooking at home without all that help, on the other hand, I'm just as happy slowly cooking the meat until tender, then picking the meat off the bones and mixing it with aromatic vegetables and cooking liquid.) When constructing a ragù, I decide what seasonings will go into the first step, slowly cooking vegetables in a little olive oil or in cured pork fat from prosciutto scraps or pancetta, then which herbs to add with the vegetables—rosemary, bay leaves, sage, as well as parsley and maybe even a little grated lemon zest. If I want a hearty southern ragù, I might crumble a couple of dried chili peppers in too. Once the vegetables have wilted and become translucent, I add water or wine, just a cup or two, perhaps with a couple of tablespoons of tomato paste diluted in the liquid, and let the vegetables cook more briskly until just a couple of spoonsful of liquid are left and the vegetables are really tender and well cooked. When the liquid is cooked away, I add the meat, raw if it's ground meat, or seared first in olive oil if it's in chunks. At this point either more liquid is needed or, in the case of the ground meat, its own juices might be sufficient. If I'm using canned tomatoes, I add them after the meat has begun to brown. Then I put a lid on the pot and either slow braise it at about two hundred degrees in the oven or simmer it slowly on top of the stove.

Our chef friend Cathy Whims, from Nostrana restaurant in Portland, Oregon, made an interesting point about ragù when she visited us in Tuscany. Looking at a gorgeously mahogany-colored ragù with a half inch of red oil on top in our local butcher shop, Cathy said, "That's how you know it's done—all the fat has been cooked out of the meat and it's just shimmering on top." It's a good point.

It all sounds simple, doesn't it? And it really is. All it takes is time, and much of that time is spent simply waiting while the ragù slowly turns from a bare assembly of raw meat and vegetables into the most sumptuous, flavorful, elegant, and seductive sauce imaginable.

NOTE *You'll find a few more recipes for hearty ragùs in the Autumn chapter as well.*

Ragù Bolognese

This is the true ragù as made by generations of cooks in Bologna. At least, it is according to Anna Nanni, the *sfoglina* (pasta maker) and supervisor of ragù production at Trattoria da Amerigo, a Michelin-starred restaurant in the little town of Savigno, tucked into the hills of the Colline Bolognese, south of Bologna itself. Other cooks may have other interpretations: Some say milk, some say no milk; some say pork and veal, some say pork, sausage, and beef. It all depends on what your very own mother and grandmother and great-grandmother did. One thing to keep in mind, however: According to everyone we talked with, a true ragù bolognese is not at all a tomato sauce, although it may have more or less tomatoes in it. But think of it as a meat sauce and you will come closer to the truth.

The simplicity of this preparation belies the rich and complex meld of flavors that results from a long, slow cooking process during which everything comes together. In the finest ragù, you should not be able to taste meat or tomatoes or carrots or wine but an amalgam, a symphony, in which the whole is far, far greater than its parts.

In Bologna ragù is usually served either with the region's handmade egg tagliatelle (see page 45) or in a multilayered lasagna, the pasta layers as thin as sheets of silk (see our directions for handmade pasta on pages 40–42, and for assembling lasagna on page 46). You could also serve it with an excellent artisanal pasta secca such as pappardelle, lasagnette, or short pastas such as casarecce or cavatappi.

Note that Anna's beginning soffritto—finely minced onion, carrot, and celery—is cooked very slowly in oil and butter over low heat for a very long time, up to 40 minutes, stirring occasionally with a wooden spoon. This, she feels, gives a richly caramelized vegetable base to the sauce, vital to its delicious success.

**MAKES 4 CUPS RAGÙ,
ENOUGH FOR 6 TO 8 SERVINGS**

¼ cup extra-virgin olive oil
2 tablespoons unsalted butter
¾ cup finely minced yellow onion
½ cup finely minced carrot
½ cup finely minced celery (use the darkest green stalks)
½ pound lean ground pork
½ pound lean ground beef

Sea salt and freshly ground black pepper
2 slices pancetta, very finely minced
½ cup dry red wine
2 tablespoons double concentrate of tomato
One 28-ounce can whole tomatoes, preferably San Marzano, with their juice
1 cup whole milk

Combine the oil and butter and set over low heat until the butter has melted. Then add the onion, carrot, and celery and cook very gently, stirring with a wooden spoon from time to time, until the vegetables have melted in the fat and are beginning to caramelize and brown. This may take as long as 40 minutes, but it's essential to the final flavors.

Stir in the pork and beef and continue to cook, stirring and breaking up the meats with a fork, until they have changed color. Add salt and pepper to taste, then stir in the minced pancetta and continue cooking until the pancetta bits have dissolved. Add the wine and raise the heat a little, continuing to stir the ingredients in the pan. Let the wine bubble and reduce, throwing off its alcohol.

Now add the concentrate (if the concentrate is very thick, dilute it in about ¼ cup hot water before adding to the pan), stirring it in. Add the tomatoes, breaking them up with your hands, along with all their juice. Turn the heat down to the lowest possible setting and cook very gently, uncovered, for 3 hours. From time to time, as the juices cook down, add a little boiling water or stock to the pan. At the end of the cooking time, add the milk and cook for another 15 to 20 minutes. The sauce will have lost its bright red tomato essence and will smell (and taste) richly of meat.

VARIATION *Some Bolognese cooks like to add a couple of chopped chicken livers with the ground meats. As you stir the meats, use your fork to crush the chicken livers into the mix.*

Tuscan Wild Mushroom and Sausage Ragù with Sagna Riccia

In winter we make this with wild porcini that were sliced and dried in the autumn sun; they have a very different flavor from fresh mushrooms, with a more intense muskiness that recalls the bosky aromas of the forest floor. But if you live in a part of the world where fresh wild mushrooms are available in winter, by all means use fresh ones instead—about one-half pound of fresh mushrooms will take the place of the dried ones in the recipe. Clean wild mushrooms very well, using a soft brush to get rid of any bits of soil, but rinse only briefly right before you are about to use them so they won't absorb too much liquid (see page 30). Add sliced fresh mushrooms to the skillet with the onion, carrot, celery, and parsley, and let them sauté gently with the vegetables before adding the tomatoes.

We use a pasta shape called sagna riccia, long, flat noodles with a ruffled edge, available from Pastificio Masciarelli; or try Benedetto Cavalieri's similar shape called lasagnotte. Pappardelle would work well here too.

SERVES 6

1½ ounces dried porcini

1 pound sweet Italian sausages

2 tablespoons extra-virgin olive oil

1 medium onion, minced

1 medium carrot, minced

1 celery stalk, minced

¼ cup minced flat-leaf parsley

One 28-ounce can whole tomatoes, preferably
  San Marzano, with their juice, chopped

½ teaspoon chopped fresh thyme

3 or 4 fresh rosemary sprigs, coarsely chopped

Sea salt and freshly ground black pepper

About 1 pound (500 grams) pasta (see
  headnote)

½ cup freshly grated parmigiano-reggiano,
  plus more to pass, if desired

Put the dried porcini in a small bowl and cover with very hot water. Set aside for 30 minutes to soften, then strain through a fine-mesh sieve, reserving the mushroom liquid. Rinse the mushrooms briefly in running water and chop coarsely.

Open up the sausage skins with a sharp knife and remove the insides. Crumble the sausage meat into a heavy skillet and set over medium-low heat. If the sausage is very dry, add a tablespoon of olive oil; otherwise, sauté the sausage slowly in its own fat until it has all changed color. Then stir in the onion, carrot, celery, and parsley and cook, again slowly, until the vegetables have softened considerably. Once the vegetables are soft, add the tomatoes and their juice, breaking the tomatoes up with your hands or using the side of a cooking

spoon to chop them in the pan. Add the thyme and rosemary and leave the sauce to simmer very gently, uncovered, until it is thickened, 20 to 25 minutes. Now stir in the reserved strained mushroom liquid and the coarsely chopped mushrooms. Continue cooking until the ragù is very thick. Taste and add salt and pepper. Keep the sauce warm while you cook the pasta.

Bring a large pot of water to a rolling boil. Add salt and the pasta and cook following the directions on page 33, until done, 10 to 12 minutes. Put about 1 cup of the ragù in the bottom of a warm serving bowl, then drain the pasta and turn it immediately into the bowl. Add another ladleful of ragù and turn the pasta in the sauce. Pour the remaining sauce over the pasta, sprinkle with the grated parmigiano, and serve immediately, passing more grated cheese, if you wish.

Pappardelle with Duck Ragù

Pappardelle are wide, flat noodles, sometimes with a ruffled edge. They are a tradition in Arezzo, our Tuscan shire town, where they're often served with wild game—hare is a local favorite. Duck makes a great accompaniment too, especially when slowly roasted for several hours with nothing but salt and pepper, until much of the fat has melted off and the meat is succulent, tender, and full of flavor, almost like a confit. Another benefit from this method: about a cup of duck fat, fragrant with salt and pepper, that can be stored in a jar in the refrigerator and used whenever sautéed potatoes are on the menu. (Julia Child always had a jar of duck fat on hand for just such an occasion.)

You could roast a whole duck for this sumptuous recipe, but we find readily available duck legs are easier to work with than the whole bird.

SERVES 6

4 whole duck legs (about 3½ pounds)
4 tablespoons extra-virgin olive oil
Sea salt and freshly ground black pepper
2 bay leaves
5 garlic cloves
2 ounces pancetta or bacon, diced small
    (about ½ cup)
½ cup chopped celery
½ cup chopped carrot
½ cup chopped red onion
2 tablespoons chopped fresh sage leaves
1 cup dry red wine, preferably a Chianti
    Rufina or Chianti Classico
One 28-ounce can whole tomatoes, preferably
    San Marzano, with their juice
About 1 pound (500 grams) pappardelle
½ cup freshly grated parmigiano reggiano
    or Tuscan pecorino, plus more to pass,
    if desired

Prick the skin of the duck legs all over with a fork. (This will help release the duck fat.) Rub 2 tablespoons of the olive oil all over the duck legs and sprinkle generously with salt and pepper. Set the duck legs in the bottom of a roasting pan in which they will just fit comfortably and add the bay leaves and 1 of the garlic cloves. Transfer to a cold oven and set the temperature on 300°F. Leave the duck legs to roast very gently for 3 hours, then raise the heat to 375°F and roast for an additional 30 minutes, or until the duck legs are brown all over and the skin is crisp. When the duck is finished, take the legs out of the fat and set aside. Strain the fat into a refrigerator container. All this may be done well ahead, but if you are not making the ragù immediately, the duck should be refrigerated until ready to use.

When ready to make the ragù, strip the duck meat away from the leg bones, discarding the bones. Chop the meat coarsely, reserving several large pieces to use for garnish.

Combine 2 tablespoons of the duck fat with the remaining 2 tablespoons olive oil in a heavy-duty saucepan and set over medium heat. Add the pancetta and cook, stirring occasionally, until brown and crisp. Meanwhile, chop the remaining 4 garlic cloves and add them to the pan with the celery, carrot, onion, and 1 tablespoon of the sage. Stir into the fat. Let cook briefly, until the vegetables are softened, then add the wine and cook briskly until the wine has reduced by half. Stir in plenty of ground black pepper and the tomatoes, breaking them up in your hands or with a spoon. When the tomatoes are simmering, lower the heat and let the ragù cook gently for about 20 minutes, then stir in the chopped duck meat, except for the pieces reserved for garnish. Let the duck meat simmer in the ragù for another 20 minutes, during which time it will thicken and grow richer in flavor. At the end, taste and add salt if necessary and the remaining 1 tablespoon sage.

While the ragù is cooking, bring a large pot of water to a rolling boil. Add salt and the pasta and cook following the directions on page 33. Pappardelle should be done in 8 to 10 minutes, but start testing earlier in order not to overcook.

Add a ladleful of duck ragù to a warm serving bowl.

When the pasta is al dente, drain it quickly and add to the bowl. Spoon another couple of ladlesful of ragù over the top and turn the pasta briskly in the sauce, adding a handful of the cheese as you do so. Finally, top the pasta with the remaining ragù, sprinkle with the remaining cheese, and garnish with the reserved pieces of duck. Serve immediately, passing more grated cheese if you wish.

Ragù del Macellaio

Butcher's Ragù, with a Mix of Meats

A hearty ragù, this one is traditionally made with what the butcher has left at the end of the day—veal, pork, and lamb all mixed together. Add red chili pepper (Aleppo pepper is good for this) to give it an authentic flavor of southern Italy. And if you can't get veal, beef is fine to use in its place.

Any shape of pasta will go well with this, though it's traditional to use small, stubby cuts. It is also good with handmade semolina pastas, such as pasta alla chitarra (see page 49).

SERVES 6

1 large onion, halved and thinly sliced
½ cup extra-virgin olive oil
½ pound lean veal, coarsely ground
½ pound lean pork, coarsely ground
½ pound lean lamb, coarsely ground
1 cup dry red wine
One 28-ounce can whole tomatoes, preferably San Marzano, with their juice
1 small dried hot red chili pepper, or ½ teaspoon ground red chili, or more if desired
5 or 6 whole cloves
Sea salt and freshly ground black pepper
2 bay leaves
About 1 pound (500 grams) pasta (see headnote)
Freshly grated cheese (optional)

Combine the onion and oil in a saucepan large enough to hold all the sauce ingredients and gently sauté the onion over medium-low heat until very soft and just starting to turn golden. Add the ground veal, pork, and lamb, a little at a time, raising the heat slightly. Cook, stirring constantly, until the meats are brown. Add about a third of the wine, stirring to scrape up any brown bits from the bottom of the pan. When the wine has been almost fully absorbed, add another third, and then the final third. The meat should be quite soft.

Strain the tomatoes, reserving their juice, and add to the sauce, breaking the tomatoes up in your hands. Stir in the chili, cloves, and a little salt, then lower the heat so the sauce simmers gently. Add the bay leaves and several grinds of black pepper and cover the saucepan. Leave to simmer very gently for 2 to 2½ hours, adding some of the juice from the tomatoes from time to time if necessary. If you use up all the tomato juice, add a little boiling water as necessary to keep the sauce from getting too thick.

When the sauce is done, thick and unctuous, the meats and tomatoes practically melted together, taste and adjust the seasoning. Remove and discard the bay leaves and cloves.

Bring a large pot of water to a rolling boil. Add salt and the pasta and cook following the directions on page 33. Put a ladleful of sauce in the bottom of a warm serving bowl. Drain the pasta and add to the sauce in the bowl, mixing well, then add the rest of the sauce on top. Serve immediately, passing grated cheese, if you wish.

Ragù di Maiale

Simple Pork Ragù

U p in the mountains between Tuscany and Umbria where we have our Italian home, every family used to keep a pig or two—and sometimes many more. The breed was nothing special. Called, even in Italian, "large white," they were a standard porker, but their flesh was notably delicious, probably because they grazed in the mountain forests on a steady diet of acorns, chestnuts, roots, and grubs. The ones marked for slaughter were usually dispatched in early winter, sometime between December 6 (Saint Nicholas Day) and January 17 (feast day of Saint Anthony Abbot, patron saint of swineherds). The meat of these prized animals was quickly converted into hams, as well as all manner of cured meats—sausages, salami, capocolla, pancetta, guanciale, finocchiona, coppa di testa (head cheese). Together with the rendered lard from the pork fat, this made up a good part of each family's protein supply for the winter.

But of course some part of the pig got consumed fresh, and in the days before refrigeration, that meant a feast, one feature of which might well be this stunning ragù of fresh pork, which could be started on the day of the pig slaughter and cooked all night in the dying heat of the wood-fired oven outside each farmhouse. Sauced over pappardelle or tagliatelle, it makes a magnificent introduction to a meal, but it is also sufficiently meaty and robust to stand on its own as *pasta e basta.* This is an extraordinarily simple sauce, given elegance by the long, slow method of cooking and the bundle of herbs from just outside the kitchen door.

Pork shoulder, with its nice balance between fat and lean, is an excellent choice for this.

Note that the recipe makes 8 to 10 abundant servings, so you should plan on 1½ packages (about 1½ pounds) of pasta.

**MAKES 7 TO 8 CUPS SAUCE,
ENOUGH FOR 8 TO 10 SERVINGS**

2 pounds yellow onions, thinly sliced (10 to
    12 cups)
5 plump garlic cloves, crushed with the flat
    blade of a knife and chopped
½ cup extra-virgin olive oil
Sea salt and freshly ground black pepper
1 cup dry white wine
2 pounds pork shoulder, cut in small cubes

About ½ bunch flat-leaf parsley
2 or 3 bay leaves
2 sprigs fresh sage
2 sprigs fresh rosemary
Chopped flat-leaf parsley, for garnish

Set the oven on 250°F.

Combine the onions, garlic, and oil in a large, heavy, oven-proof saucepan and set over low heat. Cook very slowly, stirring, for 15 to 25 minutes as the onion slices start to soften and give up some of their liquid. When the onions are soft, sprinkle with salt and pepper, cover the pan, and continue cooking for another 15 minutes. At this point, the onions should be very soft and limp, but with no color at all.

Add the wine and raise the heat slightly. Cook the wine until the alcohol has burned off, then stir in the pork, along with the herbs (except for the parsley garnish). Mix everything together well, adding more pepper if you wish (the ragù should be quite peppery), cover with a tight lid, and set in the preheated oven. Bake for 3 to 4 hours. When done, the meat should be almost falling apart in the oniony sauce, while the onions themselves will have reduced to a cream.

Bring a large pot of water to a rolling boil. Add salt and the pasta and cook following the directions on page 33. Pappardelle should take 8 to 10 minutes. Drain the pasta and turn it into a warm serving bowl. Top with the pork ragù, garnish with parsley, and serve immediately.

Pasta al Forno con Ragù e Ricotta

Oven-Baked Pasta with Ragù and Ricotta

A Neapolitan favorite, rich with meaty ragù, tamed by cool ricotta, this is usually baked in the oven. But you could also serve the ragù simply as a sauce for spaghetti or other long, thin pasta, and top it with ricotta. Note that this makes up to 10 servings—or more, if serving light eaters. We find it's perfect for a cold-weather buffet table.

SERVES 8 TO 10

¼ cup extra-virgin olive oil, plus a little more
*   for oiling the dish*
1 medium onion, chopped fine
2 garlic cloves, sliced thin
1 dark green celery rib, finely chopped
1 medium carrot, finely chopped
2 pounds very meaty ("country-style")
*   pork ribs*
1 pound beef shank (osso buco)
Sea salt and freshly ground black pepper
1 cup dry red wine
One 28-ounce can whole tomatoes, preferably
*   San Marzano, with their juice*
1 tablespoon tomato paste, dissolved in
*   ½ cup hot water*
Freshly grated nutmeg
Crushed dried red chili pepper
2 tablespoons plus ¼ cup finely minced
*   flat-leaf parsley*
2 tablespoons finely minced fresh basil, if
*   available*
1½ pounds fusilli, rigatoni, penne rigate, or
*   farfalle*
1¼ pounds ricotta (2 cups plus 2 tablespoons)
½ cup freshly grated pecorino or parmigiano-
*   reggiano*

Combine the oil, onion, garlic, celery, and carrot in a large heavy-duty saucepan and set over low heat. Cook gently, stirring often, until the vegetables are softened but not brown.

Push the vegetables out to the edges of the pan and add the pork and beef to the center. Add salt and black pepper to the meat, raise the heat to medium, and brown the meat on all sides, turning frequently. Add the wine and let it cook until the wine is reduced by half, then stir in the tomatoes, crushing them with your hands, and the dissolved tomato paste. Add the nutmeg and chili to taste (the sauce should have a little bite from the chili but it should *not* be hot as an American chili sauce) and bring to a simmer. Cover and cook at a bare simmer for up to 3 hours, stirring from time to time, and adding a tablespoon or so of hot water if the sauce gets too thick and starts to stick.

Remove the meats from the pan, scraping off the sauce. Shred the meats with a fork, discarding the bones and fat, and return to the sauce. Stir in 2 tablespoons of the parsley and the basil (if using). Taste and adjust seasoning, if necessary. You should have about 5 cups of sauce. (The sauce may be prepared well ahead and refrigerated for 3 or 4 days before continuing the recipe. It should be at room temperature or a little warmer when you're ready to assemble the pasta al forno—that is, neither chilled from the refrigerator nor hot from the stove.)

Set the oven on 375°F.

Bring a large pot of water to a rolling boil. Add salt and the pasta and cook for just 5 minutes, then drain. Do not overcook at this point. The pasta will finish cooking in the oven.

Lightly oil the bottom and sides of a 4-quart baking dish, preferably a casserole dish with a lid. Spread about 1½ cups of the ragù over the bottom of the dish.

Mix 2 cups of the ragù with the ricotta. Taste and add salt, if necessary. Combine this mixture with the drained pasta and spoon over the bottom layer of plain ragù. Spoon the remaining plain ragù over the thick layer of pasta. Sprinkle with the grated pecorino and the remaining ¼ cup parsley.

Cover the dish, using aluminum foil if you don't have a lid. Bake for 20 minutes, then uncover, raise the oven temperature to 400°F, and continue baking for an additional 5 to 10 minutes, or until the cheese is lightly browned on top. Remove from the oven and let settle for 10 to 15 minutes before serving.

Spaghetti con le Vongole

Classic Pasta with Clam Sauce

Winters in Rome, we escaped from the city for Sunday lunch. If it was sunny and warm, our destination was Fregene, a beach town not far from the airport. The beach strip was dotted with trattorie that specialized in seafood, specifically spaghetti con le vongole, pasta with tiny telline, a delicious clam no bigger than your thumbnail that in those days was scooped up in the sand along the edge of the water. The harvest of sweet telline is now prohibited, but the dish is still made with *vongole veraci*, which are similar to what we call Manila clams. Serving clams in their shells is proof that they are fresh.

At its heart, this is a classic Aglio-Olio-Peperoncino (page 55) with clams tossed in. No white wine is added, just shake the pan as the clams steam open so their juices mix with the oil to make an unctuous dressing. It's a recipe that goes quickly, so have your ingredients prepped, chopped, and ready to go before you put the water on to boil.

SERVES 6

⅓ cup extra-virgin olive oil
4 plump garlic cloves, crushed with the flat
*   blade of a knife*
Sea salt
About 1 pound (500 grams) spaghetti or
*   linguine*
3 pounds Manila clams, rinsed (see page 14)
½ cup coarsely chopped flat-leaf parsley
Pinch dried red chili pepper

Bring a large pot of water to a rolling boil.

While the water is coming to a boil, assemble all the ingredients and have them ready to go.

Combine the oil and garlic in a skillet large enough to hold all the pasta with the clams. Set over medium-low heat and cook, stirring, until the garlic is melting and starting to turn golden. If it starts to get brown, remove from the heat immediately.

By now the water should be boiling. Add salt and the pasta and cook following the directions on page 33.

While the pasta cooks, return the garlic and oil to medium heat and as soon as it starts to sizzle, tip in the clams. Cook rapidly, tossing and stirring the clams to expose them all to the heat. The clams will start to open and release some of their juices into the pan, and the juices will emulsify with the oil to make an unctuous sauce. Continue tossing and stirring until the pasta is almost al dente. If necessary, add a tablespoon or so of the pasta water to the pan.

Just before you drain the pasta, add about ¼ cup of the pasta water to the clams. Drain the pasta and turn immediately into the clams, along with the parsley and dried red chili. Continue cooking, tossing and stirring, until the pasta is fully al dente. Transfer to a warm serving bowl and serve immediately.

Tubettini con Cozze e Fagioli

Pasta with Mussels and Beans

Imagine you've taken a length of macaroni or bucatini and cut it into short, quarter-inch lengths—that's tubetti or tubettini. Little pasta shapes like this are often cooked with beans, as in this recipe. If you can't find tubettini, penne will do—the smallest you can find. For more information about mussels, see page 14.

SERVES 6

1 cup dried white beans, soaked several hours
  or overnight, drained
1 carrot, coarsely chopped
1 celery stalk, coarsely chopped
4 garlic cloves, coarsely chopped
4 quarts (about 5 pounds) mussels
¼ cup dry white wine
¼ cup extra-virgin olive oil
1 cup canned whole tomatoes, preferably San
  Marzano
Sea salt and freshly ground black pepper
¾ pound (about three-quarters of a 500-gram
  package) tubetti, tubettini, or penne
¼ cup finely minced flat-leaf parsley
Fresh basil, if available, slivered

Combine the beans, carrot, celery, and about one-quarter of the chopped garlic in a heavy saucepan over medium heat. Add water to cover and bring to a boil. Simmer, covered, until the beans are tender, 45 minutes to 1 hour. Check from time to time and add more boiling water as needed.

While the beans are cooking, rinse the mussels under running water. Discard any with gaping shells or any that feel suspiciously heavy—they're probably full of mud.

Set the mussels in a broad pan, add the wine, and bring to a boil over high heat. Cook, tossing frequently, until all the mussels have opened. As the mussels open, remove them from the pan and transfer to a deep plate or bowl. (Any that don't open after 10 or 15 minutes should be discarded.) Strain the mussel liquid through several layers of cheesecloth to get rid of any grit. (All of the above may be done ahead of time.)

When you're ready to continue, add the remaining garlic to a soup kettle or large saucepan along with the oil. Sauté very gently until the garlic is soft but not brown, then stir in the tomatoes but not their liquid, breaking them up in your hands. Cook for about 10 minutes, or until the tomatoes are very soft and starting to disintegrate into a sauce. Stir in the cooked beans, with all their liquid, and continue gently simmering.

Now prepare the pasta. Bring a large pot of water to a rolling boil. Add salt and the pasta and cook following the directions on page 33. When it is almost done, in 8 or

9 minutes, drain it and add to the beans. Stir in the strained mussel liquid. The dish should be saucy rather than soupy—if it's too soupy, before you add the mussels, cook it down a little to thicken. Once the mussels are added, cook very gently for about 5 minutes, or until they are hot and the flavors have combined. (Do not overcook the mussels—they will toughen.) Stir in the parsley and basil (if using), salt to taste, and plenty of pepper.

Nodi Marini con Scungilli alla Marinara

Pasta with Whelks in a Nontraditional Tomato Sauce

If you're of Italian descent, you might know whelks as scungilli, a favorite for the Feast of the Seven Fishes, the Christmas Eve celebration beloved of Italian Americans. Around Christmas, then, is a good time to find whelks at local fishmongers', but they are not strictly seasonal and fishermen find them throughout the year. In New York they're occasionally sold by fishmongers in the Greenmarkets. In Maine we get them from friendly lobstermen who bring them up in their traps.

To prepare whelks, rinse them carefully to rid them of any detritus, then poach for about 10 minutes in a large pot with heavily salted water to which you have added the grated zest of a lemon and a couple of bay leaves. A small dried red chili pepper is also good in the cooking water. Once the whelks are done, remove them from their cooking liquid but *do not discard the cooking liquid.* When the whelks are cool enough to handle, remove them from their shells by piercing them with a skewer or a lobster pick and twisting gently in the direction of the shell's spiral. They should slide easily out of the shells. Now clean the whelks by removing the operculum, the fingernail-like disk that closes the whelk's opening, then cutting away the intestinal sac, the darkish brown sac at the end of the body (sometimes this sac gets left behind in the shell when you remove the critter). Large whelks should be cut into three or four pieces before adding to the sauce. If you're not ready to consume them right away, store them in the refrigerator with a little of their cooking liquid to keep them moist. (This may be done a day or two ahead.) Strain the cooking liquid through cheesecloth or a fine-mesh sieve to get rid of any sand or other bits, then set aside to add to the pasta water (or to any kind of seafood preparation).

Nodi marini ("sailor's knots") are tense curls of pasta, a shape made by Pastificio Setaro and not, as far as we can tell, by anyone else. It's a nice culinary pun to serve them with the whelks, tightly curled in their shells. But lacking nodi marini, you could use lumache (snails—another nice pun), small shells (conchiglie), fusilli spirals, or any other type of twisted pasta that will capture bits of the sauce.

Marinara is a traditional sauce to serve with whelks in Italian American restaurants, but in this case we've made it a good deal less traditional by adding aromatics—ground fennel seeds, ground dried red chili pepper (piment d'Espelette is what we prefer), cinnamon, and a hint of cumin.

SERVES 4 TO 6

FOR THE MARINADE
1½ tablespoons finely minced flat-leaf parsley

1 garlic clove, crushed with the flat blade of a knife

24 to 36 whelks, cooked, cleaned, and sliced (see headnote)

FOR THE SAUCE

3 tablespoons extra-virgin olive oil

¼ cup finely diced pancetta

½ medium onion, chopped fine

*2 garlic cloves, crushed with the flat blade of
    a knife*

½ teaspoon sea salt

*One 14-ounce can whole tomatoes, preferably
    San Marzano, with their juice*

1 cup dry white wine

*1 cup liquid left from cooking the whelks or
    plain water*

1 teaspoon fennel seeds, crushed in a mortar

Pinch ground cumin

*Pinch ground dried red chili pepper (piment
    d'Espelette or similar)*

2 bay leaves

One 2-inch cinnamon stick

Sea salt and freshly ground black pepper

*About 1 pound (500 grams) pasta (nodi
    marini, shells, fusilli; see headnote)*

Prepare the marinade: Chop together the parsley and garlic to make a fine mince. Sprinkle this over the whelks and toss to coat them entirely. Set aside, covered, to marinate for several hours or overnight.

While the whelks are marinating, prepare the sauce: Combine the oil and pancetta in a heavy saucepan and set over medium heat. Cook gently just until the fat in the pancetta is starting to run and the cubes are beginning to brown on their edges. Add the onion and garlic with a little salt and stir. As the onion bits start to soften, stir in the tomatoes with all their juice, breaking up the tomatoes into smaller pieces. Add the wine and whelk poaching liquid, along with the fennel seeds, cumin, chili pepper, bay leaves, cinnamon, and salt and black pepper to taste.

Let the sauce come to a simmer, then turn it down so that it barely bubbles. Cook for 1½ to 2 hours, or until it has reduced by half. If the sauce starts to catch and burn on the bottom, stir in a little more liquid—wine, poaching liquid, or plain water. At the end of the cooking time, the sauce should be very thick. If not, raise the heat and cook a little longer, until it has thickened. Taste and adjust the seasoning. Remove the cinnamon stick and bay leaves from the sauce.

Add water to the remaining whelk poaching liquid to bring it up to 6 quarts. Bring to a rolling boil, add the pasta (salt may not be necessary in this case), and cook according to directions on page 33.

While the pasta is cooking, stir the sliced whelks, with their marinade, into the sauce and set over gentle heat just to warm the seafood through.

As soon as the pasta is done, drain and tip it into a warm serving bowl. Add most of the sauce and toss well, then serve with the remaining sauce garnishing the top.

Fettuccine with Scallops in a Lemony Cream

Look for untreated fresh scallops, called dry scallops, as opposed to wet ones. Wet scallops have been treated with phosphates to extend their shelf life; they have no flavor and, moreover, will not cook properly. Sweet little bay scallops are best in this recipe, but if you can find only big sea scallops, cut them into quarters before cooking. If scallops are unavailable, you could substitute fresh shrimp, cutting them in half the long way, head to tail, if they are very large.

Chervil adds a wonderful, slightly aniselike flavor to scallops, but it is not always easy to find. If unavailable, use flat-leaf parsley.

SERVES 6

1 pound scallops (see headnote)
4 tablespoons extra-virgin olive oil
3 tablespoons finely minced shallots (1 or
  2 plump shallots)
¼ cup heavy cream
Sea salt and freshly ground black pepper
About 1 pound (500 grams) fettuccine or
  linguine
2 tablespoons freshly grated lemon zest
2 tablespoons freshly squeezed lemon juice
2 tablespoons finely minced fresh chervil, if
  available; otherwise use flat-leaf parsley

Prepare the scallops and dry thoroughly with paper towels.

Heat 2 tablespoons of the oil in a sauté pan over medium-high heat. Let the oil get very hot, add the scallops, and sear on both sides, turning once. As the scallops finish cooking, remove and set aside in a warm place.

Turn the heat down to medium-low and add the remaining 2 tablespoons oil to the pan, along with the minced shallots. Cook, stirring, until the shallots are soft and melting, but do not let them brown. Add the cream, stirring it in, and bring to a simmer. Set aside but keep warm while you make the pasta.

Bring a large pot of water to a rolling boil. Add salt and the pasta and cook following the directions on page 33.

While the pasta is cooking, bring the shallot cream to a simmer once again. Add the lemon zest, lemon juice, chervil, and a ladleful of pasta water. Cook just long enough to thicken the sauce, then stir in the scallops. Add salt and pepper to taste.

When the pasta is al dente, drain and transfer it to a warm serving bowl. Combine with the scallop sauce, mixing and turning the pasta to coat it with the lemon cream. Serve immediately.

Conchiglie with Shrimp and Orange Sauce

O range zest and juice add freshness to this sauce, which we like to make with small Maine shrimp, when available in their winter season. But you could use larger shrimp as well, cutting them into bite-size pieces after peeling. We use Gaeta olives in this dish, but other types will do, as long as they don't come with a lot of additional seasonings.

To roast sweet peppers, see page 14.

SERVES 6

½ *medium yellow onion, finely chopped*
1 *garlic clove, finely chopped*
¼ *cup extra-virgin olive oil*
1 *pound medium-large (25-count) shrimp, peeled*
12 *black olives, preferably Gaeta (see headnote), pitted and coarsely chopped*
½ *dried red chili pepper, not too hot (New Mexico or Anaheim), chopped*
1 *red sweet pepper, roasted, peeled, and cut into long, thin strips*
¼ *cup dry white wine*
3 *tablespoons freshly grated orange zest*
3 *tablespoons freshly squeezed orange juice*
Sea salt and freshly ground black pepper
About 1 pound (500 grams) medium conchiglie (shells)

Over medium-low heat in a pan large enough to hold all the ingredients except the pasta, gently sauté the onion and garlic in the oil, stirring frequently, until very soft but not brown. While the onion is cooking, slice the shrimp in half lengthwise. (Smaller shrimp may be left whole.)

Add the olives, chili pepper, and sweet pepper to the pan, raise the heat slightly, and toss in the oil for 2 to 3 minutes. Pour in the wine and cook, stirring frequently, until the liquid is slightly reduced. Stir in orange zest and orange juice and simmer for another 2 to 3 minutes. Keep the sauce warm while you cook the pasta.

Bring a large pot of water to a rolling bowl. Add salt and the pasta and cook following the directions on page 33, until al dente, about 9 minutes.

While the pasta is cooking, reheat the sauce until it is simmering, then add the shrimp, tossing and stirring, just until the shrimp pieces turn pink—it's important not to overcook and toughen the shrimp. The sauce should be thick enough to coat the pasta. If it seems a little thin, add a ladleful of starchy pasta water and cook down slightly to thicken the sauce. Taste and add salt and black pepper, if you wish.

As soon as the pasta is done, drain and turn into a warm serving bowl. Add the hot shrimp sauce and toss to combine. Serve immediately.

Mezze Rigatoni con Pesce Spada e Olive

Mezze Rigatoni with Swordfish and Black Olives

Swordfish is rich and meaty and stands up beautifully to the strong flavors of olives and capers, but you could substitute another firm-textured white fish instead. Halibut or cod would work well.

SERVES 6

One ¾-pound swordfish steak, about 1 inch
    thick
Sea salt and freshly ground black pepper
4 tablespoons extra-virgin olive oil, or more
    if needed
½ medium onion, thinly sliced
1 garlic clove, thinly sliced
2 cups canned whole tomatoes, preferably
    San Marzano, drained and coarsely
    chopped
½ teaspoon crumbled dried red chili pepper
⅓ cup coarsely chopped pitted black olives,
    preferably Gaeta, niçoise, or taggiasca
2 tablespoons salted capers, rinsed and chopped
About 1 pound (500 grams) mezze rigatoni or
    other short, stubby pasta
½ cup mixed chopped flat-leaf parsley and
    fresh basil

Pat the swordfish dry with paper towels and season generously with salt and black pepper. Heat a cast-iron skillet until very hot. Add 2 tablespoons of the oil and immediately set the swordfish in the pan, cooking for 3 to 4 minutes until a beautiful golden sear has formed on one side. Then turn over the steak and cook for 3 more minutes, by which time the swordfish should be cooked through but not overcooked. When the fish is done, remove it from the pan and set aside.

In a separate large skillet big enough to hold all the ingredients, including the pasta, combine the remaining 2 tablespoons oil with the onion and garlic and set the skillet over low heat. Cook, stirring, until the vegetables are soft, but do not let them brown. As soon as the onion and garlic are soft, add the chopped tomatoes to the pan, raise the heat, and cook rapidly until the tomatoes are thoroughly softened and melting into a sauce. Stir in the chili pepper, olives, and capers, along with about 2 cups of water. Cover the pan and simmer gently for about 30 minutes.

While the sauce is cooking, break the swordfish into bite-size pieces.

As the tomato sauce finishes cooking, bring a large pot of water to a rolling boil. Add salt and the pasta and cook following the directions on page 33.

Stir ¼ cup of the parsley-basil mix into the tomato sauce, taste, and adjust the seasoning. Add the swordfish pieces to the sauce and continue simmering the sauce gently while the pasta cooks. Let the pasta cook for just 6 minutes. Drain, toss the pasta in the sauce, and cook for another 5 minutes. Serve immediately, garnished with the remaining ¼ cup parsley-basil mixture.

Manicotti with Four Cheeses

Curiously enough, manicotti seems to be missing from Italian cooking traditions. We've never seen it on a restaurant menu, never encountered a recipe in an Italian cookbook, never been served manicotti in an Italian home. But it was one of the first truly Italian dishes Nancy ever had, in little restaurants in Boston's North End where even students could afford the prices. We may have been underage, but the proprietors of these places took pity on us and cheerfully served us something they called Chianti that came in raffia-wrapped bottles. It was as close as we could get to Italy itself, and if the *cucina* was not as *genuina* as it would be in the mother country, we were sufficiently versed in Italian films to pretend we were Marcello Mastroianni and Monica Vitti. At least for one evening.

Manicotti are hollow tubes about four inches long and an inch in diameter, large enough for filling with a delicious mix of cheeses. They usually come in half-pound boxes that contain fourteen shells or tubes. Barilla makes them, but if you can't find manicotti, use instead lasagna sheets, either dried or freshly made, cut to the right size. In fact the sheets are easier since you can simply pipe the filling down the middle of the cooked pasta sheet, then roll the sides around it.

The manicotti should be cooked just before they are to be filled. Filling the shells is easy with a pastry bag. Be sure to have the tomato sauce ready before you boil the manicotti.

SERVES 4 TO 6

½ cup freshly grated Asiago cheese

½ cup freshly grated aged pecorino

½ pound mozzarella, freshly grated

1 pound fresh ricotta

¼ cup coarsely chopped walnuts

2 or 3 tablespoons finely chopped flat-leaf parsley or basil

1 garlic clove, finely minced

3 large eggs

Sea salt and freshly ground black pepper

One 8-ounce (250 grams) package manicotti shells (14 shells)

6 cups tomato sauce (page 176)

½ to ¾ cup freshly grated parmigiano-reggiano

2 to 3 tablespoons unsalted butter

Bring 5 to 6 quarts of water to a rolling boil in a large pot.

While the water is heating, prepare the filling: Mix together the Asiago, pecorino, half the mozzarella, and all the ricotta cheese and fold in the walnuts, parsley, and garlic. Beat the eggs together with a fork, then fold them into the cheese mixture. Add a pinch of salt and plenty of pepper and set aside.

When the water has reached a rolling boil, add a spoonful of salt and tip in the manicotti shells. Bring back to a boil and let cook for just about 5 minutes, or until the manicotti are supple enough to fill but by no means cooked through. Remove with a slotted spoon and set aside on kitchen towels to drain.

Set the oven on 375°F. Using a little oil, oil the bottom of a 9 x 13-inch baking dish. Spread half the tomato sauce over the bottom of the dish.

Using a teaspoon or a pastry bag, fill the manicotti tubes with several spoonsful of the cheese filling and set them side by side on top of the layer of tomato sauce in the dish. When all the tubes have been filled, spoon the remaining tomato sauce over the top, covering every bit of the pasta. Sprinkle liberally with grated parmigiano and the remaining mozzarella. Dot all over with the butter.

Bake for 30 to 35 minutes, until the sauce is bubbling all around and blistering on top. Remove from the oven and let rest for 5 to 10 minutes before serving.

Fresh Cannelloni with a Savory Ragù

What's the difference between cannelloni and manicotti?

Truly, they are first cousins once removed; the former are a much-loved staple of banquets, especially wedding banquets, in Italy, while the latter are featured on Italian American restaurant menus. Manicotti are usually made with preformed and packaged pasta tubes (although there's no rule that says you can't make the pasta yourself from scratch), while cannelloni are almost always made with fresh pasta, rolled out in a sheet and cut to size. Because they're made with fresh pasta, cannelloni tend to be lighter and somewhat more elegant than manicotti, but that all depends on the hand that rolls the pasta. Both are essentially pasta tubes with savory fillings, but manicotti are usually filled with a cheese mixture, while cannelloni are apt to have a filling of meaty ragù. Honestly, we have to say, one man's manicotti is another man's cannelloni and leave it at that.

Have the ragù ready before you start making the pasta. We suggest the Ragù Bolognese (page 78), Mita's Oxtail Ragù (page 287), or the wild mushroom ragù on page 80 for a vegetarian presentation. Whatever you choose, you should have about 5 cups of ragù in all. Make the pasta, and while it is resting, mix the peas, onions, and cheese into half the ragù. Then roll out the pasta, cut it to size, fill it, and most of your work will be done.

SERVES 6

1¼ pounds fresh pasta (page 43)

5 to 6 cups ragù (see headnote)

1 medium yellow onion, finely chopped

1 tablespoon unsalted butter

2 to 3 tablespoons extra-virgin olive oil, plus more for the baking dish

1 cup frozen green peas

1 cup freshly grated parmigiano-reggiano

Sea salt

¼ cup torn fresh basil, if available

1 pound thinly sliced fresh mozzarella

Following the directions on page 43, make the pasta.

While the pasta dough is resting, heat the ragù to just barely simmering.

Combine the onion with the butter and 1 tablespoon of the oil in a skillet. Cook over low heat just until the onion bits soften. Do not let them brown. Stir in a teaspoon or two of water and add the frozen peas. Cover the pan and cook until the peas are tender, adding a little more water, if necessary.

Divide the ragù into two roughly equal portions. Stir the onion-pea combination into one portion and add ½ cup of the grated cheese, mixing well. Keep both portions of ragù warm while you work the pasta.

Using half the dough at a time, roll the pasta out on a lightly floured board to a broad, thin sheet, not more than $\frac{1}{16}$ inch thick. Cut the pasta in large regular rectangles, about 4 x 5 inches each. When you're done with both portions of dough, you should have at least 16 pasta rectangles. (You may not use all of them, but some may tear while you're working so it's best to have a few extra.)

Bring a large pot of water to a rolling boil and add a big spoonful of salt. Have ready a bowl of cold water next to the stove into which to drop the pasta squares to stop the cooking. Next to the bowl, or on a nearby counter, have clean, lightly dampened kitchen towels spread out on which to lay the pasta squares.

Drop 3 or 4 of the pasta rectangles into the boiling water and cook for just about 1 minute, then remove with a slotted ladle and drop them into the cold water. Remove the squares from the cold water and lay them out delicately on the kitchen towels.

Proceed with the remaining pasta squares.

Butter or oil a 9 x 13-inch baking dish. Set the oven on 375°F.

Spread half the plain ragù over the bottom of the baking dish. Then, using the ragù mixed with peas and onion, take one of the pasta rectangles and spread several spoonsful of ragù down the long side of the rectangle. Roll the pasta around the filling, jelly-roll fashion, to make a loose tube or cigar. Set the tube, seam side down, in the baking dish on top of the plain ragù, and continue with the remaining pasta and filling. You should have enough pasta tubes to fit comfortably side by side in the baking dish. Spoon the remaining plain ragù sauce over the top, scatter the basil (if using) over it, and layer the mozzarella slices on top. Sprinkle generously with the remaining ½ cup grated cheese and dribble oil over the top.

Bake for about 20 minutes, or until the sauce is bubbling and blistered on top. Remove from the oven and let rest for 10 or 15 minutes before serving.

NOTE *If you lack time or inclination to make the pasta from scratch, Rustichella d'Abruzzo makes cannelloni shells that do not require precooking. You will need some sort of pastry bag or piping tube to fill them with the stuffing.*

Turkish Pasta with a Garlic-Yogurt Sauce and Brown Butter

A quick-and-easy recipe, this brings slightly different flavors, all the way from the eastern Mediterranean, into the pasta kitchen. Turks are as enthusiastic about their pasta as Italians are, and this dish is a great example of what lamb and yogurt can add to the table. If you can get your hands on tart, lemony sumac, available from Middle Eastern shops as well as good herb-and-spice dealers, sprinkle some over the top. Crushed sumac with its deep red berries makes a handsome contrast to the alabaster yogurt. Another essential spice in this dish is za'atar, the Middle Eastern mixture of wild thyme, sumac, and sesame seeds, often with olive oil too; za'atar is available from online markets such as www.penzeys.com and www.kalustyans.com, which offers Syrian, Jordanian, and Lebanese versions of the spice mix. Or you can buy Palestinian za'atar at www .canaanfairtrade.com and support a cooperative of Palestinian farmers.

If you do not have Greek-style yogurt, you can easily make it by straining about 2 cups regular whole milk yogurt through a fine-mesh sieve lined with cheesecloth. Leave the yogurt to drain overnight and in the morning you will have a nicely thickened yogurt to use in this dish. Note that the yogurt should be at room temperature, not chilled from the fridge.

SERVES 6

2 plump garlic cloves, crushed with the flat
   blade of a knife
Sea salt and freshly ground black pepper
1½ cups thick Greek-style yogurt or strained
   yogurt, at room temperature
2 tablespoons extra-virgin olive oil
1 medium yellow onion, finely minced
¾ pound ground lean lamb
About ⅓ cup coarsely chopped flat-leaf
   parsley
Middle Eastern dried red chili pepper (such as
   Aleppo pepper)
2 tablespoons freshly squeezed lemon juice
About 1 pound (500 grams) farfalle (bow ties)
8 tablespoons (1 stick) unsalted butter
1 to 2 tablespoons za'atar
Big pinch sumac, if available
2 tablespoons pine nuts, toasted

In a small mortar, combine the garlic and about ½ teaspoon salt. Crush to a paste with the pestle. Or put the garlic and salt in a small bowl and crush to a paste with the back of a soupspoon. Stir the garlic paste into the yogurt. Set aside at room temperature.

Set a large skillet over medium-low heat and add the oil and onion. Cook until the onion is translucent, but do not let it brown. Stir in the lamb and cook, crumbling the meat, until it is brown. Add a pinch of salt and plenty of black pepper, along with the parsley. Finally, add a good pinch of Middle Eastern chili pepper.

Keep the meat warm while you prepare the pasta.

Bring a large pot of water to a rolling boil. Add salt and the pasta and cook following the directions on page 33.

While the pasta is cooking, melt the butter in a small saucepan over medium heat. Let it cook until it starts to brown, then remove from the heat and stir in the za'atar.

As soon as the pasta is ready, drain and turn it into a warm serving bowl. Add the ground lamb mixture and toss; then add a little more than half the yogurt sauce and toss again. Spoon the rest of the yogurt sauce over the top, then top that with the browned butter and finally a sprinkle of sumac (if using) and the pine nuts. Serve immediately, mixing at the table.

Spring

What does spring mean in your part of the world? In Tuscany it's the first tender shoots of wild asparagus spotted in some woodlot, or the quiet chuckle of hens in the farmyard as they start once more to provide their eggs. It's the sight of flocks of sheep cruising the green hills and lowlands in search of fresh grass. Above all, it's great mounds of fava beans and peas piled in our markets, so tender, so compelling that easily half of them get consumed, raw from the shell, on the drive home. In Maine it means wild fiddleheads and dandelion greens, while in New York it's a mad Greenmarket explosion of everything from new greens, bright with flavor, to wild ramps, that peculiar cross between a leek and an onion, that are so much in demand.

Spring comes very early to some parts of the Mediterranean. By February the almond trees are already in blossom in Sicily and Andalusia, their flowers like pink-white cotton puffs along the gray branches; later in March, it's time for mimosa, drooping clusters of bright yellow flowers that carpet hillsides in Liguria and Provence and shine like neon in the soft spring rain. And on the slopes of Mount Lebanon wild anemones, windflowers, carpet the forest floor.

It's a time too when country gardens and city markets fill with new green vegetables called *primeurs* in France, *primizie* in Italy, *proima* in Greece: fava beans so young and tender they need no shucking but are eaten whole straight from the pod; slender shoots of wild asparagus and constellations of wild chicory, gathered by the roadside and in abandoned fields; early peas, spring artichokes, the first green shoots of garlic and onions. Young tender greens, wild or cultivated, are suddenly abundant, and after the heavy days of winter it seems right to eat green, both because your taste buds crave it and because it's what you find all over in vegetable shops, market stalls, and backyard gardens. If you follow the seasons as we do, it will have been a year since you last ate asparagus. By June we've grown weary of the woodsy flavor of the green shoots, but come the following April, when we see them again, we cannot wait to cook with them, day in and day out, blanched until tender and dribbled with olive oil, or long braised to falling-apart sweetness and tossed with pasta, butter, and lots of grated cheese. In Rome the first tiny sweet peas and fava beans of spring are prized, each one served alone or in combination, sweated out lightly with chopped spring onion and salty cured pork, pancetta, or guanciale—delicious as a side dish but even better tossed with tiny shells or cavatelli.

Right around the world spring is also lamb season and lamb never seems tastier than when paired with fresh young peas or fava beans. Great flocks of snowy sheep forage the rolling green of the Crete Senesi near our home farm. Sad to say, it's also time to cull the flocks of their young, but it provides lush lamb and kid for Easter markets. Upside down, their naked carcasses hang from hooks in the butcher shops lining via Dardano in Cortona. And along with tender meat comes a fresh supply of milk for all the wonderfully savory pecorino cheeses, fresh and aged, plus ricotta, all of which find roles to play in pasta sauces and garnishes.

As the days grow longer and the light softens, spring pastas mirror the balmy air, engendering an instinctive desire for more fresh vegetables. Banned from our tables are the deep rich braises and sumptuously meaty ragùs of colder seasons, replaced by tender young vegetables, just barely cooked, paired with newly sprouted chives and tarragon, mint and thyme, perhaps blended with fresh ricotta. Whole sweet snap peas are slivered and tossed with butter and prosciutto to complement little shells of pasta, or pureed to fill ravioli for a simple dish topped elegantly with fresh cream and mint. Plain spinach is barely steamed and mixed with ricotta. Wild stinging nettles, carefully harvested, are transformed into green lasagna or a simple sauce for handmade tagliatelle. Or in a spectacular spring dish called *la vignarola* in Rome and *la frittella* in Sicily, a myriad of sweet young vegetables are combined and tossed with pasta, a version of pasta alla primavera that simply sings of the delights of this awakening season.

Pasta and Parmesan Broth with
Peas and Pea Shoots

Le Virtù: A Spring Minestrone
from the Abruzzi

Pennette with Roman-Style
Artichokes with Mint and Garlic

Rigatoni ai Carciofi
Rigatoni with Artichokes and Savory Sausage

Tagliatelle with Grilled Asparagus, Goat
Cheese, and Crisp Prosciutto

Pappardelle with Long-Cooked
Asparagus and Basil

Conchiglie alla Primavera con Fave,
Piselli Freschi, e Ricotta
*Springtime Shells with Fava Beans,
Fresh Peas, and Ricotta*

Pasta Primavera (Fusilli alla Vignarola)
Corkscrew Pasta with Green Spring Vegetables

Sweet Pea Ravioli with Mint, Cream,
Parmigiano, and Black Pepper

Shells with Snap Peas and Pea Shoots
in a Peppery Cream

Maccheroncini with Tiny Fava Beans
(or Peas) and Fresh Ricotta

Bavette with Fresh Spring Herb Pesto and
Bread Crumbs

Fusilli with Spinach and Ricotta

Gnudi di Erbette
*Fresh Herb-Ricotta Gnudi with
Brown Butter and Sage*

Lasagna Verde
Green Nettle Lasagna

Bucatini with Nettles and Cream

Pennette ai Funghi con Burro e Rosmarino
*Pasta with Wild Mushrooms, Rosemary,
and Brown Butter*

Pasta alla Carbonara

Ragù di Rigaglie di Pollo
Chicken Liver Ragù for a Spring Feast

Cavatelli del Pastore
Cavatelli with Braised Lamb and Ricotta

Lamb Meatballs in Spicy Tomato
Sauce with Elicoidali

Pasta Colle Sarde
Pasta with Wild Fennel and Fresh Sardines

Linguine with Fresh Shrimp and Arugula

Tagliolini with Fresh Shucked Oysters,
Crème Fraîche, and Chives

Fusilli with Salmon, Lemon,
and Fresh Spring Greens

Spaghettini with Lemon Butter and Bottarga

Moroccan Couscous aux Sept Légumes
*Couscous with Seven (or More)
Vegetables—A Vegetarian Dish*

Pasta and Parmesan Broth with Peas and Pea Shoots

When you come to the end of a wedge of parmigiano-reggiano cheese, take a tip from the Italian farmwife's native frugality and save the rind to use later in soups and stocks. It will keep, well wrapped, in the refrigerator for several weeks, or store it in the freezer for longer periods. Then just toss it into the mix for a chicken or vegetable stock, where it will add subtle richness and meaty flavor. When the stock is finished, extract the rind and discard it.

Ditalini are small tube-shaped pastas, as if you took a strand of bucatini and chopped it into half-inch bits. You could substitute elbow macaroni or any other type of small pasta shape here—keeping in mind that this is a soup, so any shape too big to fit on a soupspoon is not advised.

This is a splendid way to announce the first fresh green peas of the season, and if you can find pea shoots, the leafy tops of young pea plants, along with their soft curly tendrils, they make a handsome addition. Lacking pea shoots, you could use watercress, although the flavor is a bit spicier. If you use watercress, we advise changing the quantities—3 cups shucked fresh peas and 3 cups loosely packed watercress should do it.

SERVES 6

10 cups homemade chicken stock (see page 9)

½ pound, more or less, parmigiano-reggiano rinds (see headnote)

Sea salt

About ¾ pound ditalini

2 cups tender young peas, freshly picked and shucked

4 loosely packed cups pea shoots

Freshly grated zest of 1 organic lemon

Coarsely ground black pepper

½ cup freshly grated parmigiano-reggiano

Combine the chicken stock and parmigiano rinds in a saucepan and bring to a simmer over medium-low heat. Reduce the heat to low. The liquid should just barely bubble up from the bottom; use a flame tamer if necessary. Simmer, uncovered, until the stock is reduced to 8 cups, about 2 hours. Strain the stock and discard the rinds. (This may be done ahead of time; the stock is fine for an hour or so, depending on ambient temperature, but for a longer time, it should be refrigerated.)

When you're ready to continue with the soup, return the stock to a simmer over medium-low heat. Add salt and the ditalini and cook according to the instructions on the package. (Ditalini should take about 10 minutes.) When the ditalini are almost al dente, add the peas (they will take about 2 minutes to cook).

When the peas are done, add the pea shoots and the lemon zest to the simmering stock. Taste for salt, adjust if necessary, add plenty of pepper and the grated parmigiano-reggiano, and serve immediately.

Le Virtù: A Spring Minestrone from the Abruzzi

Nicolina Sergiacomo told us about le virtù, a pasta-bean-vegetable minestrone from the Abruzzi. The doyenne of Rustichella d'Abruzzo, a family pasta company in the town of Pianella (currently managed by her offspring, Gianluigi and Stefania Peduzzi), Nicolina is a legendary home cook who cherishes her kitchen heritage. *Le virtù*, the virtues, is a ritual dish made just once a year on May Day. Her description of using up all the pasta, the beans, the preserved meats, left over from winter, and stirring them into a sumptuous blend, reminded us of similar rites, especially the Passover ritual of cleansing the house of every trace of last year's wheat, for instance.

Why is it called le virtù? It's a reminder of the seven virtues requiring seven shapes of pasta, seven types of legumes, seven fresh vegetables, and seven kinds of salted meat, all of which derive from the pig. We have abridged the recipe a bit and left out the salted pig's ears and the pig's foot, feeling they might be a bit tricky to source.

There's no real recipe for le virtù—it's based on what's at hand. The following is our interpretation of what we found in our own pantry, but don't be afraid to add, subtract, and adjust. If you happen to have a ham bone, it's a great addition to the bean stock. And if you live near an Italian market, a piece of *cotiche* (a type of salted pork rind available in Italian groceries) will add flavor and texture.

Note that le virtù should always be made for a crowd—no point in assembling all this for fewer than ten people.

SERVES 10

1 to 1½ cups dried legumes (beans of various kinds and colors; chickpeas; dried fava beans, if available; or whatever is in your pantry cupboard), soaked overnight

1 ham bone, if available

1 or 2 pieces cotiche (see headnote), if available

4 ounces pancetta, diced small

¼ cup extra-virgin olive oil

2 celery stalks, including green tops, chopped or diced

2 medium carrots, chopped or diced

1 large yellow onion, chopped

1 medium fennel bulb, diced

Sea salt and freshly ground black pepper

2 garlic cloves, crushed and chopped

4 ounces prosciutto, diced small

Two 28-ounce cans whole tomatoes, preferably San Marzano, with their juice

½ to ¾ cup small lentils

1 pound fresh peas, shelled, to make about 1 cup

1½ pounds fresh fava beans, shelled, to make about 1 cup (see page 22)

½ cup finely chopped mixed herbs (parsley, sage, thyme, wild fennel, mint, borage, nettles)

Small pinch dried red chili pepper, or 1 whole small dried red chili pepper (optional)

About 2 pounds fresh greens, including wild greens, if available, but also dandelion greens, beet greens, chard, spinach, broccoli rabe

2 medium zucchini, diced

*2 cups mixed pasta, mostly short chunky
cuts (such as fusilli, farfalle, cavatelli, or
whatever is in your pantry cupboard)*
*Freshly grated aged pecorino or parmigiano-
reggiano, to pass*

Put the drained legumes in a saucepan
with water to cover by 1 inch. If you have a
ham bone, add it to the beans. If you have
cotiche, cut it into slivers and add to the
beans. Simmer over medium-low heat,
covered, until the legumes are not quite
done, still with a little resistance to the
bite. Add boiling water from time to time as
necessary to keep the beans from drying
out. In the end, take the saucepan off the
heat but leave the beans in their cooking
water until they are added to the rest of
the ingredients. Discard the ham bone and
cotiche if you used them.

In another larger pot, combine the
pancetta with the oil over medium-low
heat. Cook, stirring, until the pancetta has
rendered its fat and started to crisp and
brown. Stir in the celery, carrots, onion, and
fennel and add a pinch of salt and plenty
of black pepper. Cook, stirring, until the
vegetables are soft, then stir in the garlic and
prosciutto.

When the garlic starts to take on a little
color, add 3 to 4 cups of the tomatoes,
with their juice, breaking the tomatoes up

in your hands as you add them. Let the
liquids come to a simmer, then add the
cooked beans with their cooking liquid and
the (uncooked) lentils. There should be
sufficient juice to cover all the ingredients,
but if not, add a little more juice from the
remaining tomatoes, or add boiling water.
Continue cooking until the beans and lentils
are fully tender—another 20 to 30 minutes
should be sufficient.

Bring 2 cups water to a boil in a separate
small saucepan and add the peas and fava
beans, along with a pinch of salt. Cook until
the vegetables are bright green and tender,
then add to the soup, with the cooking water.
Stir in the mixed herbs and the chili (if using).

Pick over and rinse the greens,
discarding any yellow or faded ones. For
some (dandelion greens, for instance), strip
them and discard the stiff ribs. Sliver the
well-rinsed greens and stir into the soup.
Let cook for another 20 minutes, or until the
greens are softened. Stir in the zucchini.

Bring 3 to 4 quarts of water to a rolling
boil in a separate large pot. Add a spoonful
of salt and the pasta and cook until the
pasta is almost done. Remove it with a
slotted spoon or skimmer and add to the
soup, adding some of the pasta water if
necessary. When the pasta is tender, le
virtù is ready to serve, with plenty of grated
pecorino to put on top.

VARIATION *Some Abruzzese cooks like to garnish the soup with fried
meats or vegetables: tiny meatballs, for instance (see page 279), or thick slices
of zucchini or artichoke hearts, dipped in a flour-and-water batter and fried to
a crisp in oil. The meatballs may be added with the beans and lentils; the fried
vegetables should be dropped onto the hot soup right at the end so they stay crisp
for serving.*

Pennette with Roman-Style Artichokes with Mint and Garlic

Carciofi alla romana, slowly braised artichokes with mint and garlic, are classics of early spring in Rome when big fat *mammole* artichokes show up in the stalls at Campo de' Fiori and other open markets. We love this Roman combination of flavors—slightly bitter artichokes, sharp fresh spring garlic, salty anchovies, and earthy mint to bring it all together. The artichokes often retain a little taste of lemon from the lemon water they sit in as you clean them, lending just the right touch of acidity to cut through the richness.

Artichokes are amazingly versatile. They can be eaten raw, lightly steamed, or deliberately overcooked, and they present different flavor profiles at each stage. Slow cooking, as in this recipe, brings out the sugars, to contrast nicely with the artichoke's natural bitterness.

California artichokes are as big as mammole, even if they're not precisely the same variety. Use 4 to 6 of those; or, if you find baby artichokes, you will need 12 to 16. Judge accordingly: You should have 1 to 1½ pounds of artichokes, once they are trimmed.

Instead of pennette, use penne, or any other of the great variety of short tubular pasta shapes.

SERVES 6

1 lemon, for preparing the artichokes

12 to 16 baby artichokes or 4 to 6 big
  artichokes

¼ cup plus 2 tablespoons extra-virgin olive
  oil

Sea salt and freshly ground black pepper

2 garlic cloves, smashed with the flat blade of
  a knife

2 oil-packed anchovy fillets

6 or 7 fresh mint sprigs, plus 2 tablespoons
  chopped fresh mint leaves

4 or 5 fresh thyme sprigs, plus 2 tablespoons
  fresh thyme leaves

½ bunch flat-leaf parsley

About 1 pound (500 grams) pennette or penne

½ cup freshly grated pecorino or parmigiano-
  reggiano, plus more to pass (optional)

Prepare the artichokes as described on page 13. Cut larger artichokes into quarters or even eighths and scrape away the spiny choke at the heart. If you're using baby artichokes, slice them in half lengthwise. (The point is to have pieces of artichoke sized to marry well when tossed with the pasta.) As you finish each artichoke, toss it into the bowl of acidulated water. (The artichokes may be prepared an hour or two before making the pasta.)

Heat ¼ cup of the oil over medium heat in a large heavy sauté pan—large enough to hold the artichokes and the pasta at the end. While the oil is heating, pat dry the artichoke pieces and add them to the oil, seasoning liberally with salt and pepper. Feed the pan slowly, not adding all the artichokes at once, and keep turning and tossing the pieces. You are looking to get a lot of nice crisp brown texture.

When all the artichokes are in the pan, raise the heat and brown, turning and tossing the slices as you do so. As the artichokes brown, slide in the smashed garlic to brown a little in the oil. Now reduce the heat to low and add the anchovy fillets and the whole sprigs of mint and thyme, along with 1 cup water. Give the contents of the pan a stir.

When the water is simmering, cover the pan and braise the artichokes for about 15 minutes, or until they are tender. The liquid in the pan should be just simmering. If the pan dries out, add a little more boiling water— just a few tablespoons. (You may do this up to 2 hours or more before making the pasta; reheat when you're ready to cook the pasta.)

Bring a large pot of water to a rolling boil.

While the water is heating, chop together the thyme leaves, chopped mint, and parsley. Raise the heat under the artichokes to boil away any residual cooking liquid, leaving 2 to 3 tablespoons of liquid in the pan. Remove and discard the herb sprigs.

Add salt and the pasta to the boiling water and cook following the directions on page 33. When done, set aside about ¼ cup of the pasta water, then drain and toss the pasta in the pan with the artichokes. Add the chopped mixed herbs and the remaining 2 tablespoons oil. If the pasta seems dry, add a little of the hot pasta water and toss again, adding the grated pecorino as you do so. Taste and adjust the seasoning.

Transfer to a warm serving bowl and serve immediately, passing more grated cheese, if you wish.

Rigatoni ai Carciofi

Rigatoni with Artichokes and Savory Sausage

Once the artichokes are trimmed and set in a bath of lemony water, this recipe goes very quickly. A lot of the flavor in the dish comes from the sausage. We use fresh pork sausages, Italian style, from our favorite butcher, but if you prefer, veal sausages would be just as tasty. Our list calls for 5 or 6 artichokes, but if you are using small ones, sometimes sold as baby artichokes, you might need as many as 10. Use your judgment—there should be a nice balance between sausages and artichokes.

If you don't have rigatoni, use another short, stubby pasta, such as penne rigate, casarecce, cavatelli, or garganelli.

SERVES 6

*5 or 6 artichokes, trimmed as described on
   page 13*
*3 Italian-style fresh pork sausages (about
   1 pound), either sweet or hot, as you wish*
2 tablespoons extra-virgin olive oil
*1 fat leek, trimmed, rinsed, and chopped
   (¼ cup)*
¼ to ½ cup finely minced flat-leaf parsley
Sea salt and freshly ground black pepper
*About 1 pound (500 grams) rigatoni, penne
   rigate, or similar shape pasta (see headnote)*
*Freshly grated parmigiano-reggiano
   (optional)*

Bring a saucepan of water to a rolling boil. Make sure all the tough leaves have been removed from the prepared artichokes, then slice them lengthwise into ¼-inch-thick slices. When the water is boiling, add the artichoke slices and cook briefly, about 5 minutes, just to soften them slightly.

While the artichokes are boiling, open the sausages and discard the skins, breaking up the meat inside. Combine the oil and sausage meat in a large skillet and cook, breaking up the sausage with a fork and stirring until the bits are brown and have released some of their fat. Stir in the leek and parsley and continue cooking, stirring occasionally, until the leek pieces start to soften, but do not let them brown.

When the artichoke slices are done, drain and add them to the skillet, mixing well. Lower the heat and continue to cook until the artichoke slices are quite tender. Add salt and pepper to taste.

Bring a large pot of water to a rolling boil. Add salt and the pasta and cook following the directions on page 33, but be prepared to drain the pasta before it is fully al dente. Have the skillet with the artichoke-sausage mixture ready over medium heat. If the sauce looks a little dry, add a ladleful or two of pasta water.

Drain the not-quite-done pasta and transfer immediately to the skillet. Toss and stir the ingredients together and let the pasta finish cooking and absorb the flavors of the artichoke-sausage sauce. When done, serve immediately, passing grated parmigiano if you wish.

Tagliatelle with Grilled Asparagus, Goat Cheese, and Crisp Prosciutto

We love to grill vegetables on a cast-iron stovetop grill. It's a terrific way to sear asparagus, although if you have the time and space, a charcoal grill, heated very hot, can also do nicely for this recipe. And if you don't have either one, you can achieve somewhat the same result, without the grill marks, by using a heavy cast-iron skillet over medium-high heat.

SERVES 4 TO 6

About 4 ounces (½ cup) soft goat cheese (chèvre), at room temperature
Slivered zest of 1 organic lemon, plus a few drops of lemon juice if needed
1 tablespoon very finely chopped fresh dill or rosemary
1½ to 2 pounds fresh tender asparagus
¼ cup plus 2 tablespoons extra-virgin olive oil
Sea salt and freshly ground black pepper
1 medium red onion, cut into ¼-inch-thick slices
About 1 pound (500 grams) tagliatelle or pappardelle
6 slices prosciutto
Freshly grated parmigiano-reggiano (optional)

Combine the softened goat cheese, lemon zest, and dill in a small bowl. Mix with a fork to a fine cream. Taste, and if you think it needs it, add a few drops of lemon juice and mix well. Set the goat cheese cream aside at room temperature. (Don't worry if it seems too thick; you will add pasta water to thin it later.)

If you are using a stovetop grill, set it on medium-high heat while you prepare the asparagus.

Trim the asparagus by snapping off the stems where they offer the least resistance. Rinse the asparagus carefully and dry by wrapping in a kitchen towel.

In a flat-bottomed bowl or baking dish, combine ¼ cup of the oil with salt and plenty of pepper. Roll the asparagus spears in the oil to coat them liberally. When the stovetop grill is hot, add the asparagus spears and cook over high heat, turning, until tender and starting to brown.

While the asparagus is cooking, turn the red onion slices in the same oil. As soon as the asparagus is done, remove from the heat and set in a low (200°F) oven to keep warm while you continue with the dish.

Add the oiled onion slices to the grill and cook, turning, until they start to soften and turn brown. (The onion slices should remain a bit crunchy.) Remove when done and combine with the asparagus.

Bring a large pot of water to a rolling boil. Add salt and the pasta and cook following the directions on page 33.

While the pasta is cooking, heat the

remaining 2 tablespoons oil in a skillet over medium heat. Sear the prosciutto slices until they are crisp, then drain on paper towels.

Before the pasta finishes cooking, extract ¼ cup or more pasta water and beat it into the goat cheese cream. Drain the pasta and transfer to a warm serving bowl. Add the asparagus and onion and toss to mix, then spoon the goat cheese cream over the top. Serve immediately, topping each serving with a slice of crisped prosciutto. If you wish, pass some parmigiano-reggiano to grate over the top.

Pappardelle with Long-Cooked Asparagus and Basil

Asparagus is a delight when freshly picked and barely blanched, with a little fine extra-virgin olive oil dripped over the top. Its sweet vegetal flavors are a welcome herald to spring. But as the season winds on and the spears get fatter and a little tougher, we like to cook it thoroughly, breaking down the tough fibers and pulling out a little extra sweetness along the way. A splash of cream and verdant basil will tie everything together. It's great served over pappardelle or any other kind of long, broad noodles—fettuccine, for instance, or tagliatelle.

SERVES 4 TO 6

2 pounds fresh asparagus
2 tablespoons unsalted butter
2 tablespoons extra-virgin olive oil
1 large shallot or 1 small fresh spring onion,
*   finely minced (2 tablespoons)*
Sea salt and freshly ground black pepper
½ cup loosely packed basil leaves, in fat
*   slivers*
¼ cup heavy cream
About 1 pound (500 grams) pappardelle
½ cup freshly grated parmigiano-reggiano or
*   grana padano*

Trim the asparagus by snapping off the bottoms, which break where the stem starts to get woody. Cut the stalks into 2-inch lengths, setting the tips aside.

Combine the butter and oil in a saucepan or deep skillet over medium heat. When the butter begins to foam, add the shallot and the asparagus pieces, except for the tops, along with a good pinch of salt. Cook briskly until the shallot and asparagus take on a little color, 8 to 10 minutes. Then turn the heat down and add the cream, 2 tablespoons water, the asparagus tips, and half the basil leaves. Cover the pan and continue cooking until the asparagus is very soft and the liquid in the pan is reduced by half.

In the meantime, bring a large pot of water to a rolling boil. When the asparagus sauce is ready, add salt and the pasta to the water and cook following the directions on page 33, until it is al dente.

Have ready a warm serving bowl. Drain the pasta and toss in the bowl with the asparagus, the remaining basil, and the parmigiano-reggiano. Add more pepper to the top and serve immediately.

Conchiglie alla Primavera con Fave, Piselli Freschi, e Ricotta

Springtime Shells with Fava Beans, Fresh Peas, and Ricotta

We've had this brilliant spring confection served with all sorts of pasta shapes, from cavatelli to spaghetti and flat tagliatelle, but honestly it seems to go best with any shape that, like conchiglie (small shells) or fusilli (twisted ribbons), features little traps for bits of the sauce.

The dish is all about exquisitely perfect ingredients: the lean flavor of true ricotta made from whey left over after the cheese is made, contrasting with the sweet bitterness of tiny fresh-picked favas so young they don't need their inner skins peeled, and peas just picked and shucked without a chance to get stale and starchy. When you find these ingredients, through a farmers' market or your own garden (fresh peas and favas are reason enough to have a garden), and you also have a local maker of real ricotta or a cheese store that brings in fresh sheep's-milk ricotta from Italy, that's when you want to make this dish. If one of these ingredients is missing, just increase the others and it will still be a delicious spring presentation.

SERVES 6

2 pounds fresh fava beans in the pod
1 pound fresh peas in the pod
2 tablespoons diced pancetta, guanciale, or prosciutto
2 to 3 tablespoons diced fresh spring onion
2 tablespoons extra-virgin olive oil
1 tablespoon unsalted butter
Sea salt and freshly ground black pepper
About 1 pound (500 grams) pasta (see headnote)
¼ cup fresh ricotta, plus a bit more for garnish
1 tablespoon finely minced flat-leaf parsley or mint leaves
Freshly grated parmigiano-reggiano, for garnish

Shell the fava beans and, if necessary, blanch and peel them (see page 22 for directions). Shell the peas, if using fresh.

In a saucepan large enough to hold all the vegetables, combine the pancetta and onion with the oil and set over medium-low heat. Add the butter and cook very slowly for 5 to 7 minutes, just to melt the pancetta and onion in the buttery oil. Be very attentive—any hint of browning will spoil the dish.

When the onion bits are tender, add the fava beans and peas, along with boiling water to just barely cover the vegetables. Raise the heat to medium and bring to a simmer. Add a small spoonful of salt. Let cook, uncovered, for about 5 minutes, or until the beans and peas are tender. The liquid in the pan will reduce and thicken.

Be careful not to let it boil away—have boiling water ready to add if necessary.

While the beans and peas are cooking, bring a large pot of water to a rolling boil. Add salt and the pasta and cook following the directions on page 33, checking the package recommendations for cooking time.

When the pasta is almost done, the vegetable liquid should be reduced almost to a syrup. Remove the beans and peas from the heat and add the ricotta, along with about ¼ cup of the pasta water. Stir and toss to mix well.

Drain the pasta and transfer to a warm serving bowl. Immediately top with the vegetable mixture. Add another dollop or two of ricotta to the top and garnish with pepper, the parsley, and grated parmigiano before serving.

Pasta Primavera (Fusilli alla Vignarola)

Corkscrew Pasta with Green Spring Vegetables

Pasta alla primavera, a much loved dish of the 1980s, actually originated in Rome as a wonderful springtime treat called la vignarola, a combination of seasonal fava beans, green peas, and either asparagus or artichokes—but not both, the idea being to keep the flavors clean and green. La vignarola is traditionally served on its own, as a vegetable mix, but we like this with pasta—twisted loops of fusilli or farfalle (bow-tie or butterfly pasta), or any shape that catches bits of pancetta-flavored sauce and vegetables.

Other early spring vegetables could be substituted, but keep the combination as simple and pure as possible, so that the fresh flavors really come through.

SERVES 6

About 2 ounces prosciutto, pancetta, or
*   guanciale, diced small*
2 tablespoons extra-virgin olive oil
1 medium spring onion, chopped fine
2 pounds fresh fava beans (1½ cups shelled
*   beans; see page 22)*
2 pounds fresh peas (2½ cups shelled peas)
1 pound fresh asparagus trimmed and cut
*   into 2-inch lengths*
Sea salt and freshly ground black pepper
1 pound (500 grams) fusilli or other pasta (see
*   headnote)*
Handful fresh mint leaves, chopped
½ cup freshly grated parmigiano-reggiano,
*   grana padano, or pecorino toscano*

In a skillet large enough to hold all the vegetables, combine the prosciutto with the oil and set over medium-low heat to melt and soften.

Bring a large pot of water to a rolling boil for the pasta.

Add the onion to the skillet and stir. Let the onion cook briefly, just to soften it, and then add the fava beans, peas, and asparagus. Raise the heat to medium and stir and cook briefly. As the vegetables start to soften, add 1 cup of the boiling pasta water, along with salt and pepper to taste. Cook, uncovered, at a rapid boil so that the vegetables retain all their bright color and flavor. By the time the vegetables are tender, there should be just a few spoonsful of syrupy liquid left in the bottom of the pan.

Meanwhile, add salt and the pasta to the boiling water and cook following the directions on page 33. As the pasta cooks, add another ladleful of pasta water to the vegetables in the skillet, along with the mint. Bring to a simmer.

When the pasta is al dente, drain it and combine with the vegetables in a warm serving bowl, turning the pasta and vegetables together. Sprinkle a little parmigiano-reggiano over the top and serve immediately with the remaining cheese to pass at the table.

Sweet Pea Ravioli with Mint, Cream, Parmigiano, and Black Pepper

A surprising turn—delicate ravioli filled with the fresh flavors of sweet green peas with mint, then sauced with a mint-and-parmigiano cream and lots of cracked black pepper to offset the sweetness. First make the filling, then roll out the pasta dough, fill the little ravioli, simmer, drain, and sauce with the rich cream.

These are best made with the first, fresh young green peas, the kind the French call *primeurs*, when they're so sweet you want to eat them raw, like candy. But we have a confession to make: We have also made these with frozen peas and, while they are not quite as delicious as the fresh variety, they work well when the younger peas are no longer available.

MAKES 36 RAVIOLI, TO SERVE 6

1 recipe Basic Pasta Fresca Dough, made using 3 cups flour and 3 large eggs (see page 43)
2 tablespoons unsalted butter
2 plump shallots, finely minced
3 pounds fresh young peas (3 cups shelled peas)
Sea salt and freshly ground black pepper
2 tablespoons finely minced fresh mint
1 pint heavy cream
½ cup freshly grated parmigiano-reggiano
1 egg beaten with 1 tablespoon cool water
All-purpose flour, for dusting
Semolina or fine cornmeal, for the sheet pan

Have the pasta dough ready but do not roll it out until the filling has been prepared.

Add the butter to a saucepan and set over medium-low heat. As soon as the butter melts, stir in the minced shallots and cook gently, just until they have softened slightly. Stir in the peas and mix well. Add 2 or 3 tablespoons hot water—just enough to keep the peas from catching—along with a pinch of salt and a little pepper. Cover the pan and cook the peas for about 10 minutes, or until they are tender. (If you're using frozen peas, 2 minutes will be sufficient.) Stir in 1 tablespoon of the mint and the cream. Bring the cream to a simmer and then remove from the heat.

Use a slotted spoon to strain out the peas from the cream. Transfer the strained peas to the bowl of a food processor and add about ¼ cup of the cream. Blend until smooth. If the mixture seems too stiff, add in another tablespoon or two of cream. Taste and adjust the seasoning, adding salt and/or pepper, if necessary.

Stir ¼ cup of the grated parmigiano into the cream remaining in the saucepan and heat just enough to melt the cheese. Keep the mixture warm while you make the ravioli.

Working with half the pasta dough and keeping the other half covered, roll it out in the pasta roller until the sheet is a

Dabs of pea puree, each about 1 tablespoon, placed ½ inch apart on one half of an egg-washed sheet of pasta. The dabs of pasta are covered with the other half of the sheet, and the two sheets are pressed together using the side of the cook's hand. A round ravioli cutter is used to cut out each ravioli.

long rectangle, about 4 inches wide and approximately 1⁄16 inch thick. Stretch the dough sheet out on a lightly floured board. Using a pastry brush, brush the egg wash over the left half of the sheet. Put the pureed pea filling into a piping bag and pipe dabs of filling, about 1 tablespoon each and approximately 1⁄2 inch apart, on the egg-washed half of the pasta sheet. You should be able to get at least 18 dabs on the sheet. Now fold the other half of the pasta sheet over the dabs to cover them completely. Press down with the side of your hand along the edges and in between each of the filling dabs to make 18 ravioli, about 1 1⁄2 by 2 inches, each one filled with pea puree. Use a round ravioli stamp to cut out the ravioli, making sure that each one is sealed well. Sprinkle a tray with a layer of semolina, pick up the ravioli and gently lay them, one by one, on the tray without touching. Continue with the remaining pasta and filling.

When you have finished with all the ravioli, bring a large pot of water to a rolling boil and add a big spoonful of salt. Turn the heat down to a very gentle boil and add the ravioli, a few at a time. Cook the ravioli in batches. They will be done in 2 to 3 minutes, when they float to the top of the water. Remove with a slotted spoon to a warm serving bowl.

When all the ravioli are done, plate them in warm dishes, spoon the cream mixture over the top and garnish with the remaining 1 tablespoon minced mint and the remaining 1⁄4 cup cheese. Crack a couple of turns of pepper over the top and serve immediately.

Shells with Snap Peas and Pea Shoots in a Peppery Cream

Another celebration of early spring, this one brings together the crispness of sugar snap peas (aka edible-pod peas) and the grassiness of pea shoots, both of which should be available in good farmers' markets and well-stocked supermarket produce sections.

Pea shoots are the tender early leaves of pea plants—green and juicy with a distinctive fresh pea flavor. They should be just wilted into the pasta at the end, right before serving. If you can't find pea shoots, simply increase the quantity of snap peas to 1½ pounds.

SERVES 6

1 pound fresh sugar snap peas
Sea salt
2 tablespoons unsalted butter
2 tablespoons extra-virgin olive oil
4 scallions or 1 spring onion, including green
    tops, slivered
¼ cup heavy cream
About 1 pound (500 grams) pasta shells
1 cup pea shoots, if available
½ cup grated grana padano or parmigiano-
    reggiano cheese
About 1 teaspoon freshly ground black
    pepper, or more to taste

Trim the snap peas, breaking off and discarding the stem ends.

Set about 4 quarts of water on high heat and bring to a rolling boil. Have ready a bowl filled with ice water to shock the peas. When the water is boiling, drop the peas in and blanch them for 4 minutes, or just until they turn bright green, then remove with a slotted spoon or a pasta basket, without discarding the cooking water. Turn the peas into the ice water.

Add a large spoonful of salt to the water in which the peas cooked and keep it on reserve for cooking the pasta.

In a skillet large enough to hold all the ingredients including the pasta, melt the butter in the oil over medium heat, then lower the heat to very low and add the slivered scallions with a pinch of salt. Let the scallions wilt into the pan without taking any color. When they are soft, add the cream and 2 tablespoons water. Let come to a simmer and reduce the liquid by half, watching carefully not to over-reduce.

Meanwhile, slice the blanched peas on the bias in about ½-inch pieces.

Bring the pasta water back to a rolling boil. Add the pasta and follow the directions on page 33. After the first 3 minutes of cooking, add the snap peas to the skillet with the scallion cream. Set over low heat and let the peas just warm up. (If you cook it too long, the snap peas will lose their bright color.)

Just before the pasta is ready, add the pea shoots to the skillet. Quickly drain the pasta and add to the skillet with the other ingredients. Toss together, along with the grana padano. Taste and add salt if necessary and plenty of pepper. Serve immediately.

Maccheroncini with Tiny Fava Beans (or Peas) and Fresh Ricotta

This is a dish for when you find absolutely perfect fresh tiny fava beans, one of the first green vegetables to appear in the spring in Italy—and in California, where they're usually available in late February. In the northeastern United States, they don't show up in farmers' markets until June. If you can find only larger ones, you will have to shell them, then blanch the beans and peel off the tough outer skin from each individual bean (see page 22). But when fava beans are young, tender, and freshly picked, they just need shelling. Marjoram's delicate piney flavor goes beautifully with fava beans, and mint is also a classic pairing, while the ricotta makes a gentle, creamy sauce that, rich as it looks, is actually light and delicate.

If fava beans are not available, this is also very good with fresh green peas.

SERVES 6

2 cups best-quality fresh ricotta, ideally from sheep's milk (see page 23)
¼ cup freshly grated parmigiano-reggiano
2 tablespoons chopped fresh mint
1 tablespoon minced fresh marjoram
Sea salt
2½ pounds fava beans (about 3 cups shelled)
About 1 pound (500 grams) maccheroncini
2 to 3 tablespoons extra-virgin olive oil
Freshly ground black pepper

Put the ricotta through a food mill or food processor to break down the curds, then mix in a bowl with the grated parmigiano, mint, and marjoram. Taste for salt, adding if necessary.

Bring 2 cups water to a rolling boil in a small saucepan. Add the beans and cook, uncovered, just long enough to tenderize the beans—4 to 6 minutes, depending on the size of the beans. When the beans are done, drain and set aside.

Bring a large pot of water to a rolling boil. Add salt and the pasta and cook following the directions on page 33, checking the package recommendations for time. A few moments before the pasta is done, pull out ¼ cup of the pasta water and stir it into the ricotta to smooth and soften it.

Drain the pasta and transfer immediately to a warm serving bowl. Toss with the oil and then with about two-thirds of the ricotta. Pile the remaining ricotta on top and scatter the fava beans over it, along with plenty of freshly cracked pepper. Serve immediately.

Bavette with Fresh Spring Herb
Pesto and Bread Crumbs

In times of deepest poverty in the not-too-distant past, toasted bread crumbs were used as a substitute for cheese when there was nothing else to put on the pasta. It's an interesting textural contrast—soft pasta and crisp fried bread crumbs—and strangely satisfying. Even in very poor country districts, however, there was often a source of wild foraged herbs to add distinctive flavors to the mix. Children who were sent out to tend a flock of sheep or herd the family pigs down through the forest were expected to return home with a handful of wild mint or oregano, and perhaps a few mushrooms when they were in season, to add to the family pot. In our Tuscan kitchen we have a collection of cultivated herbs right outside the kitchen door—rosemary, sage, parsley, thyme—as well as plenty of wild nepitella (a type of mint), wild fennel, and lemon balm growing under the olive trees, to add to the pot. Sometimes, a small crumbled dried chili might be added as well.

The following recipe is a takeoff on the idea—the butter enrichment is obviously not something you'd find in a poor country farmhouse, but it helps the herbs cling to the pasta. Use at least four different herbs to give a good variety of flavors. Some are in season at one time, others at another. Make a selection based on what you have in your garden and what's available from local farm stands or supermarket produce sections.

Grate bread crumbs from a slightly stale loaf of crusty, country-style bread, preferably whole grain if you have it. You may do this on the large holes of a box grater or dice the bread and reduce it to crumbs in a food processor. The texture will be best if it is somewhat irregular.

Bavette, long, slightly convex pasta, is a good choice for this, but linguine, tagliatelle, or maccheroni alla chitarra would be equally good choices.

SERVES 6

1½ to 2 cups mixed chopped fresh herbs, using any four of the following: tarragon, marjoram, flat-leaf parsley, sorrel, thyme, chives, garlic chives, lemon balm, lovage, mint, basil, dill, winter savory

Freshly grated zest of 1 large lemon, preferably organic

1 fresh spring onion or 2 fat shallots, finely chopped

⅓ cup extra-virgin olive oil, plus a little more if necessary for the top

1 cup fresh, unflavored, coarsely grated bread crumbs

1 small dried red chili pepper, crumbled (optional)

½ cup freshly grated parmigiano-reggiano

3 tablespoons unsalted butter

Sea salt

1 pound (500 grams) bavette or linguine pasta

Bring a large pot of water to a rolling boil.

Finely chop all the herbs together with the lemon zest and onion. Combine the chopped herb mixture in a bowl with ¼ cup of the oil.

Heat another 2 tablespoons of the oil in a skillet over medium-low heat. Add the bread crumbs and the crumbled chili (if using). Fry gently, stirring constantly, until the crumbs are golden and crisp, about 10 minutes. Remove from the heat and let cool. Mix about 2 tablespoons of the bread crumbs with 2 tablespoons of the grated parmigiano and set aside to garnish the top of the pasta.

Put a big spoonful of the herb mixture in the bottom of a serving bowl, along with 2 tablespoons of the butter, cut into chunks.

Add salt and the pasta to the boiling water and cook following the directions on page 33 until the pasta is al dente.

Drain and transfer the pasta to the serving bowl. Toss briefly to mix the herbs and butter in the bowl, then add the rest of the herbs, the remaining bread crumbs, and the remaining cheese. Toss vigorously to mix well, then top with the reserved crumb-cheese mixture and the final 1 tablespoon butter. Serve immediately.

Fusilli with Spinach and Ricotta

Good spinach, fresh from the garden, brings incredible flavor to the springtime table. It's often overlooked, perhaps because it requires several rinses in water to rid it of the mud and sand that sometimes cling to the leaves. But it's worth the effort. You can indeed buy bags of prewashed spinach, but that's not going to be the best choice. So buy spinach in bunches, rinse and rinse again, and you'll be very glad you did for the flavor.

SERVES 6

2 pounds spinach, trimmed, washed, and
    dried
3 tablespoons extra-virgin olive oil
4 small scallions, chopped (¼ cup)
1 small garlic clove, chopped
Sea salt and freshly ground black pepper
1 cup ricotta, preferably made from sheep's or
    goat's milk
½ cup whole milk
Pinch freshly grated nutmeg (optional)
½ cup freshly grated parmigiano-reggiano,
    plus more to pass
Freshly grated zest of ½ lemon, preferably
    organic
1 tablespoon unsalted butter
1 teaspoon freshly squeezed lemon juice
About 1 pound (500 grams) fusilli

Bring a large pot of water to a rolling boil.

While the water is warming, prepare the spinach-ricotta mixture: Pile up several of the spinach leaves and sliver them into strips ¼ to ½ inch wide. You should have about 8 packed cups of spinach.

Add 2 tablespoons of the oil, along with the scallions and garlic, to a large deep skillet and set over medium-high heat. Cook, stirring, until the vegetables are softened, about 5 minutes. Add the spinach in handfuls, stirring and mixing. As the spinach softens and cooks down, add more handfuls. The whole process should go very quickly and all the spinach should be done in about 5 minutes. Stir in salt and pepper to taste and set the skillet aside, but keep the spinach warm.

In a bowl, whisk together the ricotta, milk, nutmeg (if using), parmigiano, lemon zest, and the remaining 1 tablespoon oil, mixing until smooth. Stir about half this mixture into the spinach along with the butter. (Don't try to blend the spinach and ricotta thoroughly—a streaky mixture makes a more handsome presentation.) Return the skillet to medium-low heat and simmer the spinach gently for about 2 minutes, just long enough to meld the flavors. Add the lemon juice, taste, and adjust the seasoning, adding more salt, pepper, or lemon juice if it seems necessary.

Add salt and the pasta to the boiling water and cook following the directions on page 33.

When the pasta is al dente, set aside about ½ cup of the pasta water. Drain the pasta in a colander and return it to its cooking pot. Set the pot over very low heat. Add the spinach mixture and toss. If the mixture seems a little dry, add a couple of tablespoons of the reserved pasta water. When the pasta is well sauced, transfer it to warm serving plates and set a spoonful of the remaining ricotta mixture atop each serving. Serve immediately.

Gnudi di Erbette

Fresh Herb-Ricotta Gnudi with Brown Butter and Sage

Hard to pronounce (say NYEW-dy) but lovely to taste, *i gnudi* are gnocchi by another name, light little puffs of ricotta, spinach, and fresh garden herbs. So what are these dumplings doing in a book about pasta? The explanation is simple: In Tuscany, gnudi are "nude" ravioli, that is, ravioli without the pasta envelope on the outside. Think of these as pasta without pasta.

We can't stress enough the importance of using well-drained ricotta in this recipe. It's best if you can let the ricotta sit in a sieve over a bowl overnight.

Gnudi are traditionally made with spinach and ricotta, but in springtime when garden herbs start to poke out of the dark earth and turn green, when they are at their most delicate and the flavor is not yet fully pronounced, that's when we like to make these gnudi with a big handful of what's available—chives, sorrel, lovage, thyme, parsley, basil, mint, tarragon—growing in the garden, or on display at the produce stand. Be a little cautious with strongly flavored herbs such as mint, lovage, and basil—too much of them will dominate the mixture.

Pick over the herbs carefully, discarding any brown leaves and tough stems. Rinse the herbs thoroughly and dry before chopping. Chop very fine.

SERVES 6

About 1 pound ricotta, well drained, to make
  1½ cups
2 cups or more finely chopped mixed herbs
  (see headnote)
¾ cup freshly grated parmigiano-reggiano
6 tablespoons unbleached all-purpose flour,
  plus a little more for flouring the gnudi
Sea salt and freshly ground black pepper
1 large egg
6 tablespoons (¾ stick) unsalted butter
6 fresh sage leaves, or 3 tablespoons freshly
  grated parmigiano-reggiano

Combine the ricotta and mixed herbs in a bowl and beat together with a fork; or use your hands to combine thoroughly. Add the ¾ cup grated parmigiano and mix again. Sift 4 tablespoons of the flour over the mixture and combine. (The remaining flour may be added if necessary after you've added the egg.)

Taste for salt and add if necessary, keeping in mind that the cheese may be quite salty. Add pepper too, and stir in the egg. Take up a spoonful of the mixture and shape it into a gnudo the size of a walnut. The mixture should hold together; if it doesn't, add another tablespoon of flour, but be careful not to make it too dense.

Bring about 3 quarts of water to a rolling boil over medium-high heat. When the water boils, add a spoonful of salt. Test a couple of gnudi to make sure they are holding together. If they don't hold, mix in a little more flour, a tablespoon or so at a time.

Once you are sure the dough is working, prepare the gnudi: Spread a layer of flour on a dinner plate or platter. Shape the ricotta mixture into walnut-size balls, slightly flattened, and set them on the floured plate, then sift or shake more flour over the tops to cover them lightly.

When the water is boiling, turn the heat down to maintain a steady simmer. Gently roll the balls in the flour and drop, a few at a time, into the boiling water. Let the gnudi poach until they rise to the surface, then leave them to cook a few minutes longer. Remove each one with a slotted spoon and set aside in a warm place while you finish with all the gnudi.

Pile the gnudi in a warm serving bowl, or serve them on separate warm plates, 4 to each serving.

Heat the butter in a small skillet until it starts to brown, then add the sage leaves (if using), and continue cooking just a minute or two until the sage leaves start to crisp. Pour the brown butter and sage over the gnudi and serve immediately. Or pour the brown butter over and add a small handful of grated cheese, passing more at the table.

Lasagna Verde

Green Nettle Lasagna

Wild nettles are one of the earliest spring greens, in Italy as in North America. Packed with iron and other nutrients, they are really good for you, a spring tonic after a long winter of grains, beans, and salted meat. Wild foraged greens, brought to the table long before the first peas or fava beans were ready, brought new vitality to subsistence farmers who were often running out of stored food in the early spring. Nowadays, nettles are often to be found in farmers' markets right across the country. But truth to tell, almost any cooking greens work in this recipe, whether common spinach, beet greens, radish or turnip tops, even destemmed Swiss chard leaves. Use what you find, or use a mixture of greens. Flavors will change, but they all work deliciously.

You could use packaged lasagna for this, but, like most Italian cooks, we find that even the best pasta brands can't produce the kind of silken-textured lasagna that the finest cooks of Emilia-Romagna and Tuscany make. Don't be intimidated—this is actually the easiest handmade pasta to produce and is a fine way to gain confidence in the art of pasta making. To make green pasta, *pasta verde*, you simply add to the dough about a half pound of whatever greens you are using (see page 45): Blanch them in boiling water, drain them thoroughly, chop them fine, then drain again, squeezing to get out as much of the liquid as possible. Mix with the eggs into the dough.

Make the pasta dough and let it rest while you make the béchamel and filling. Then roll the dough out, poach it briefly, and you're ready to go.

SERVES 6

1 recipe Pasta Verde (Green Pasta) (page 45)
5 to 6 cups béchamel (page 11)
2 pounds fresh nettles, or nettles and spinach, or nettles and chard, or other combination of greens
1 medium yellow onion, finely chopped
2 tablespoons extra-virgin olive oil
Sea salt and freshly ground black pepper
2 to 3 tablespoons unsalted butter
1 cup freshly grated parmigiano-reggiano

First make the pasta dough, using the green pasta recipe on page 45. (Note that the dough can be made ahead of time and refrigerated for up to 24 hours, but if it is refrigerated, bring it back to room temperature before rolling it out.)

While the dough is resting, make the béchamel.

Now make the filling: Pick over the greens (if using nettles, before handling with bare hands, blanch them to remove the sting), removing any yellow or wilted greens and stripping leaves away from tough stems. Slice the greens into ribbons.

Combine the onion and oil in the bottom of a heavy-duty saucepan and set over medium-low heat. Cook, stirring, until the onion is soft, then stir in the greens by handfuls, letting each handful collapse and wilt slightly before adding more. If necessary, add a few tablespoons of boiling water to keep the greens from catching. Add salt and pepper and cook until the greens are done, 8 to 10 minutes.

Now you're ready to roll out the pasta, which you may do with a rolling pin and board or with a pasta machine. Follow the lasagna instructions on page 46, laying the cooked lasagna sheets out on damp kitchen towels as described.

Set the oven on 450°F. Use a little butter to grease the bottom of a 9 x 13-inch baking dish or lasagna pan.

Spread a couple of tablespoons of the green filling over the bottom of the dish, then set a layer of pasta sheets over the filling. Cover the pasta sheets with about a third of the remaining filling, then spread some of the béchamel over that. Sprinkle with parmigiano. Add another layer of pasta strips and cover again with filling, béchamel, and cheese. Keep doing this until all the pasta sheets are used up. The topmost layer should be béchamel and grated cheese, dotted with the butter.

Bake for 15 to 20 minutes, until the top is bubbling and lightly golden. Remove from the oven and leave to set for 15 minutes before serving.

About Nettles

Nettles are often called stinging nettles, with good reason—and it's a reason to be careful when harvesting them. In contact with the skin, the leaf hairs sting and burn and the sensation does not go away quickly. Nettles should be harvested and handled with care, then blanched to remove the sting. For harvesting, wear a long-sleeved shirt and gloves and clip the leaves with shears to fall into a basket or plastic sack. Harvest the tender tops of the plants and carry them home in the basket. Once in the kitchen, rinse them under running water (still using gloves or tongs) to get rid of any undesirables. You can then get rid of the sting by blanching: Bring a pot of water to a rolling boil, dump in the nettles, and give a stir so all are covered by the hot water. Have ready a bowl of ice water. Blanch the nettles for 30 seconds or so, drain, and plunge them into the ice water. This should rid them entirely of their sting.

Bucatini with Nettles and Cream

Please see About Nettles (page 140). Despite their sting, we love nettles for their musky, dusky flavor, sort of like a deeper-flavored spinach. It's true they sting when they're raw, but cooking takes that away, leaving a deep green vegetable that is as good for you as it is delicious. If you can't find nettles, spinach or another cooking green, such as Swiss chard, could be substituted.

SERVES 4 TO 6

About 3 pounds fresh nettles
3 tablespoons unsalted butter
2 garlic cloves, finely minced
½ cup heavy cream
Sea salt and freshly ground black pepper
Whole nutmeg, for grating
About 1 pound (500 grams) bucatini or any
*   long, thick pasta*
½ cup freshly grated parmigiano-reggiano

Wearing rubber gloves, remove the leaves from the nettle stems and discard the stems. Rinse the nettle leaves in abundant cold water and drain. Handle the nettles with rubber gloves until they are cooked.

In a heavy saucepan large enough to hold all the leaves, melt the butter and add the garlic. Cook the garlic very gently in the butter without letting it brown. Add the cream and nettles and let wilt, pushing the nettles down into the cream and turning with a wooden spoon. Add a pinch of salt, and when the leaves have wilted, grate nutmeg into the sauce—several gratings, or as much as you want. (This sauce can be prepared several hours ahead and reheated when you're ready to serve.)

When ready to serve, bring a large pot of water to a rolling boil, Add salt, tip in the pasta, and cook until al dente. Have ready a warm serving bowl. When the pasta is ready, drain and turn it into the bowl. Add the sauce and mix vigorously, then add a little parmigiano and serve immediately, passing more grated cheese at the table.

Maccheroncini ai Funghi con Burro e Rosmarino

Pasta with Wild Mushrooms, Rosemary, and Brown Butter

This is the simplest mushroom pasta dish we know. (For a slightly more complicated—and more autumnal—preparation, see the mushroom ragù on page 300.) Although we use maccheroncini, pennette, or another short, stubby pasta, when it's wild mushroom season in Tuscany and Umbria the mushrooms are often served with rich, handmade tagliatelle. If you have the time, making your own pasta will take this rustic dish up a notch and turn it into something truly elegant (directions are on page 43). Morels are a favorite for this, but chanterelles and black trumpets are delicious as well. In Tuscany the most commonly used, most highly valued mushrooms are porcini, foraged in the chestnut and oak forests traditionally in the fall, but when conditions are right, they appear in late spring as well.

SERVES 6

2 to 3 pounds fresh wild mushrooms (morels, chanterelles, black trumpets, porcini, or a combination)
4 tablespoons (½ stick) unsalted butter
Sea salt
1 tablespoon finely chopped fresh rosemary
About 1 pound (500 grams) pennette, maccheroncini, or other short, stubby pasta
¼ cup finely chopped flat-leaf parsley
½ cup freshly grated parmigiano-reggiano

Trim and clean the mushrooms: Wipe chanterelles or porcini carefully, using a soft mushroom brush to get into all the crevices. We don't rinse them because they absorb too much water and don't cook well. But with black trumpets or morels, a quick soak is necessary to get the dirt out. Soak them no more than 5 minutes in cold water. Scoop the mushrooms off the top of the water, giving them a swish, so the grit that has fallen to the bottom is left behind. Pat dry, then spread out on a dry kitchen towel and let the mushrooms air-dry for about 45 minutes. Cut in half lengthwise, or in quarters if the mushrooms are very large.

Bring a large pot of water to a rolling boil.

In a skillet large enough to hold the mushrooms and the pasta, melt the butter over medium heat until foaming. Add the mushrooms and a pinch of salt and turn the heat up to high. Sauté the mushrooms, and as they crisp up and the butter browns, add the rosemary and toss. Turn off the heat and reserve.

When the pasta water is boiling, add salt and the pasta and cook following the directions on page 33, checking the package recommendations for time. When the pasta is al dente, drain and add to the pan with the mushrooms and butter. Toss to mix well. Sprinkle with the parsley and a little parmigiano and toss again. Transfer to a warm serving bowl and serve immediately with the rest of the cheese.

Pasta alla Carbonara

Sara loved pasta alla carbonara during the years we lived in Rome. It's the first dish she began to cook for herself when she went away to school, even if sometimes that meant making it with bacon and cheddar cheese. It's a great dish for anyone trying to introduce small children to the art of the kitchen. It fits a springtime pasta menu because as the days grow longer and the sun grows stronger, the chickens start to lay again and there is plenty of material for this lush Roman classic. With that in mind, you want to use the freshest eggs you can find, preferably with dark yellow yolks, from hens that are truly free to range and graze and eat the things hens love.

Bucatini is the most traditional pasta to use in this typical Roman dish, but some cooks prefer spaghetti or even—sacrilegiously—short, stubby cuts like penne or rigatoni. But never, ever, says our friend Giovanni, with linguine. Why? "Because you don't do carbonara with linguine," says Giovanni, in an unassailably Roman argument.

Diced guanciale, cured pork cheek, is the preferred meat in Rome, but most of us will use the more commonly available pancetta or even slab bacon—the slight smokiness of good bacon gives an added luxury to the dish.

Pasta alla carbonara is one of those lightning rods of controversy in Italy over how it is made and what is traditional, any deviation being scorned. Sara sometimes likes to add minced onion to it, but that is unacceptable in most Roman trattorie; Nancy thinks chopped parsley brightens the dish visually and in your mouth, but that disqualifies it in Roman eyes. Even the smoked bacon we suggest as an option would be frowned on in Trastevere. But these are all modifications we have made over the years because we believe they add good flavor to the dish and we don't really like to be tied to tradition simply for tradition's sake.

See the variation below, equally traditional, called pasta alla papalina (papish pasta), which includes spring peas and diced ham instead of the guanciale in the original.

SERVES 4 TO 6

¼ pound guanciale or pancetta, diced small
  (about ½ cup)
2 tablespoons extra-virgin olive oil
4 or 5 large fresh eggs (the fresher the better)
1½ cups freshly grated pecorino romano
1½ cups freshly grated parmigiano-reggiano
Sea salt and freshly ground black pepper
1 pound (500 grams) bucatini or other long,
  slender pasta
¼ cup finely minced flat-leaf parsley
  (optional)

Combine the guanciale and oil in a skillet and sauté over medium-low heat until the meat is slightly crisp and brown. When done, set aside but keep warm.

While the guanciale is cooking, beat the

eggs together in a medium bowl. Combine the pecorino and parmigiano and set aside about 1 cup. Beat the rest of the cheese into the eggs.

Bring a large pot of water to a rolling boil. Add salt and the pasta and cook following the directions on page 33, until the pasta is al dente, 9 to 10 minutes.

While the pasta is cooking, get ready a warm serving bowl—ladle in some of the pasta cooking water to heat it.

As the pasta finishes cooking, have everything lined up and ready so you can act fast: colander in the sink, skillet with guanciale, bowl with eggs and cheese, warm bowl for serving pasta.

Okay, now: Acting quickly, set the skillet with guanciale back over medium heat, add a small ladleful (about ½ cup) of the pasta water, and bring to a simmer. Empty the hot water out of the serving bowl. Drain the pasta in the colander and immediately turn it into the heated bowl. Straight away, *immediately*, pour the egg mixture over the pasta, followed by the guanciale and its liquids. Start turning the pasta, over and over, vigorously, using two big spoons or a serving fork and spoon—the heat of the pasta and the guanciale mixture will slightly cook the eggs so that they thicken and coat the pasta well. Finally, sprinkle with a couple of spoonsful of the reserved grated cheeses, a lot of freshly ground pepper, and the minced parsley (if using). Serve immediately, passing the remaining cheeses to be added at the table.

VARIATION *Fettuccine alla papalina is basically a carbonara to which fresh sweet spring peas, cooked in butter with a little minced onion, and diced cooked ham (not raw prosciutto) are added. Toss the peas and ham with the pasta just before adding the final grated cheese and pepper.*

Ragù di Rigaglie di Pollo

Chicken Liver Ragù for a Spring Feast

This is a real peasant dish, a *piatto contadino*, from the farmhouse kitchens of Tuscany and Umbria, famous for never wasting a thing that is edible. Properly made, the sauce uses the livers, hearts, kidneys, stomachs, even the unborn eggs and the crests of farmyard birds (chickens, ducks, guinea fowl, and the like), trimmed, chopped, and braised in a simple tomato sauce flavored with fresh herbs—sage, rosemary, thyme, and in summer, perhaps a little basil. Often a pasta al ragù di rigaglie will be the primo, the first dish in a feast, followed by the same birds roasted in the wood-burning oven of the farmhouse. It's the kind of food our Tuscan neighbor Mita always prepared for the celebration that followed the daylong efforts of the *trebbiatura*, the threshing of wheat that took place around the middle of July, but she would also make this for the great spring feast of Easter when she fed as many as fifteen or twenty people around the long farmhouse table.

This sauce is good with almost any kind of pasta, although we like to serve it over short, twisted pasta shapes.

If you keep chickens or know someone who does, you can make ragú di rigaglie with all the innards, carefully cleaned and chopped. But for most of us, we'll make do with the chicken livers we find in any good meat counter or butcher shop. We insist on livers from organic, genuinely free-range chickens that have been raised with a certain amount of freedom.

You should have a good two cups of chopped vegetables—a reminder of the importance of vegetables in Italian country cooking. They aren't always obvious—meat is seldom served, as it is in North America, garnished with sides of vegetables on the plate. But the vegetables are always there, often like these hiding in a sauce. Note that the passata di pomodoro should be simply pureed tomatoes with nothing added but perhaps a little salt.

SERVES 6

1 pound chicken livers, carefully picked over
    and trimmed
Sea salt and freshly ground black pepper
1 medium carrot, chopped
1 medium onion, chopped
1 celery stalk, chopped
1 garlic clove

2 tablespoons diced pancetta or guanciale
¼ cup extra-virgin olive oil
¼ to ½ cup chopped flat-leaf parsley
½ cup dry white wine
One 14-ounce can whole tomatoes, preferably
    San Marzano, with their juice
½ cup passata di pomodoro (pureed tomatoes)
Leaves from 3 or 4 fresh thyme sprigs
3 or 4 fresh sage leaves, torn

Leaves from 1 fresh rosemary sprig
About 1 pound (500 grams) fusilli or other
  shape of your choice
1 cup or more freshly grated parmigiano-
  reggiano, aged pecorino toscano, or other
  grating cheese

Rinse the chicken livers and pat dry with paper towels. Salt and pepper them generously and set aside.

Combine the carrot, onion, celery, and garlic and chop further to make a fine mixture. You should have about 2 cups of chopped vegetables

Add the pancetta and oil to a large skillet and set over medium heat. Cook, stirring, until the meat starts to melt and brown slightly along the edges. Stir in the vegetables, lower the heat to medium-low, and cook, stirring frequently, for 10 to 15 minutes while the vegetables start to soften. Stir in the parsley and push the vegetables out to the edge of the skillet.

Add the chicken livers to the middle of the skillet and raise the heat slightly. Cook the livers until brown on all sides. As they brown, crush them in the pan juices with a fork. Once the livers are brown and crushed, mix them with the vegetables. Add the wine and raise the heat again to medium or medium-high. Cook briskly, stirring the contents of the skillet as the wine cooks down and releases its alcohol, about 5 minutes. Add the whole tomatoes along with their juice, breaking the tomatoes up as you add them to the skillet. Add the pureed tomatoes, along with the thyme, sage, and rosemary. Stir everything together and lower the heat so the sauce is just simmering. Cover and cook for 1½ hours, adding, if necessary, a little water from time to time to keep it from getting too thick.

When the sauce is done, remove from the heat. It may be served as is, or if you wish, puree it just slightly, either in a food processor or using an immersion blender. It should not be a smooth sauce, but rather have lots of bits and pieces to cling to the pasta. (The sauce may be made ahead a day or two and reheated just before serving.)

When ready to serve, bring a large pot of water to a rolling boil. Add salt and the pasta and cook following the directions on page 33. When the pasta is al dente, drain and turn it into a warm serving bowl. Add the hot sauce and mix vigorously, then add a little parmigiano and serve immediately, passing more cheese at the table.

Cavatelli del Pastore

Cavatelli with Braised Lamb and Ricotta

C avatelli del pastore (shepherd's pasta) features the shepherd's two prize ingredients, spring lamb and fresh sheep's-milk ricotta.

You have to imagine great flocks of sheep, guarded by a shepherd, a *pastore*, and a pair of fierce dogs, marching slowly across the spring hillsides of the Abruzzi, moving steadily higher as the season advances, always seeking fresh pasture. When they reach the grassy upper slopes, the ewe's milk is at its sweetest, and then the shepherd's wife spends her days making it into cheese, using the whey to make fresh creamy ricotta. Many of the fine pecorino cheeses of Italy come from homely, hands-on production like this. Up until the middle of the last century, flocks still traveled on foot between the high Abruzzi mountains, rich in summer pasture, down to the plains of northern Puglia where winter grass was abundant. It was an amazing spectacle, they say, as flocks numbering in the hundreds if not thousands moved slowly, munching their way along the *tratturi*, broad, grassy highways, some of which dated to Roman times. Sheep are, or were, a major part of the economy of southern Italy and naturally of the cuisine as well. Lamb and mutton are featured dishes whenever it's time for a feast.

Southern Italy's great sheep's-milk cheeses (*pecorino*, the name comes from the Italian for a female sheep, *pecora*) are easier to find in North America than they used to be. Sharp, strong pecorino romano has been around for some time, but subtler, sweeter pecorinos from Sicily, Sardinia, and other parts of the south are increasingly available. (See page 23 for more information on pecorino and ricotta.)

Cavatelli is often made by hand, the pasta disks rolled with a flick of the fingers. Cooks talk about one-finger, two-finger, or three-finger cavatelli, depending on the size. But there are excellent brands of artisanal pasta secca cavatelli; if you cannot find them, use small shells, orecchiette, or any other small, cup-shape pasta instead.

A slow, steady simmer is the key to making the meat so tender it almost disappears into the sauce.

SERVES 8

4 tablespoons extra-virgin olive oil

About 1 ounce pancetta, diced small (¼ cup)

About 2 pounds lamb (shoulder is a good choice), bone in, in 1 piece

2 Italian-style fresh pork sausages, sweet or hot, your choice

2 medium yellow onions, diced small (1 cup)

2 medium carrots, diced small

2 celery stalks, diced small

1 garlic clove, crushed with the flat blade of a knife

About 2 tablespoons chopped flat-leaf parsley

1 tablespoon minced fresh rosemary

1 small dried red chili pepper, broken, or a
pinch crushed red pepper flakes
2 bay leaves
1 cup flavorful red wine (Montepulciano
d'Abruzzo would be perfect)
One 28-ounce can whole tomatoes, preferably
San Marzano, with their juice
Sea salt and freshly ground black pepper
1 cup fresh ricotta, drained, if necessary, for
a few hours
½ cup freshly grated aged pecorino toscano,
pecorino sardo, or grana padano
About 1 pound (500 grams) cavatelli

Combine 2 tablespoons of the oil and the pancetta in a large heavy saucepan and set over medium heat. Cook, stirring frequently, until the pancetta starts to melt and give off its fat. Add the lamb and continue cooking, turning the lamb to brown on all sides.

While the lamb is browning, open the sausages, discarding the skins, and crumble the sausage meat with a fork. Remove the browned lamb from the saucepan, setting it aside, and add the sausage meat. Cook and stir until the sausage meat has browned.

Now lower the heat to medium-low and stir in the onions, carrots, celery, garlic, and parsley. Continue cooking and stirring until the vegetables start to soften and give off their aroma. Add the rosemary, chili pepper, and bay leaves, along with the wine. Raise the heat to medium and cook rapidly, scraping up any brown bits from the bottom of the pan. Return the lamb to the saucepan.

Let the wine bubble and reduce by at least half, then add the tomatoes, breaking them up in your hands as you do so, along with their juice.

Lower the heat to just barely simmering, cover the pan, and cook for about 2 hours, or until the meat is so soft it's falling apart in the sauce. Lift the lid from time to time and give the contents a stir, adding water if the sauce is cooking down too much.

When the sauce is ready, combine the drained ricotta with the grated pecorino and plenty of freshly ground black pepper. Beat with a fork or a wire whisk to combine thoroughly, adding the remaining 2 tablespoons oil (or more) as you beat. Set aside.

Remove the lamb from the sauce and break it up into smaller pieces, discarding the bones. Discard the bay leaves. Return the lamb to the sauce and continue cooking while you prepare the pasta.

Bring a large pot of water to a rolling boil. Add salt and the pasta and cook following the directions on page 33.

Just before adding the pasta to a warm serving bowl, put about a third of the sauce into the bottom.

When the pasta is done, drain and turn it immediately into the bowl. Toss with the sauce in the bottom of the bowl, then mound the remaining sauce on top and cap it all with the ricotta mixture. Serve immediately, tossing at the table to mix the sauce, ricotta, and pasta together.

COOK'S TIP *If a rind is attached to the pancetta or guanciale, remove it in one piece and add it to the sauce after you've added the tomatoes. It will add considerable richness. But remove it, for appearance's sake, before you serve the sauce.*

Lamb Meatballs in Spicy Tomato Sauce with Elicoidali

Spring is lamb season in the pasta kitchens of the Mediterranean. We love lamb just about any way you slice it, but these meatballs, made from ground shoulder of lamb, are particularly enticing. The flavors of cumin, coriander (the seeds of green cilantro), and cinnamon are decidedly eastern—think Turkey and Lebanon—but the chili-spiced tomato sauce is definitely from the Italian south. Put them together and you have a pan-Mediterranean dish that is perfect for a spring evening.

Elicoidali are short lengths of hollow pasta with spiral ribbings, but you could use rigatoni, or any other short, stubby pasta instead.

The meatballs may be prepared ahead of time and kept until you're ready to make the sauce. And the sauce itself may also be made ahead and kept, refrigerated if necessary, until ready to use.

SERVES 6

FOR THE MEATBALLS
1 pound ground lamb shoulder
2 large eggs
About ½ cup finely chopped red onion
1 teaspoon or more ground cumin
½ teaspoon or more ground coriander
¼ teaspoon or more ground cinnamon
Sea salt and plenty of freshly ground black pepper
1½ cups soft dry bread crumbs
½ cup extra-virgin olive oil

FOR THE SAUCE
2 tablespoons extra-virgin olive oil
½ cup diced pancetta
½ cup finely chopped red onion
¼ cup finely chopped flat-leaf parsley
One 28-ounce can whole tomatoes, preferably San Marzano, with their juice
½ cup dry white wine
1 small dried red chili pepper, or to taste
Sea salt and freshly ground black pepper
About 1 pound (500 grams) elicoidali or other short, stubby pasta
Freshly grated pecorino romano or parmigiano-reggiano, for garnish

Prepare the meatballs: Combine the lamb, eggs, onion, cumin, coriander, cinnamon, salt, and black pepper in a bowl and mix together well using your hands. The mixture will be very wet.

Set aside at least ½ cup of the bread crumbs for breading the finished meatballs. Add another ½ cup to the meat mixture, mixing well. If the mixture is still too wet, add more bread crumbs, a tablespoon at a time, until the mixture will hold together nicely when you form it into balls. Set the mixture aside, covered, for about 30 minutes, so the crumbs will more fully absorb the moisture. Any leftover crumbs should be added to the reserved bread crumbs.

When the meat mixture is ready, shape it into small balls about the size of a walnut. You should have 30 to 36 balls in the end. Roll each ball in the reserved bread crumbs to coat completely. Be prepared to fry the meatballs as soon as they are coated with crumbs.

Add the oil to a skillet and set over medium-low heat. When hot, add the meatballs, a few at a time, and cook, browning them on all sides. As the meatballs brown, set them aside. (You can do this a day or more in advance, refrigerating the meatballs.)

Prepare the sauce: Combine the oil and pancetta in a saucepan and cook over medium-low heat until the fat in the pancetta starts to run. Stir in the onion and parsley and continue cooking, stirring, until the onion is soft, but do not let the onion brown. Add the meatballs and mix, then add the tomatoes, reserving the juice and breaking up each tomato in your hands as you add it to the pot. Stir in the wine and cook briefly to absorb any brown bits that have adhered to the bottom of the pan. As soon as the fragrance of alcohol has dissipated, stir in the tomato juice left in the can. Add the chili pepper, a good pinch of salt, and plenty of black pepper and cook, covered, until the tomato sauce has reduced and thickened. Stir the sauce occasionally to make sure it doesn't stick to the bottom. When the sauce is done, taste and adjust the seasoning. (If using a whole chili pepper, remove it before serving.)

Bring a large pot of water to a rolling boil. Add salt and the pasta and cook following the directions on page 33.

Have the meatball sauce simmering as the pasta cooks. Remove and set aside about a dozen of the meatballs to garnish the dish.

Add a big spoonful of tomato sauce, minus the meatballs, to the bottom of a warm serving bowl.

As soon as the pasta is al dente, drain and turn it into the bowl. Add a handful of pecorino romano and toss with the pasta and sauce. Turn the remaining meatball sauce over the top of the pasta, garnish with more of the grated cheese and the reserved meatballs, and serve immediately.

Pasta Colle Sarde

Pasta with Wild Fennel and Fresh Sardines

The Feast of Saint Joseph on March 19 comes right before the vernal equinox, and all around the Christian Mediterranean it's a welcome to spring. On the island of Sicily, it's marked by this splendid dish, which requires two ingredients that are almost impossible to find in North America—wild fennel greens and fresh sardines. But we want to include pasta colle sarde, first of all because it's an important harbinger of spring, and second, for our friends on the West Coast where wild fennel, doubtless brought by Italian immigrants generations ago, grows in some profusion and the wild sardines have returned, in part through the admirable efforts of the Monterey Bay Aquarium (see www .seafoodwatch.org).

Gather the tender stalks and feathery fronds of wild fennel, taking care to harvest only in places that have not been sprayed or subjected to exhaust pollution (that is, not along highway edges). If you can't cut the stalk easily with a paring knife, it will be too tough to use in the dish. Cut the stalks into inch-long pieces. You should have about 4 well-packed cups of stalks and greens. Rinse the fennel several times in a basin of water, swishing it to rid it of undesirable dust or critters.

If your fishmonger is not willing to clean the sardines, you'll have to do it yourself. Fortunately it's easier to do than to describe. Don't worry about getting every last little bone, apart from the backbone. Sardine bones are soft and fine—just think of them as extra calcium. Using a sharp paring knife, slice the sardine from head to tail along the belly and butterfly open the two fillets. With the point of the knife, dig under the spine by the tail and gently pull up until it starts to lift free. Pull the skeleton up along the body and discard with the head and tail of the fish. Clean any guts away and keep the fillets cold until ready to cook.

SERVES 4 TO 6

About 4 cups packed fennel greens and tender stalks (see headnote)

1 pound fresh sardines (see headnote)

Pinch saffron threads

About ½ cup extra-virgin olive oil, preferably Sicilian

1 large onion, coarsely chopped

4 anchovy fillets, chopped

2 tablespoons tomato puree

¼ cup dry white wine

2 tablespoons golden sultana raisins, steeped in warm water to soften and drained

3 tablespoons pine nuts

Sea salt and freshly ground black pepper

½ cup unbleached all-purpose flour

About 1 pound (500 grams) bucatini, perciatelli, or maccheroncini

½ cup toasted coarse unflavored bread crumbs

Bring 3 quarts of water to a rolling boil in a large pot. Add the fennel greens and stalks. Boil for 15 to 20 minutes, or until the thickest pieces of stalk are tender.

While the fennel is cooking, prepare the sardines. Cut each fish into two fillets and rinse quickly in cool water. Set aside about a quarter to a third of the sardines to be fried. (Each serving will be garnished with at least one fried fillet.) Chop the remaining sardines into bite-size pieces and pat them dry with paper towels.

When the fennel is done, use a slotted spoon to pull it out of the cooking water and set aside. *Do not discard the cooking water.* At this point you should have about 2 cups of cooked greens. Chop the greens coarsely, as soon as you can handle them.

Remove ½ cup of the cooking water and transfer to a small bowl. Add the saffron and set aside to steep.

Add 2 to 3 tablespoons of the oil to a skillet and set over medium-low heat. Add the onion and cook gently, stirring frequently, until the onion is soft and golden. Do not let the onion get brown. Stir in the chopped anchovies and cook, pressing with a fork to mash the anchovy bits into the oil. Add the tomato puree and wine, raise the heat slightly, and simmer for 2 to 3 minutes to combine the flavors.

Add the chopped sardines to the skillet and cook, stirring, until they have turned opaque, then stir in the chopped fennel. Add the drained raisins, pine nuts, and saffron water, stirring them in. Let the sauce simmer very gently while you fry the sardines and cook the pasta. If the sauce appears to be drying out too much, add a little of the fennel cooking water. (You may prepare the recipe ahead of time to this point and hold the sauce, refrigerated if necessary, reheating when ready to continue with the recipe.)

Dry the reserved whole sardine fillets once more with paper towels. Spread the flour on a plate and lightly coat the fillets with flour. Add about ¼ cup of the remaining oil to a skillet and set over medium heat. When the oil is hot, brown the fillets on both sides, then transfer to a rack covered with paper towels to drain.

Add water to the fennel cooking liquid to make about 6 quarts and bring to a rolling boil. Add salt and the pasta and cook following the directions on page 33. Bucatini take about 12 minutes, but start testing the pasta after 8 or 9 minutes.

When the pasta is al dente, drain and immediately turn it into a warm serving bowl, dressing it with the hot sardine-fennel sauce. Top with the toasted bread crumbs and garnish with the fried fillets. Serve immediately.

Linguine with Fresh Shrimp and Arugula

Sweet shrimp and spicy bitter arugula is a combination we never tire of. The shrimp and white wine cook together and the hot pasta then wilts the arugula, keeping its texture and spicy flavors intact. Small shrimp may be left whole, but medium or large shrimp should be cut in half after peeling and deveining; very large shrimp should be cut into bite-size pieces. No matter what size you use, the shrimp should be peeled and deveined before you start cooking.

SERVES 4 TO 6

2 or 3 garlic cloves, finely minced
2 or 3 tablespoons extra-virgin olive oil
1¼ pounds shrimp, fresh if possible, peeled,
*   cut smaller if necessary (see headnote)*
¼ cup dry white wine
Pinch ground red chili pepper or crushed red
*   pepper flakes*
Freshly grated zest of ½ lemon, preferably organic
Sea salt
About 1 pound (500 grams) linguine or other
*   long, slender pasta*
2 tablespoons freshly squeezed lemon juice
2 tablespoons unsalted butter, cut into small
*   pieces*
2 cups fresh peppery arugula, rinsed and dried

Bring 6 quarts of water to a rolling boil in a large pot.

While the water is heating up, prepare the shrimp sauce: Combine the garlic and oil in a skillet large enough to hold the shrimp and set over medium-low heat. Cook the garlic gently—do not let it burn. When it is soft, remove it from the oil with a slotted spoon and set aside. Raise the heat under the skillet and add the shrimp. Cook quickly, tossing as if stir-frying, just until the shrimp change color. With small shrimp, this is a matter of seconds, not even a minute. Larger shrimp will take a bit longer, but be careful not to overcook. Remove the shrimp and add to the garlic.

Add the wine to the pan and continue cooking as you stir in the chili pepper and lemon zest. Reduce the wine to a couple of tablespoons, then return the garlic and shrimp to the pan, give it a swirl, and remove from the heat. Keep warm while you cook the pasta.

By now the pasta water will be at a rolling boil. Add salt and the pasta and cook following the directions on page 33. As soon as the pasta approaches the al dente stage, turn on the heat under the skillet and stir in the lemon juice and butter. Drain the pasta and turn immediately into a warm serving bowl. Add the shrimp sauce and the arugula and toss to mix well. Serve immediately.

VARIATIONS *In early spring, you could add a handful of tender young asparagus stems, cut into 1-inch lengths and steamed until soft. Later in the summer, a handful of little grape tomatoes, halved, can be stirred in so that the hot pasta melts them slightly and pulls out some of their juices.*

Tagliolini with Fresh Shucked Oysters, Crème Fraîche, and Chives

Elegant and delicate in flavor, this is another great way to use handmade egg-rich tagliolini (see page 45). The slightly cooked oysters retain a briny hint of the sea that is repeated in the tang of crème fraîche. The chives add color and more flavor to the dish.

In Maine we use oysters from Pulpit Harbor on North Haven Island or from the brackish waters of the Bagaduce near Castine. But all up and down the East Coast are really fine oyster grounds, from Prince Edward Island to South Carolina and beyond. Just make sure you get the freshest you can find, from as close to home as possible.

Open the oysters ahead of time, then just heat them in the crème fraîche and you're good to go. (And if you have a good source of freshly made egg pasta, by all means use it, if you wish.)

SERVES 6

36 fresh oysters
Sea salt and freshly ground black pepper
½ cup crème fraîche
2 tablespoons minced chives
Freshly grated zest of 1 lemon, preferably
    organic
1 pound fresh egg tagliolini (see page 284)

Scrub the oysters in cold running water. Set a cast-iron pan over medium-high heat and heat to hot, then add the oysters to the pan and roast dry just until the shells pop open. Shuck the lightly cooked oysters into a bowl with all their juices. Scoop the oysters out and set aside. Strain the liquid of any sand or bits of shell—you should have about ½ cup strained oyster liquid.

Bring about 6 quarts of water to a rolling boil in a large pot and add a big spoonful of salt.

While waiting for the water to boil, combine the oysters and their strained liquid in a saucepan and poach gently over medium-low heat for a minute or so, just long enough to be cooked through without becoming tough and overcooked. Remove from the heat.

Have ready a warm serving bowl. Add the crème fraîche and chives to the bowl. Strain the oyster liquid into the crème fraîche and whisk together, then fold in the oysters and lemon zest. Keep warm while the pasta cooks.

When the water is boiling, tip the pasta in, give it a stir with a long-handled spoon, and cook—if fresh, it will be ready when it starts to float. Otherwise, cook according to the package directions. Scoop out or drain the pasta and add to the crème fraîche and oysters and toss to coat the strands of pasta with the oyster cream. Add plenty of pepper. Taste for salt—the oysters themselves may provide enough salt. Serve immediately.

Fusilli with Salmon, Lemon, and Fresh Spring Greens

Once upon a time, salmon was a strictly springtime treat, when that sleek and graceful fish was in such abundance that whole schools ran up rivers on both sides of the Atlantic to spawn. But that was long ago, before dams, pollution, and overfishing wiped out the Atlantic salmon population. Nowadays, the only legal Atlantic salmon is farmed. But don't knock it. Farmed salmon is a wise and healthy choice, as long as it is farmed sustainably—and most salmon is indeed farmed sustainably nowadays. You could, of course, use wild Pacific salmon in this dish, but the texture of the flesh is dry and less unctuous than that of the true Atlantic salmon.

Because salmon was always so closely identified with springtime, we think it belongs in the Spring section of recipes—but the dish is delicious almost any time of the year.

You could use any spring greens for this, including spinach, chard, pea shoots—or the mixture called braising greens. But be sure to select young, fresh, tender greens in their prime. Six cups may seem like a lot, but fresh spring greens cook down rapidly. This will be adequate for the number of servings.

SERVES 4 TO 6

One 1-pound piece fresh salmon
4 to 5 tablespoons extra-virgin olive oil
Sea salt and freshly ground black pepper
½ cup chopped scallions, small, thin leeks, or
    a combination
¼ pound fresh mushrooms, sliced (optional)
6 cups braising greens (see headnote)
Grated zest of 1 lemon, preferably organic
2 tablespoons freshly squeezed lemon juice
About 1 pound (500 grams) fusilli or other
    curly pasta

Rinse the salmon and pat dry with paper towels. Heat 2 tablespoons of the oil in a skillet over medium heat. When the oil is hot, add the salmon, skin side down, and adjust the heat so the fish is cooking steadily but not burning; cook until the fillet is cooked through and the flesh has turned from translucent red to opaque pink. (Do not turn the salmon during cooking. If necessary, you can run it under a broiler for a minute or two to finish the top.) When the salmon is done, remove it from the skillet, sprinkle the fish with salt and pepper, and set aside.

Discard the burned fat in the skillet and when the skillet is cool enough to handle, wipe it out. Add 2 more tablespoons of the oil to the skillet. Add the scallions and mushrooms (if using) and set over medium-low heat. Cook, stirring occasionally, until the scallions and mushrooms are soft. Add the greens with the water clinging to their leaves and a good sprinkle of salt. Cook until the greens are thoroughly wilted, stirring frequently and combining with the scallion mixture. When the greens are done, remove the skillet from the heat. Add the lemon zest and lemon juice and mix them in.

Remove and discard the salmon skin. Flake the cooked salmon and combine with the greens. Taste and add more salt and pepper or a little more lemon juice, if you wish. Keep the salmon and greens warm while you cook the pasta. (This may be prepared ahead to this point, but the salmon and greens should be hot when the pasta is ready.)

Bring a large pot of water to a rolling boil. Add salt and the pasta and cook following the directions on page 33. When the pasta is al dente, add ¼ cup of the pasta water to the greens and salmon and bring to a simmer. Drain the pasta and turn it into a warm serving bowl. Toss with the greens and salmon and serve immediately.

Spaghettini with Lemon Butter and Bottarga

S ara speaking: "Getting invited to wine lunches with visiting winemakers or vineyard owners is probably one of the best perks of my job as restaurant chef. We often wind up talking about food, and one Sicilian winemaker told me about this incredibly simple yet tasty dish. It's the sort of thing that you make when you don't have anything else, and at the same time it's so complex in flavor it will dazzle anyone you serve it to."

Bottarga is salted and dried fish roe (see page 22). It used to be something we had to smuggle back from Sicily or Sardinia, but it is now so common that it's even available at www.amazon.com. It's not cheap, but a little goes a long way. There are two types of bottarga—bottarga di muggine, which is made from the roes of gray mullet, and bottarga di tonno, from the roes of tuna. We prefer the former, mostly because the bluefin tuna from which the latter is made is threatened with extinction.

SERVES 6

8 tablespoons (1 stick, or ½ cup) unsalted butter

¼ cup freshly squeezed lemon juice, or more to taste

Sea salt

About 1 pound (500 grams) spaghettini or spaghetti

¼ cup finely minced flat-leaf parsley, or a handful of arugula

8 ounces bottarga, preferably bottarga di muggine, grated

2 tablespoons extra-virgin olive oil

Freshly grated zest of ½ lemon, preferably organic

Bring a large pot of water to a rolling boil.

While the water is heating, melt the butter over gentle heat, and when it is creamy, whisk in the lemon juice. Turn off the heat but keep the lemon butter warm.

Add salt and the pasta to the boiling water and cook following the directions on page 33. Thin spaghettini should take about 6 minutes, but start to test at 5 minutes.

When the pasta is al dente, drain and turn it immediately into a warm serving bowl. Toss with the lemon butter, parsley, and half the bottarga. Add the oil and lemon zest and toss again. Top the pasta with the rest of the bottarga and serve immediately.

Moroccan Couscous aux Sept Légumes

Couscous with Seven (or More) Vegetables—A Vegetarian Dish

*C*ouscous aux sept légumes is a traditional Moroccan dish that is often more attractive in the imagination than in the reality, which is all too frequently a rustic dish of lamb shanks with overcooked vegetables. Sara re-proposes it as an elegant, delicate vegetarian presentation that is completely about the vegetables and not the meat at all. She developed the recipe originally for vegetarian customers at her restaurant—and as a way to play with some of the beautiful spring vegetables to be found in New York's Greenmarket. Make it with the aromatic vegetable broth on page 10 and whatever vegetables you find in season that are freshest and most beautiful. If you can't find something on our list below, just substitute another seasonal addition.

Pulverizing the cauliflower and mixing it in with the couscous is a party trick stolen from a modernist chef whose food we would normally scorn as too technical, overly restaurant-ish, but in this case it seems like a fun way to incorporate the vegetable. You could probably do the same thing with green broccoli florets, but they wouldn't be so disguised in the couscous.

Note that you will need a total of 8 cups of cooked vegetables to accompany the couscous, approximately 4 cups of leafy greens and 4 cups of assorted other vegetables. Try to include some colorful carrots and radishes in the latter group to make a handsome presentation.

SERVES 6 TO 8

½ medium head of cauliflower, broken into florets (about ½ pound cauliflower)

2 cups plain couscous

4 tablespoons extra-virgin olive oil

Bay leaf

1 teaspoon ground turmeric, or one 1-inch nob fresh peeled turmeric

One 2-inch cinnamon stick

5 cloves

4 cardamom pods

1 small dried red chili pepper

1 teaspoon sea salt, plus more to taste if needed

4 cups Vegetable Broth (page 10)

4 cups trimmed assorted vegetables, such as: whole snap peas; shucked fava beans; green beans cut into 2-inch lengths; scallions cut into 2-inch lengths; baby turnips, peeled; baby carrots, peeled; radishes; okra

4 pounds tender, leafy greens, such as spinach, chard, bok choy, baby kale, trimmed and coarsely chopped

1 teaspoon finely minced cilantro, plus 12 sprigs for garnish

¼ to ½ teaspoon vinegar

¼ cup harissa, or to taste

Put the cauliflower florets in the bowl of a food processor and pulverize, pulsing until the florets are reduced to a fine grain, about the size of the couscous grains. Set aside.

Combine the dry couscous and 2 tablespoons of the oil in a mixing bowl. Rub and knead the couscous grains until the oil has been fully incorporated. In a saucepan, combine 2 cups water with the bay leaf, turmeric, cinnamon, cloves, cardamom, chili, and salt, and bring to a boil. Strain the spiced water over the couscous, give it a quick stir, and cover immediately with plastic wrap. Set aside to steam for 10 minutes. Then fluff the couscous with a fork and stir in the remaining 2 tablespoons oil and the pulverized cauliflower. Cover again and set aside.

Set the oven on 375°F.

Bring the vegetable broth to a simmer in a large saucepan and cook the vegetables one at a time as long as needed to just tenderize. If using radishes, set aside 3 or 4 to shave over the top of the couscous as a final garnish. Different vegetables will take different amounts of time, with roots taking longer than vegetables such as peas, beans, and okra. As each vegetable finishes cooking, skim it out and reserve. Add the chopped leafy greens at the last, cooking them until they're very tender, then strain from the stock and chop again until fine.

Mix the chopped greens into the couscous and cauliflower and set in the oven to reheat, uncovered, for 10 minutes.

Meanwhile, bring the vegetable stock back to a simmer and add back all the remaining vegetables except the reserved radishes. Simmer briefly, just long enough to warm them thoroughly. Taste the stock and add salt if necessary, along with the minced cilantro and a few drops of vinegar.

To serve, mound the couscous and greens in a large, warm serving bowl and arrange the vegetables all around. Spoon the broth over the vegetables and couscous. Shave the reserved radishes over the top, add a good dollop of harissa, and garnish with sprigs of cilantro.

Serve immediately.

Summer

Henry James said it most succinctly: "Summer afternoon, summer afternoon; to me those have always been the two most beautiful words in the English language." Words that call up long, languid days; afternoon picnics in the bee-loud glade beneath the chestnut trees in a Tuscan garden; late-night suppers on a trattoria terrace in sleepy Rome; children chasing fireflies through a Maine twilight while their elders dip bread crusts into the last of the pasta sauce; sunny mornings at the beach foraging for clams, lobsters, mussels, and crabs; bare feet curling into the warm earth of a friend's garden as he plies us with tomatoes and cucumbers, sweet and spicy peppers, fresh beans and early corn. "Take, take," he says, "it's too much for me, it's summer's bounty."

Summer in New England, summer in California, summer in Italy, summer in far-off, upside-down Australia—wherever summer happens, it's a brilliant time of year as gardens, farm stands, and produce markets alike explode in a dazzling selection of gorgeous vegetables. And we want them all, tossed on our

In Tuscany's Arno valley, a friend makes a great pesto using wild fennel greens and pistachios—California cooks might forage for wild fennel growing in abandoned plots in that state where the wild plant emigrated centuries ago from its Mediterranean homeland.

plates of pasta, one after the other or in sensational combinations. The earliest harbingers of this seasonal abundance fade away in the bright warmth of early July, and asparagus, fava beans, and peas are banished as zucchini, eggplants, and tomatoes march into our kitchens; then the drowsy heat of high summer arrives, bringing with it sweet corn, grilled and grated into pasta; tiny new beets, new potatoes, and sweet peppers in rainbow colors; skinny French haricots and flat green romano beans, and our favorite, fresh shelling beans, whether cranberry, cannellini, or any of the myriad heirloom beans, adding a healthful note to robust pastas.

Roasted, steamed, grilled, sauced, pureed, or chopped, raw summer vegetables brighten up the pasta menu. Sometimes, cruising a farmers' market or a roadside farm stand, we snatch up just one or two fresh greens that catch our eye and simply toss them into a frying pan together with a healthy glug of olive oil, a bit of garlic and onion, some salt and pepper, to make a spontaneous *pasta al orto*, pasta fresh from the garden. Whenever we can, we add from that other summer sweet spot, the bright array of crisp fresh herbs, foraged in the wild, cultivated in gardens, or carefully nourished in pots on city window ledges. Parsley, sage, rosemary, and of course thyme, but also basil, summer savory,

delicate chervil and chives, cilantro, mint, and tarragon—not all of them, not all at once, but each one or two will find a role to play in the kitchen, enhancing the flavors of the summer vegetables we love.

Thinking about herbs reminds us of basil and inevitably of pesto. We aim to convince ambitious cooks to try at least once to make real old-fashioned Pesto Genovese (page 195), using a mortar and a pestle. The texture is surprising, almost unctuous in the way the sauce coats the pasta. But don't restrict pesto to the basil–pine nut version we know best, the one that goes so well with a combination of pasta, potatoes, and green beans. Once upon a time, the Ligurian original from Italy's Riviera was made with walnuts and parsley instead—a splendid idea to try. And we love the brilliant pesto from Trapani on the west coast of Sicily using Sicilian almonds, basil, and tomatoes (see page 192), traditionally served over intricately curled busiate, a regional favorite. In Tuscany's Arno valley, a friend makes a great pesto using wild fennel greens and pistachios—California cooks might forage for wild fennel growing in abandoned plots in that state where the wild plant emigrated centuries ago from its Mediterranean homeland. Or just use your imagination and combine fresh herbs with nuts (hazelnuts also work well) in a food processor and beat in olive oil until the mixture is the right consistency. Add a little cheese, a little garlic, maybe a tiny pinch of chili pepper, then toss with pasta hot from the pot and serve it up immediately. Summertime in a bowl!

Eggplant is another harbinger of summer, roasted or grilled and tossed with tomatoes and mozzarella, or charred into a sweet-smoky filling for ravioli. It's true, eggplant is in supermarket produce sections year-round, but nothing beats the fresh flavor of eggplant right out of the garden—something you won't get from supermarket varieties that have been chilled and shipped thousands of miles. (Refrigeration is not good for this summer favorite.) Zucchini are ubiquitous throughout the year too, but their blossoms, pale and delicate, are purely a summer treat.

If you've been thinking about eating less meat (and who hasn't these days?), summer is an ideal time to amp up your vegetable consumption—with so very many vegetables to choose from, meat won't even be missed. But it's also a perfect time to practice being a locavore—maybe not for every meal, nor even for every day, but once in a while take up the challenge of eating nothing that hasn't been grown within, say, a fifty-mile radius of your house. Impossible?

Not really, not with the burgeoning of farmers' markets all over the country.

The warm, days of summer call naturally for lighter meals so it's also a time when we crave fish and seafood. Our Maine holidays always include lobster—it wouldn't be summer in Maine without it—but other types fit summer menus too, even those that are in abundance all year round. Seafood means lightness, as in alluring seafood pastas made with clams or lobster or sweet white fish sparked with tart lemon and fresh herbs.

So much of summer cooking is about quick and easy—quick in order not to heat up the kitchen, easy in order to get back outside in the sunshine—but we're also passionate about two slightly more complex summertime pasta dishes that we think are spectacular, especially for summer entertaining. One is Cuscussù Trapanese (page 227), the Sicilian dish that's a takeoff on North African couscous but easier and fun too, with its range of seafood. The other is a great tradition from Catalonia, on Spain's east coast, where Mediterranean seafood stars in a brilliant version of paella—but paella made not with rice as usual, but with *fideos*, or Spanish pasta (see page 229).

L'IMPORTANZA DEL POMODORO (THE GIFT OF SUMMER: ON THE IMPORTANCE OF TOMATOES)

If sweet corn spells high summer for Americans, in other parts of the world it's the tomato that reigns as the emblem of the summer kitchen. The warmth, the sunshine,

the very energy of summer brings to mind fresh, quick tomato sauces bursting with the taste of ripe fruit, sweet and tart with a bitter edge at the end. It's hard not to

Don't be afraid to use any and all of these tomato varieties, whether Italian or Chinese or native Mexican, in our tomato recipes.

believe that god invented tomatoes just to go with pasta. (And then invented basil to go with tomatoes.)

Raw or cooked, embellished with leaves of fresh green basil and parsley or just a dribble of olive oil, smoothed to a puree or chopped into chunks, tomatoes in any form give pasta a reason for being. We're content to eat all sorts of things on our pasta the rest of the year, but at the height of summer, give us fresh, ripe tomatoes to make us truly grateful. Then, after we've licked the bowl of pasta al pomodoro clean, we'll be off to the kitchen to make tomato sauce, la pomarola, putting it up in jars for our winter pantry.

And not just any tomatoes. In open-air markets all over Italy, from Genova to Catania and everywhere in between, we look for the finest specimens from local farms—plum-shaped San Marzanos, perfect for sauce; deeply ridged costolutos, looking like a tomato in a Baroque still life; heart-shape cuor di bue, or oxhearts; little grape-clustered datteri growing like the dates for which they are named; and last, but hardly least, pomodorini del piennolo del Vesuvio, the small, tough-skinned but tasty cluster tomatoes that are grown in the south, often harvested vine and all, and hung in an airy pantry to last through the winter, growing ever sweeter as they concentrate their flavors.

But here's something odd: Although it is dead easy to find fabulous tomatoes at the height of the season throughout Italy, there is not the range of choice that we have come to experience in North America, where we can add to all of the above-mentioned such old-timey, newly popular favorites as green zebras with their delicate lime-green stripes; black krims, which are actually purple-red in color; big, beefy Amish paste tomatoes, so perfect for sauce; greeny-yellow German cherry tomatoes; sweet orange Wellingtons; and old-fashioned ones with curious names like Mortgage Lifter and Arkansas Traveler. In fact, to the delight of American shoppers and gardeners, we have available tomatoes from all over the world—the Crimea, China, Spain, India, the Middle East, Scandinavia, and of course Italy—brought back to the tomato's birthplace in the New World by early and more recent settlers from all those places to which the tomato has migrated over the course of its history. Once upon a time tomatoes in North America were a uniform round red fruit that you either sliced into a salad or cooked in a sauce—and unless it came from your own garden, you probably bemoaned its lack of flavor. Nowadays, tomatoes come in all shapes and sizes and tastes to suit all comers.

Don't be afraid to use any and all of these tomato varieties, whether Italian or Chinese or native Mexican, in our tomato recipes. You'll quickly discover that some varieties are better for long-cooked sauces, while others work best raw in salads or quickly cooked to yield up all the bright taste of summer. But it could be that a brilliant orange Earl of Edgecombe would be just fine in a spicy ripe tomato sauce, giving it a beautiful color too. In other words, just because our recipes usually call for ripe "red" fresh tomatoes doesn't mean you can't use another color, another size— as Shakespeare reminds us, "Ripeness is all." In general, juicier tomatoes are better for quick-cooking pasta sauces, while thick-walled paste tomatoes are what we look for when we're making long, slow-cooked ragùs and sauces to put up for the winter pantry.

We love our summer pasta with tomatoes—fresh cherry tomatoes, blistered in a pan so that the fruits collapse and the juices brown and caramelize, or plump plum tomatoes, skinned, seeded, and chopped, sautéed in oil with a pinch of salt and slivers of basil, spooned over ricotta ravioli or tossed in a bowl of spaghetti. One of the best of these summer treatments is a curious dish of hot pasta with raw tomatoes called pasta alla checcha, which we discovered many years ago in Rome. It was a dish to be consumed on hot nights in the Eternal City when we lingered at tables in little trattorie and osterie on back streets, arriving late in the evening when the heat had finally risen from the cobblestones and a cool breeze off the Tiber freshened the torpid air. Pasta alla checca is a brilliant answer to summer's heat—fresh tomatoes, chopped with slivered red onions and basil, olive oil, maybe a splash of wine vinegar, the cold sauce turned over hot pasta.

A boon too to the cook in hot weather, requiring no more energy than a quick, easy boil up of the pasta before serving.

A quick glance through our recipes will confirm that not every pasta sauce by any means has tomatoes in it. Nonetheless, tomatoes are almost ubiquitous; sometimes, even when they don't stand up and shout, their presence will be noted as a touch, often nearly invisible, like the mere edge of a spoonful of tomato paste, estratto di pomodoro, that blends into everything else and raises the flavor profile of a meaty ragù. Not just a star of the summer table, tomatoes, whether preserved in a pomarola sauce, or sun-dried to a paste, or just tossed whole into the freezer, are integral to the winter table as well.

Having said all this, we offer a small selection of recipes for producing great tomato sauces. The first is a quick, barely cooked, easy sauce for when the best tomatoes are in season. The second, la pomarola, is equally to be prepared with fresh seasonal tomatoes but it's cooked a little longer and is similar to what Italian cooks might preserve for the winter pantry—and we've included directions for doing just that. Finally, we offer a way to boost the flavor of fresh tomatoes that are perhaps not at an ideal stage of ripeness.

Pasta alla checca is a brilliant answer to summer's heat—fresh tomatoes, chopped with slivered red onions and basil, olive oil, maybe a splash of wine vinegar, the cold sauce turned over hot pasta.

Sugo di Pomodoro

Fresh Tomato Sauce

Made from deep-red, sun-ripened tomatoes fresh from the garden, this sauce, or *sugo*, is as good on top of a pizza as it is with pasta. For that reason, think about doubling quantities and serving it on pasta one day, on pizza the next.

Children adore basic tomato sauce. Even finicky eaters, we've found, will submit to its appeal. But grown-ups love it too. Quick and easy to prepare, it goes straight to the heart of what you want on the table when the weather is warm and no one wants to spend time in the kitchen. In Italy, it's traditional to serve this with spaghetti, linguine, or any other kind of long, skinny pasta, but don't feel bound by tradition—it's just as good with short curlicues or shells, any of which might be more fun and easier for kids to eat.

Peel the tomatoes and seed, if you wish, following the directions on page 13.

Sugar brings out the flavor in tomatoes as it does with most fruits, but a little goes a long way. We're not making ketchup here, but a fresh-tasting tomato sauce. If your sauce is bitter, just a half teaspoon or so of sugar can make a difference.

MAKES 3½ TO 4 CUPS SAUCE, ENOUGH FOR 4 TO 6 SERVINGS OVER PASTA

1 tablespoon unsalted butter
1 tablespoon extra-virgin olive oil
2 garlic cloves, thinly sliced
2½ to 3 pounds ripe fresh tomatoes,
preferably plum tomatoes, peeled, seeded
(optional), and coarsely chopped
Sea salt and freshly ground black pepper
½ teaspoon sugar (optional)
Handful of basil leaves, slivered

Combine the butter and oil in a heavy saucepan and set over medium-low heat. When the butter has melted, add the garlic and cook slowly until the slices are almost melted in the oil. Do not let the garlic brown (it will give an acrid flavor to your sauce).

When the garlic is soft, add the tomatoes with their juice to the saucepan. Raise the heat slightly and cook rapidly so that the tomatoes give off a lot of their liquid. Stir in salt and pepper to taste and the sugar, if you wish. Continue cooking until the tomato bits start to soften and fall apart, thickening into a sauce. Most of the liquid will have cooked down and you can start to crush the tomatoes further using a fork.

Taste the tomato sauce and adjust the seasoning. You should have 3 to 4 cups of sauce. At this point you may decide to serve the tomato sauce as is with its lovely chunks of tomato, or to puree it coarsely, using an immersion blender, or to puree it into a completely smooth sauce using a food processor or a vegetable mill. The basil should be stirred in at the last minute before serving.

VARIATIONS *Add (or substitute for the basil) other fresh herbs—parsley, chervil, lovage, chives, all spring to mind; dried herbs such as oregano to give a more southern flavor; a touch of cumin to give a North African taste. Let your imagination be the guide, but keep in mind that the sauce is really about fresh tomatoes—thus, enhance the flavors, but don't try to mask them.*

For a sweeter sauce, add about a pound of finely chopped yellow onions along with the garlic and cook them down very, very slowly before adding the tomatoes.

For a creamier sauce, puree the tomatoes completely and beat in ½ cup cream, then reheat gently before serving.

For a spicier sauce, add one or more whole dried red chili peppers, crumbled, with the tomatoes.

Marcella Hazan famously made a simple tomato sauce by cooking tomatoes as above, pureeing them, then simmering them again for 45 minutes with just a halved onion and a large lump of butter. Discard the onion when the sauce has finished cooking—it will have done its job of flavoring the sauce.

For a Moroccan sauce, to the tomatoes, add an inch of fresh ginger, peeled and coarsely chopped; a cinnamon stick; a few cloves; and a pinch of ground cumin. After pureeing the sauce (first removing the cinnamon stick and the cloves), add some chopped fresh cilantro and, if you have it, half a salt-preserved lemon, chopped into bits. This is surprisingly delicious over spaghetti, or with couscous.

When you have a good supply of fresh tomatoes, this very basic sauce can be made in quantities and put up in pint or quart jars (see page 177 for more information), or frozen in pint containers to provide a great resource for the winter kitchen.

La Pomarola (Salsa di Pomodoro per la Dispensa)

Basic Tomato Sauce for Preserving, or for Serving Fresh

This is the tomato sauce in every Tuscan farmwife's repertoire, made fresh for the day's pasta and preserved in jars and bottles for the *dispensa*, the pantry. Please use it as a free-flowing model. Don't feel you must have exact ingredients in the precise quantities we have listed. If you reach into the fridge and discover the celery has gone bad, just leave it out. If you have only one onion, don't worry. The glory of Italian cooking is its adaptability to every imaginable circumstance. Really the only thing you must have for a basic tomato sauce is . . . tomatoes.

But what kind? We prefer plum tomatoes, because they are dense, with a greater ratio of flesh to juice, than round, juicy salad tomatoes. San Marzano and Roma are two plum varieties widely grown in North America. In Italy plum tomatoes are for cooking, round tomatoes (often slightly underripe) for salad, and cherry tomatoes, like the famous Pachinos from the deep south of Sicily, are a whole other category used in both sauces and salads. If salad tomatoes are all that's available, use them by all means, but remember that it will take longer to cook down the juices and there will be a consequent diminishing of flavor. The most important factor is that the tomatoes must be full of fragrance and flavor, perfectly ripe—and moreover, ripened on the vine and not in some gassy warehouse.

And, really, the riper the better: At farm stands and farmers' markets, you may find a bargain in overripe tomatoes that are slightly bruised or with split skins, the kind that won't last more than a day longer. Those are exactly what you want for this. Take them home, rinse them off, peel them, cut away the bruised sections, and chop very coarsely.

We give quantities for 5 pounds of tomatoes to make 4 to 5 pints of sauce, but if you simply want sauce for tonight's pasta, halve the quantities except for the olive oil. And if you come across a tomato bargain at your farm stand and wish to put up or preserve tomato sauce for the winter (directions follow), the recipe is easily doubled or even tripled.

MAKES ABOUT 8 TO 10 CUPS SAUCE, TO FILL 4 TO 5 PINT CANNING JARS

3 garlic cloves, coarsely chopped

1 or 2 medium yellow onions, coarsely chopped

2 celery stalks, coarsely chopped

2 medium carrots, coarsely chopped

½ bunch flat-leaf parsley, leaves and stems, coarsely chopped

¼ cup extra-virgin olive oil

Sea salt and freshly ground black pepper

5 pounds ripe red tomatoes, preferably plum tomatoes, peeled and seeded (optional), coarsely chopped

½ cup water or dry white wine if needed

Pinch sugar (optional)

Combine the garlic, onions, celery, carrots, and parsley with the oil in a large heavy saucepan. Add salt and pepper to taste and set the pan over medium-low heat.

uncovered, to evaporate the juice and reduce the tomatoes to a thick sauce. (This step may not be necessary if the sauce is already thick.)

When the tomatoes are done, put them through the large holes of a food mill, or use a handheld immersion blender to blend to the texture you want. Taste the sauce and add more salt and pepper if desired, or a pinch of sugar to bring out the natural sweetness of the fruit.

You should have 8 to 10 cups of sauce in the end. The sauce freezes very well: Put it in 1-cup containers for a supply that will last in your freezer for several months and provide a quick pasta sauce throughout the winter. Or preserve la pomarola in canning jars—tomatoes have so much natural acid that they don't need more than 5 or 10 minutes in a boiling water bath and they will keep all winter.

...s of sauce, have ready five scrupulously clean glass ... them. Stand the jars on a wooden counter or board so ... teakettle of water to a rolling boil and fill each canning ... owl and fill the bowl with boiling water. ... ring it back to simmering. Carefully tip the water out of ... ght up to the top, leaving about ¼ inch of space. Screw ... ars are filled, put them in a deep kettle or a canning ... pot (your pasta cooker is ideal for small quantities like ... hen towels to keep the jars from banging about. Set the ... t water to cover the jars. Set over medium-high heat and ... 0 minutes. Turn off the heat and let the water cool down ... n the wooden counter, and when they are thoroughly ... licating a complete seal. At this point the jars can be ... ready to use.

Roasted Tomato Sauce

A quick cure for not-quite-ripe tomatoes, this is an easy sauce for those anxiety-ridden late-summer weeks we often experience in Maine when it seems as if the tomatoes in the garden are just not going to ripen before the first frost. It will also boost the flavor of "fresh" tomatoes in winter produce markets, if you must use them.

MAKES 2 TO 3 CUPS SAUCE, ENOUGH FOR 4 TO 6 SERVINGS OVER PASTA

½ cup extra-virgin olive oil
1 medium red onion, sliced not too thin
2 garlic cloves, crushed and coarsely chopped
Sea salt and freshly ground black pepper
1 teaspoon Greek or Sicilian dried oregano
    (optional)
About 2 pounds ripe-as-you-can-get tomatoes

Set the oven on 400°F.

Spread 2 tablespoons of the oil over the bottom of a roasting dish into which the tomato halves will just fit.

Combine the onion and garlic in the roasting dish. Add salt and pepper to taste and the oregano (if using). Stir vigorously to mix everything together, then spread the ingredients out to make a layer across the bottom of the dish.

Cut the tomatoes in half. Core the stem ends. Set the halves, cut side down, on top of the onion-garlic layer. Dribble the remaining 6 tablespoons oil over the tops. (You may not need all the oil.)

Bake for 45 minutes to 1 hour. At the end of that time, remove the pan and let the tomatoes cool down. Pull off the skins and discard. Combine all the roasted ingredients and, if you wish, chop or puree with an immersion blender. Or leave as is—the rustic look can also be pleasing.

Pasta alla Checca

Spaghetti with Sun-Burst Tomatoes
and Grated Bottarga

Pennette with Ricotta and
Fresh Raw Tomatoes

Spaghetti or Maccheroni alla Puttanesca

Pasta alla Norma
Pasta with Roasted Eggplant and Tomato

Candele ai Fagiolini di Sant'Anna
*Pasta Candles with Long
Green Beans and Tomatoes*

Busiate al Pesto Trapanese
Pasta Twists with Almond-Garlic Pesto

Pesto Genovese
Basil Pesto from Liguria

Corzetti al Pesto Genovese
*Pasta, Green Beans, and Potatoes
with Basil Pesto*

Garganelli al Ortolano
Garganelli with Hot Summer Vegetables

Ziti with Anchovies and Cherry Tomatoes

Sedanini con Salsicce e Peperoni
Sedanini with Spicy Sausage and Roasted Peppers

Cavatappi con Peperone
*Cavatappi with Roasted Peppers,
Anchovies, Garlic, and Capers*

Shells with Roasted Corn
and Summer Savory

Pasta Shells with Zucchini,
Blossoms, Peas, and Mint

Linguine all'Aragosta con Arance
e Peperoncini
*Lobster Linguine with Oranges
and Chili Peppers*

Spaghetti Congolese
Congolese Spaghetti with Lobster Sauce

Pasta alla Chitarra allo Scoglio
Guitar Pasta on the Rocks

Gnocchetti with Mussels
and Saffron Potatoes

Ditalini con Fagioli Freschi e Verdure
Ditalini with Fresh Shell Beans and Greens

Fettuccine Pantesca
Fettuccine from Pantelleria

Ravioli con Ricotta e Melanzane
Bruciacchiate
Ravioli with Ricotta and Charred Eggplant

Cuscussù Trapanese
Sicilian Couscous with Rich Shellfish Sauce

Fideuà
Catalan Pasta and Seafood Paella

Saffron-Orange Allioli

Pasta alla Checca

A fabulous summertime dish from Rome that you might be tempted to call pasta salad, but it is *not*! As any Roman will tell you, this is hot pasta, just drained and tossed with a room-temperature sauce of raw tomatoes, fresh basil, slivered red onions, and plenty of fine, fruity olive oil, preferably from Lazio, Rome's region. A favorite of the trattorie in the heart of Vecchia Roma, pasta alla checca is deservedly popular and so refreshing on a summer night.

We've found the dish is ideal with a mix of as many different-colored tomatoes as you can find—yellow, red, green, even purple ones. But if only red tomatoes are available, by all means go ahead, just as long as they are field or garden ripened. For this, you want fruit with a lot of juice that will be absorbed by the hot pasta when you toss it. Another summertime bonus: Prepare the tomatoes at least an hour ahead of time and let them sit, covered, to macerate and absorb the other flavors. Then it's just a question of cooking the pasta, draining it, and tossing it with the sauce.

Long or short pasta, it's up to you; we like to use handmade pasta alla chitarra (see page 49) or any long, skinny pasta secca, from spaghetti to tonnarelli.

SERVES 6

*2 to 3 pounds very ripe tomatoes, coarsely
chopped*

2 or 3 garlic cloves, finely chopped

*1 medium red onion, halved and sliced very
fine (optional)*

Sea salt

⅓ to ½ cup extra-virgin olive oil

*1 teaspoon to 1 tablespoon aged wine vinegar,
more or less as needed*

Freshly ground black pepper, if you wish

*Handful of basil leaves, slivered, plus a few
whole small leaves for garnish*

*About 1 pound (500 grams) spaghetti,
tonnarelli, pasta alla chitarra, or other
long, skinny pasta*

Combine the tomatoes, garlic, and onion (if using) with a good sprinkle of salt and toss in a bowl. Add ⅓ cup oil and toss again. Taste and add just a little vinegar to give a touch of acid to the "sauce." Cover the bowl with plastic wrap and set aside at room temperature for at least an hour before serving.

Bring 6 quarts of water to a rolling boil in a large pot. Add salt and the pasta and cook following the directions on page 33, until al dente.

Taste the tomatoes once more and adjust the seasoning, adding pepper and a bit more vinegar, if you wish. Be sure there's enough salt—salt really brings out the flavor of raw tomatoes, so if it tastes a little bland, add a pinch more. Stir in the slivered basil.

When the pasta is al dente, drain and immediately turn it into a warm serving bowl. Cover with the tomato sauce, garnish with basil leaves, and serve immediately.

Spaghetti with Sun-Burst Tomatoes and Grated Bottarga

Bottarga is the dried roe of either mullet or tuna, and an age-old Mediterranean tradition (see page 22). It is expensive but a little goes a long way. Bottarga adds complexity and depth to the basic dish, but if you don't have it, the pasta is still good with its tomato sauce. Without bottarga, however, we'd substitute basil for the arugula and garnish with grated parmigiano-reggiano or grana padano.

If possible, select from an array of little grape and cherry tomatoes, red and yellow, mixing them up for a colorful presentation.

SERVES 6

¼ cup extra-virgin olive oil
2 or 3 pints mixed small tomatoes (such as
  cherry, grape, and currant) (about 2 pounds)
Fine sea salt and freshly ground black pepper
2 garlic cloves, thinly sliced
About 1 pound (500 grams) spaghetti
Handful of chopped fresh arugula, leaves only
  (discard tough stems)
⅔ cup grated or shaved bottarga

Bring 4 to 6 quarts of water to a rolling boil in a large pot.

While the water is heating, add the oil to a large heavy skillet and set over medium-high heat. When the oil is very hot (but not smoking), add half the tomatoes, sprinkle them quickly with salt, and cook, tossing the skillet, until the tomatoes start to wrinkle and collapse. Add the rest of the tomatoes and continue cooking and tossing for another 2 minutes. (Yes, some of the tomatoes will be more cooked than others— that's the point.)

Push the tomatoes to one side and add the garlic to the pan. As the garlic starts to soften, mix it in with the tomatoes, gently pressing the tomatoes to release some of their juice. When the sauce is thick, remove from the heat and add a pinch of salt and a few turns of the peppermill. Keep the sauce warm until the pasta is done.

Add salt and the pasta to the boiling water and cook following the directions on page 33.

Drain the pasta when it's al dente, transfer to a warm serving bowl, and immediately toss with the warm tomato sauce, stirring in the arugula. Toss again, then sprinkle with the bottarga and serve immediately.

Pennette with Ricotta and Fresh Raw Tomatoes

Rich textures and subtle flavors combine in this simple summer favorite. Make the sauce, except for the tomatoes, well ahead, then fold in the diced tomatoes and basil at the end, just before serving.

For best results, look for true ricotta, made from re-cooked whey, and not vinegar-thickened milk (see page 23). The butter should be at room temperature. Combine it with the ricotta, then fold in the tomato and basil just before you're ready to serve.

If your tomatoes are very juicy, drain them in a fine-mesh sieve for 30 minutes or so before adding to the cheeses.

Pennette are usually easy to find, but if you don't see them, substitute mostaccioli, short ziti, rigatoni, elicoidali, or any type of short, hollow pasta instead.

SERVES 6

2 cups best-quality ricotta

8 tablespoons (1 stick or ½ cup) unsalted butter, at room temperature

½ to 1 cup freshly grated parmigiano-reggiano

Sea salt and freshly ground black pepper

About 1 pound (500 grams) pennette or other pasta (see headnote)

1 cup diced tomato (unpeeled), drained of excess juice

½ cup finely chopped fresh basil

Combine the ricotta and softened butter in a bowl and, using a fork, blend the two together. Don't worry if there are a few streaks of butter throughout the ricotta—it will be better that way. Add the parmigiano, then taste, and, if you wish, add more grated cheese. Taste again and add salt, if necessary. Set aside any remaining grated cheese to serve with the pasta.

When ready to cook, bring a large pot of water to a rolling boil. Add salt and the pasta and cook following the directions on page 33.

While the pasta is cooking, gently fold the tomatoes and basil into the ricotta mixture. Taste again and, if you wish, add a little salt—though there may be plenty of salt from the parmigiano. If the mixture seems very tight, stir in a couple of big spoonsful of boiling pasta water, but keep in mind that moisture from the finished pasta will also loosen the sauce a bit.

Have ready a warm serving bowl. When the pasta is al dente, drain and immediately turn it into the bowl along with about three-quarters of the ricotta sauce. Add a good quantity of pepper and toss to mix well. Serve immediately, passing the remainder of the sauce and grated cheese separately.

Spaghetti or Maccheroni alla Puttanesca

*A*lla puttanesca means, literally, "prostitute style." The theory is that hard-working ladies of the night made this dish to revive their flagging spirits. However, folks in the know claim that puttanesca was actually invented in the 1950s on the island of Ischia, off Naples, when a bon vivant and restaurateur named Sandro Petti pulled it all together to serve to his friends who were all what Italians call *i veep*—very important people. Be that as it may, it's a delicious, savory, and easy dish, perfect for spur-of-the-moment summertime cooking. Spaghetti or linguine are often used with this sauce, or maccheroni—not American elbow macaroni, but rather a short, hollow pasta, slightly curved, and often ridged on the outside.

The tomatoes used on Ischia and around Napoli are pomodori a piennolo, small tomatoes raised without much irrigation, which gives them tough skins and incredibly sweet interiors.* You might come across similar tomatoes in a farmers' market, but if not, we recommend plum tomatoes (San Marzano, Amish Paste, and Roma are popular varieties found in farmers' markets and farm stands), our standbys for most fresh tomato sauces because they have greater ratios of flesh to juice. If you can't find plum tomatoes, look for tomatoes with a heavy, dense heft to them, indicating a good quantity of flesh. And of course they must be as fresh and ripe as they get—preferably straight from the garden to the kitchen.

We like small Gaeta olives, but almost any black olives will do, including wrinkled salted black olives or Greek Kalamata olives—anything, that is, but the so-called California-style canned black olives, which have no flavor at all.

SERVES 6

1 medium red or yellow onion, finely chopped
2 garlic cloves, finely chopped
¼ cup extra-virgin olive oil
Sea salt
4 oil-packed anchovy fillets, coarsely chopped
½ cup finely chopped flat-leaf parsley
3 pounds very ripe tomatoes, peeled and chopped

½ teaspoon dried Sicilian or Greek oregano, crumbled (optional)
Pinch sugar, if needed
2 tablespoons salted capers, rinsed and chopped if very large
1 cup pitted and coarsely chopped black olives (see headnote)
Freshly ground black pepper
About 1 pound (500 grams) linguine, spaghetti, or maccheroni

---

* The Pomodorino del piennolo del Vesuvio, *raised on the volcanic slopes of Mount Vesuvius, is protected by a Slow Food presidium and has its own DOP. They are available in North America, canned in jars under the brand name Casa Barone, from* www.gustiamo.com.

First make the sauce: Combine the onion and garlic and chop together to a finer texture. Add to a skillet with the oil and a good pinch of salt, stir to mix, and set over medium-low heat. Cook, stirring occasionally, until the vegetables are soft. Do not let them brown.

When the vegetables are thoroughly wilted, add the anchovy pieces to the center of the skillet and continue cooking, pressing and crushing the anchovies into the oil in the pan. Add half the parsley, reserving the rest to garnish the finished dish.

Now add the tomatoes and raise the heat slightly. Continue cooking and stirring until the tomatoes have released their juice and then, as the juice reduces, the tomato flesh itself will collapse into a jam. About halfway through the cooking, add the oregano (if using) and stir it in. If the tomatoes are not perfectly vine ripened, a pinch of sugar will help to boost the flavors.

Remove the tomato sauce from the heat and stir in the capers and olives. Taste the sauce for seasoning, adding salt and plenty of pepper. If the sauce is finished before the pasta is done, keep it hot while the pasta cooks—the ideal, of course, is to have the pasta and the sauce ready at the same time, but it's no big deal if the sauce is done first.

While the sauce is cooking, bring about 6 quarts of water to a rolling boil in a large pot. Add a big spoonful of salt and the pasta, giving it a stir with a long-handled spoon. Cook following the directions on page 33, until al dente.

Have ready a warm serving bowl. Drain the pasta and immediately turn it into the warm bowl. Spoon the hot sauce over the top and garnish with the remaining parsley. Mix the sauce and the pasta together at the table and serve immediately.

VARIATION *When you have a good supply of fresh basil, use it instead of, or along with, the parsley.*

Pasta alla Norma

Pasta with Roasted Eggplant and Tomato

When we think of Sicily, this characteristic pasta combination immediately comes to mind. Melanzane from Sicily are among the tastiest eggplants in the world, and when they're combined with Sicilian ricotta salata and fresh summer tomatoes, it sums up the glories of summer on that island in the middle of the blue Mediterranean. Pasta alla Norma is a name given it in Catania, home of the great nineteenth-century composer Vincenzo Bellini, in honor of his opera of the same name, which was first performed in 1831. There is no reason to believe that anyone was making this version back in 1831, but the myth persists nonetheless. This is our version, and if you want to hum a little "Casta Diva" while you're whipping it together, well, why not?

We make this with a short pasta shape called mezze rigatoni, but any shape, including long, skinny bucatini or spaghetti would be fine.

When fresh tomatoes aren't in season, we happily use top-quality canned San Marzanos, but in summer fresh ones right out of the garden, or right from a nearby farmers' market, are obviously best of all.

SERVES 6

2 medium eggplants (1 to 1½ pounds), cut into roughly ½-inch cubes
7 tablespoons extra-virgin olive oil
Sicilian sea salt and freshly ground black pepper
1 red onion, chopped
2 garlic cloves, minced
1 small dried hot red chili pepper (such as de àrbol), crushed
1 teaspoon dried mint
2½ cups peeled and chopped fresh tomatoes (see page 13)
⅓ cup coarsely chopped pitted black olives
About 1 pound (500 grams) mezze rigatoni
Handful of fresh basil leaves, torn into small pieces
¼ cup freshly grated parmigiano-reggiano or grana padano
4 ounces ricotta salata, freshly grated

Set the oven on 400°F.

Toss the eggplant cubes in a bowl with 4 tablespoons of the oil. Season liberally with salt and black pepper and toss again. Spread the cubes out in a single layer on a roasting sheet and transfer to the oven to roast until brown and slightly crispy, about 20 minutes.

Bring about 6 quarts of water to a rolling boil in a large pot.

In a large heavy-bottomed pot, heat the remaining 3 tablespoons oil over medium-low heat. Add the onion and garlic and cook gently, adding a pinch of salt. Let the onions sweat out, losing their moisture and softening, for about 10 minutes, then increase the heat slightly and just as they begin to pick up a little color, add the chili and the dried mint and stir them into the mixture. Let cook together briefly, no longer

than a minute, then add the tomatoes and, using a fork or an old-fashioned potato masher, break them up as they cook into a chunky mass.

Simmer gently for about 20 minutes, or until the tomato sauce thickens and reduces slightly. Add the roasted eggplant and cook together for just a few more minutes. Stir in the olives and taste the sauce, adjusting the seasoning as needed. Keep warm until ready to dress the pasta.

Season the boiling water abundantly with salt, add the pasta, and cook following the directions on page 33.

Have ready a warm bowl. When the pasta is al dente, drain and turn it immediately into the bowl. Top with the sauce and toss the pasta and sauce together, then add the torn basil leaves and toss again. Add the parmigiano and toss, then add two-thirds of the ricotta salata and toss again. Sprinkle the remaining ricotta salata over the top and serve immediately.

VARIATION *Nancy likes to add a few capers and some toasted pine nuts to garnish the dish at the end; Sara thinks that is gilding the lily and prefers the purity of the original, which comes from the brilliant Sicilian chef Salvatore Denaro.*

Candele ai Fagiolini di Sant'Anna

Pasta Candles with Long Green Beans and Tomatoes

In Tuscany long, skinny green beans, the kind called yard-long or asparagus beans in North America, are called fagiolini di Sant'Anna because they come into season around the Feast of Saint Anne, the mother of the Virgin, on July 26. Although you may use any fresh green beans for the dish—even the flat beans called romano, or the very slender ones that gardening catalogs call French filet beans—we love mixing the long Sant'Anna beans with equally long tubes of candele pasta so the pasta and the beans sort of intertwine with each other. Both Rustichella d'Abruzzo and Pastificio Faella have candele, as does De Cecco. They really do look like long, slender candles. Bucatini are a fine substitute.

SERVES 6

2 tablespoons extra-virgin olive oil
1 garlic clove, chopped
1 small yellow onion, chopped
¾ pound very ripe fresh tomatoes, preferably
   plum tomatoes, peeled and chopped (or
   use one 14-ounce can whole tomatoes,
   preferably San Marzano, with their juice)
Sea salt and freshly ground black pepper
1 pound long green beans (asparagus beans)
1 pound (500 grams) candele or similar long
   pasta
Freshly grated parmigiano-reggiano or
   pecorino toscano cheese

Combine the oil with the garlic and onion in a skillet and set over low heat. Cook, stirring, just until the vegetables start to soften, but do not let them get brown. Add the tomatoes with salt and pepper to taste and continue cooking, stirring frequently, until the tomatoes have dissolved into a sauce, 15 to 20 minutes. If you wish, puree the sauce with an immersion blender to make it smoother, but it should be quite textured. (This may be done ahead of time, if you wish.)

While the sauce is cooking, bring a good 6 quarts of water to a rolling boil in a large pot. When the water boils, add a big spoonful of salt and the green beans and cook until done, 10 to 15 minutes. The beans should not be fully cooked as they will continue to cook in the sauce. Use a slotted spoon to remove them from the water and transfer directly to the sauce. Stir into the sauce, which should be just simmering over low heat.

Bring the bean water back to a vigorous boil and add the pasta, stirring well to immerse it. Cook, following the directions on page 33, checking the package recommendations for time. Candele should take about 9 minutes, but start testing after 6 or 7 minutes.

Have ready a warm serving bowl. When the pasta is al dente, drain and turn it into the bowl. Top with the green bean sauce and toss to combine before serving, passing grated cheese at the table.

Busiate al Pesto Trapanese

Pasta Twists with Almond-Garlic Pesto

A classic from the far western edge of Sicily, busiate are a complicated twisted pasta shape for which you may substitute gemelli or fusilli. A delicious busiate from the region, made with locally grown tumminia wheat, is available from www.gustiamo.com, which is also a source for real Sicilian almonds with their strong, almost pungent, slightly bitter flavor.

The recipe is based on what Chef Pino Maggiore makes at Cantina Siciliana in Trapani. Pino adds grated pecorino from Sicily, but the flavor, for us, seems purer without the added cheese. Instead, we top the pasta with bread crumbs crisply toasted in olive oil.

The almonds are sometimes peeled (blanched), sometimes not. We do it both ways. But if we have blanched almonds, we usually toast them in an oven set at 350°F for 15 to 20 minutes, or until they are lightly golden.

Note that in Trapani this is sometimes called *agghiata trapanisa*, or *agliata trapanese*—meaning Trapani garlic sauce. It should be heavily redolent of garlic, then of the almonds, finally of the basil; the tomatoes simply help, along with the olive oil, to turn it into a sauce.

SERVES 6

3 or 4 medium very ripe tomatoes, peeled, seeded, and chopped fine
Sea salt and freshly ground black pepper
¾ cup blanched almonds, lightly toasted in the oven (see headnote)
1 cup large basil leaves, torn into smaller pieces
Crumbled dried red chili pepper (optional)
About ⅔ cup extra-virgin olive oil, preferably Sicilian
3 garlic cloves, coarsely chopped
About 1 pound (500 grams) busiate (see headnote)
3 tablespoons dry, unflavored bread crumbs, coarsely ground

Combine the tomatoes with 1 teaspoon sea salt and set in a fine-mesh sieve to drain as much of their juice as possible. (Save the juice and toss it into any future broth, ragù, or tomato sauce.)

Chop the almonds by hand, then transfer to the bowl of a food processor. Process in spurts to make a fine, grainy almond paste. Add the basil, black pepper to taste, and chili pepper (if using) and pulse to mix all together to a deep green sauce.

Set aside 1 tablespoon of the oil to use for frying the bread crumbs.

With the processor running, add about ½ cup of the oil in a thin but steady stream, as if you were making mayonnaise. Taste at this point, remembering that you will be adding salt later with the tomatoes. If you think it's necessary, add a little more oil, but the sauce should not be notably oily.

When the sauce is just right, add the garlic and process once more, just to combine. (Why not just put everything together in the processor bowl? Garlic, if it's overworked, can be bitter—so we do this in stages, adding the garlic only for the last quick processing.) Transfer the sauce to a bowl. Just before serving, combine with the tomatoes. Taste and add more salt, if necessary. (Both the pesto and the tomatoes may be prepared well ahead, but, in order to maintain the crisp crunch of the almonds, they should be combined only at the last minute.)

Bring about 4 quarts of water to a rolling boil in a large pot.

While the water is coming to a boil, toast the bread crumbs in the reserved oil in a skillet over medium heat, stirring frequently until the crumbs are brown and crisp.

Remove from the heat and immediately transfer to a small bowl. (If left in the skillet, the crumbs will continue to brown, perhaps even to burn.)

When the water boils, add salt and the pasta and cook following the directions on page 33. Before the pasta is al dente, remove about 1 cup of the pasta water and set aside to be used to thin the sauce, if necessary. Add a big spoonful of almond-garlic pesto to the bottom of a warm serving bowl. Drain the pasta and turn it into the bowl, then add most of the rest of the pesto, reserving a little for a garnish on top. Toss the pasta with the pesto until it is well coated. If necessary, add a spoonful or two or the pasta water. Top with the reserved pesto, sprinkle with the crisp bread crumbs, and serve immediately.

VARIATION *A delicious alternative that Sara likes to serve in her restaurant Porsena is a Sicilian pesto made with pistachios, mint, and lemon zest. It's a terrific idea we learned from Chef Bonetta dell'Oglio, a tireless investigator into Sicilian food traditions. Simply follow the recipe for pesto trapanese only substitute shelled pistachios for the almonds and instead of 1 cup basil, make it half basil and half fresh mint. Add the freshly grated zest of a lemon and that's it!*

Pesto Genovese

Basil Pesto from Liguria

Pesto Genovese, fragrant with fresh summery basil, may just be the second best known Italian sauce in North America (after tomato sauce). Most gardeners we know cultivate a big patch of basil to turn into pesto toward the season's end, and cooks are quick to add a dollop of pesto to just about anything from a pizza topping to a marinade for a swordfish steak. We like it best in its purest form, as a dressing for pasta.

At Porsena, Sara often serves pesto with corzetti, another Ligurian classic, handmade pasta shaped into round disks that are stamped with a carved design that traps bits of the sauce (see page 48). Lacking corzetti, however, you may serve the pasta with traditional trofie (short, thin, twisted pasta shapes) or trenette (long, flat pasta strings)—linguine might be substituted for trenette.

We firmly believe that the classic Ligurian basil pesto, as fragrant as summer itself, served the way they do it in Genova, with new potatoes and the thinnest of fresh green beans, is probably the most elegant pasta dish Italian cooks have ever invented. And we also believe that a classic Ligurian pesto is never quite as good as when made by hand, using a mortar and a pestle. It's quick and easy to make with a food processor, and as cooks in a hurry we often resort to that technique, but nothing beats the unctuous texture of an old-fashioned handmade pesto. Do please try the old-fashioned way at least once so you'll know what we're talking about, even if you go back to the food processor occasionally just for the convenience.

Note that this recipe makes enough pesto for eight servings of pasta. Any leftover pesto may be stored in the refrigerator in a glass bowl or jar with a light film of olive oil on top. Some people freeze pesto. We don't, having found that frozen pesto in February totally lacks the appeal it had last summer.

MAKES 1½ TO 2 CUPS PESTO

2 cups packed whole, tender young basil leaves (discard stems or use them, tied in a bundle, to flavor the pasta water)
¼ cup pine nuts
1 teaspoon sea salt, plus more to taste
½ cup extra-virgin olive oil, or more to taste
½ cup freshly grated parmigiano-reggiano, plus more to taste
½ cup freshly grated pecorino sardo or pecorino toscano
2 plump garlic cloves, crushed and minced

The following directions are for using a food processor; to make pesto with a mortar and pestle, see the end of the recipe.

Working delicately, rinse and thoroughly dry the basil leaves and set aside.

In the bowl of the processor, combine

the rinsed and dried basil, pine nuts, and salt. Pulse until the mixture is coarse and grainy. With the motor running, add the oil in a slow, steady stream. Add the parmigiano and pecorino, processing just enough to mix well. If the sauce is too dry, add a little more oil; if it's too liquid, stir in a little more cheese and/or pine nuts. Finally, add the garlic and process briefly, just to mix. Taste and add more cheese or salt, if desired.

TO MAKE PESTO WITH A MORTAR AND PESTLE

To the bowl of a rough-textured stone or ceramic mortar, add a pinch of salt, the pine nuts, and minced garlic. Using the pestle, gently press and pound the ingredients to a paste. Now start adding the rinsed and *thoroughly dried* basil leaves, a small handful at a time. Change the stroke you use with the pestle, swiping the pestle diagonally down the sides of the mortar to capture stray basil leaves as they work their way up the sides of the bowl. Keep turning the mortar, a quarter turn at a time, as you swipe down the sides. If you're right-handed, you'll stroke down the bowl in a counterclockwise direction as you turn the bowl; if you're left-handed, you'll find it easier to do this in a clockwise direction. Whatever works!

Keep adding more handfuls of basil until all the basil has been incorporated. Although the pesto will still be rather liquid in texture compared with the finished product, you may be surprised at the almost creamy quality the sauce develops as you work in the basil. Set aside some of the grated cheeses to garnish the pasta. Once all the basil has been incorporated, start adding the remaining cheeses, again a small quantity at a time. When all the cheeses have been added, start adding the oil, again a little at a time. You may find that just ⅓ cup will bring the pesto up to the proper thick and viscous texture—or you may need to use the entire ½ cup. The finished sauce will be a deep green, sprinkled with bits of darker green, but it will also have more texture than the smooth pesto made in a blender or food processor. Taste the sauce and add more salt, or more of the cheeses, if you wish.

Corzetti al Pesto Genovese

Pasta, Green Beans, and Potatoes with Basil Pesto

SERVES 6 TO 8

Sea salt

*½ pound small potatoes, peeled and sliced
about ¼ inch thick*

*¼ pound tender young green beans, cut into
1-inch lengths*

*About 1 pound (500 grams) corzetti (see page
43)*

1½ to 2 cups Pesto Genovese (page 195)

Several small basil leaves, or large ones, torn

Bring 6 quarts of water to a rolling boil
in a large pot. Add at least 2 tablespoons
salt and the potato slices. Cook for about
5 minutes, or until the potatoes have started
to soften but are not cooked through. Add

the green beans and continue boiling for
another 5 minutes.

Add the pasta to the pot and stir with
a long-handled spoon. Cook following
the directions on page 33. Freshly made
corzetti should take about 3 minutes to
become al dente, dried artisanal trenette
about 8 minutes. When the pasta is al
dente, the potatoes and beans should be
tender.

Have ready a warm bowl. Drain the
pasta and vegetables and turn them
immediately into the bowl. Add the pesto
and mix thoroughly. Garnish with the basil
leaves and serve immediately, passing the
reserved grated cheese.

COOK'S TIP *To loosen the pesto and make it easier to mix with the pasta, stir about ¼ cup
of the pasta water into the pesto just as you're ready to drain the pasta.*

Garganelli al Ortolano

Garganelli with Hot Summer Vegetables

Nothing speaks more poignantly of summer in the Mediterranean than the combination of bright red and yellow sweet peppers, dark purple eggplant, and deeply colored tomatoes. They all come together beautifully in this pasta sauce. But don't feel you have to be restricted to these—zucchini would fit in nicely here and so would slivers of fresh fennel or tender green beans snapped into short lengths.

If you end up with more vegetables than you need for the pasta, not to worry: Simply set aside what's not used and serve it next day as a Mediterranean summer vegetable medley to go with grilled meat or fish.

Garganelli are traditionally made by hand in the region of Emilia-Romagna, using an egg pasta dough, but they are also widely available as dried semolina pasta.

SERVES 4 TO 6

2 medium sweet peppers, red or yellow, roasted and peeled (see page 14)
2 small eggplants (about 1½ pounds)
½ cup extra-virgin olive oil
1 garlic clove, coarsely chopped
1 medium yellow onion, chopped
3 ripe red fresh tomatoes (about 2 pounds), coarsely chopped, to make 2 cups
Pinch crushed red pepper flakes
½ cup minced fresh herbs (such as flat-leaf parsley, basil, or thyme)
2 tablespoons salted capers, rinsed and coarsely chopped
½ cup coarsely chopped pitted green olives
Sea salt and freshly ground black pepper
1 pound (500 grams) garganelli, penne rigate, or other short, stubby pasta

Trim the peppers and cut them into ¼-inch strips. Cut the eggplants into narrow rectangles, about ½ inch by ½ inch and roughly 3 inches long.

In a large skillet, combine 2 tablespoons of the oil, the garlic, onion, and pepper strips and gently sauté over medium-low heat until they are very soft. Use a slotted spoon to transfer to a bowl and set aside. Add the remaining 6 tablespoons oil to the pan and raise the heat to medium-high. Add the eggplant strips and brown quickly, removing strips as they brown and adding them to the peppers.

Once the eggplant strips are done, add the tomatoes to the pan and cook rapidly, stirring frequently, until the tomatoes have softened and released a lot of juice. (If necessary, add a couple of tablespoons of hot water to the pan when you start—just until the tomato juice starts to come out.) Add the red pepper flakes. Let the tomatoes cook down to make a thick sauce, then stir in the minced herbs.

Return the vegetables in the bowl to the skillet and stir to mix everything well, adding the capers and olives. Set aside but keep warm while the pasta cooks.

Bring a large pot of water to a rolling boil. Add salt and the pasta and cook following the directions on page 33, until not quite al dente.

Have ready a warm serving bowl.

Drain the pasta quickly, reserving about ½ cup of the pasta water. Turn the pasta into the vegetable sauce and set over medium heat to finish cooking. If necessary, add a little of the reserved pasta water to keep the sauce from drying out. When the pasta is al dente, turn it into the warm serving bowl and serve immediately.

VARIATION *Summertime is grilling time, so instead of frying the vegetables, why not fire up the backyard barbecue? Grill whole peppers, then peel and slice. Grill thick slices of eggplant, painting both sides with oil. Halve the tomatoes and grill, skin side down, then chop coarsely. Even whole onions can be grilled until the skins blacken; then the skins are pulled off and the onions coarsely chopped. Mix all these vegetables in a skillet, add the garlic, capers, and olives as above, and keep warm while the pasta cooks. Then finish the pasta in the sauce as described.*

Ziti with Anchovies and Cherry Tomatoes

This recipe, so evocative of southern Italy, comes from the Cavalieri family, who make Benedetto Cavalieri pasta, one of our favorite artisanal brands. Pastificio Cavalieri is located in Maglie, in the deep south of Puglia. The flavor combination of anchovies, black olives, and fragrant wild fennel pollen, with bread crumbs substituted for some of the grated pecorino on top, speaks directly of the way southern cooks create richness from poverty. It's a quick, easy sauce to pull together at the last minute, as long as you have all the ingredients on hand.

Cooking chili and/or garlic in oil just long enough to flavor it, then discarding the aromatics and keeping the oil, is a method widely used in southern Italy where, contrary to popular impressions, aggressive flavors aren't much appreciated.

If you don't have fennel pollen, crushed fennel seeds may be substituted.

SERVES 6

*2 garlic cloves, crushed with the flat blade of
a knife*
1 dried red chili pepper
About ½ cup extra-virgin olive oil
*1 large yellow or red sweet pepper, sliced into
thin strips*
Big pinch fennel pollen, if available
10 to 12 anchovy fillets, chopped coarsely
*18 small cherry or grape tomatoes, halved or
quartered*
¾ cup coarsely chopped pitted black olives
Sea salt
About 1 pound (500 grams) ziti
½ cup toasted coarsely ground bread crumbs
*½ cup freshly grated pecorino sardo or
pecorino toscano*

Bring a large pot of water to a rolling boil. Combine the garlic, chili, and 3 tablespoons of the oil in a skillet and set over medium-low heat. Cook, stirring, until the garlic starts to turn golden and the chili to crisp. Remove from the heat and discard the garlic and chili but keep the flavored oil.

Add the sweet pepper strips to the hot oil, along with the fennel pollen (if using), and return to medium-low heat. Cook, stirring occasionally, until the pepper strips have softened, about 10 minutes. Then stir in the anchovies, crushing them into the oil with a fork.

Add the tomatoes to the peppers and anchovies with another 2 tablespoons of the oil. Cook a few minutes, just until the tomato pieces start to collapse, then stir in the black olives.

In a separate small saucepan, combine the bread crumbs with 2 tablespoons of the oil and set over medium heat. Cook, toasting until the crumbs are golden and crisp. Set aside.

Add salt and the pasta to the boiling water and cook following the directions on page 33, until the pasta is almost al dente.

When the pasta is almost done, add a ladleful of pasta water to the skillet with the tomatoes and anchovies and bring to a simmer. Drain the pasta and turn it into the skillet, tossing to mix the pasta and sauce together. Turn into a warm serving bowl and top with the toasted bread crumbs and grated pecorino. Serve immediately.

Sedanini con Salsicce e Peperoni

Sedanini with Spicy Sausage and Roasted Peppers

The unique flavor of roasted peppers dominates this dish. While roasting and peeling take some prep time, it may be done well ahead of time and the peppers kept refrigerated until you're ready to use them. You could do a whole batch of peppers and have them on hand for delightful additions to other pasta sauces, as well as to summer salads. We are convinced that roasting your own is absolutely worth the effort and gives a sweeter flavor and more interesting texture than using commercially prepared peppers in jars.

Sedanini are short, ribbed pasta, tubular in shape and slightly curved—the name actually means "little celeries," which is sort of what they look like. If you can't find them, use any other similar shape—penne, penne rigate, or maccheroni are all good choices.

SERVES 6

3 large sweet peppers, red or yellow or a mix, roasted and peeled (see page 14)

1 large white or yellow onion, halved and thinly sliced

1 garlic clove, chopped

5 tablespoons extra-virgin olive oil

Sea salt and freshly ground black pepper

About 1 pound Italian pork sausages, sweet or hot

Pinch crushed red pepper flakes (optional)

Pinch ground fennel seeds (optional)

¼ cup Basic Tomato Sauce (page 176)

About 1 pound (500 grams) sedanini or other pasta

¼ cup minced fresh herbs (such as parsley or basil), for garnish

Grated parmigiano-reggiano, for garnish

Cut the roasted peppers into ½-inch strips, discarding any seeds or membranes inside the peppers and reserving any juices.

Combine the onion and garlic with 4 tablespoons of the oil in a large skillet and set over low heat. Add a pinch of salt and cook the onion gently, melting the slices in the oil, stirring occasionally, until the onion pieces are soft and yielding. This will take 15 to 20 minutes. Add the pepper slices and stir to mix well. Now measure the pepper juices that were set aside in a measuring cup and add water to bring it up to ½ cup. Stir this into the skillet. Cover and cook over low heat for up to 40 minutes, or until the contents of the pan are soft and melting. If necessary, add a tablespoon of water from time to time to keep the contents from browning.

Meanwhile, open the sausages, discard the skins, and crumble the meat inside. Add to another skillet along with the remaining 1 tablespoon oil and set over medium heat. Cook the sausage meat, crumbling it with a fork as it browns thoroughly. If you wish, adjust the seasoning, adding, for instance, a pinch of red pepper flakes and/or ground fennel to the mixture.

When the sausage meat is browned and the vegetables in the skillet are soft, combine the two, stirring in plenty of black pepper and the tomato sauce. Keep the sauce hot while you prepare the pasta.

Bring a large pot of water to a rolling boil. Add salt and the pasta and cook following the directions on page 33.

Sedanini should take about 12 minutes.

Add a spoonful of the pepper-sausage sauce to the bottom of a warm serving bowl. Drain the pasta and turn it immediately into the bowl, piling the rest of the sauce on top. Garnish with the minced herbs and grated cheese and serve immediately, mixing the pasta and sauce together at the table.

VARIATION *Make a vegetarian version of this recipe by simply omitting the sausage, adding the chili and ground fennel seeds, if you wish, directly to the sweet pepper sauce.*

Cavatappi con Peperone

Cavatappi with Roasted Peppers, Anchovies, Garlic, and Capers

S low-roasted peppers and anchovies recall the great antipasto from northwest Italy, bagna cauda—seasonal vegetables, both raw and cooked, served with a bubbling pot of anchovies and garlic toasting away in olive oil and butter for dipping.

SERVES 6

3 red sweet peppers
2 yellow sweet peppers
3 tablespoons extra-virgin olive oil
3 large garlic cloves, sliced very thin
Two 2-ounce cans oil-packed anchovy fillets
½ cup finely chopped flat-leaf parsley
3 tablespoons salted capers, rinsed thoroughly
Sea salt
About 1 pound (500 grams) cavatappi
½ cup freshly shredded pecorino sardo or
   pecorino toscano

First, roast the peppers following the directions on page 14. When done, trim the peppers, discarding the seeds and inner white membranes, and slice lengthwise into strips. Set aside. (This may be done in advance and the peppers kept, refrigerated if necessary, until ready to use.)

Combine the oil and garlic in a skillet large enough to hold all the ingredients, including the pasta, and set over medium-low heat. Cook gently, stirring from time to time, until the garlic is softened. Do not let it brown. Add the anchovy fillets and continue cooking, using a fork to crush the anchovies into the oil and dissolve them. Stir in ¼ cup of the parsley.

Raise the heat to medium and add all of the pepper strips, stirring to mix well with the oil and anchovies. When the peppers start to sizzle, lower the heat to low, cover, and cook gently for about 40 minutes, or until the peppers are very tender. Check occasionally and add a little boiling water, if necessary, to keep the peppers from browning. When the sauce is done, remove from the heat and stir in the capers. Keep the sauce warm until ready to use.

Bring a large pot of water to a rolling boil. Add salt and the pasta and cook following the directions on page 33.

When the pasta is al dente, set aside about 1 cup of the pasta water and drain the pasta. Add it to the pan with the peppers. Combine the pasta and sauce by tossing and gently stirring, adding in some of the pasta water, if necessary, to make a creamier sauce. Stir in ¼ cup of the pecorino and the remaining ¼ cup parsley and toss again. Taste and adjust the seasoning, adding salt, if necessary. Transfer the dressed pasta to a warm serving bowl. Sprinkle the remaining ¼ cup shredded cheese on top and serve immediately.

Shells with Roasted Corn and Summer Savory

Applying Italian techniques and food philosophy to a favorite American ingredient results in this unusual dish. Corn in Italy is almost always dried for polenta or animal feed and almost never eaten fresh. But in late-summer New England, when nighttime chills intensify and set the fresh flavors of sweet corn, pairing this seasonal vegetable with pasta seems like the most Italian thing in the world. It's a wonderful combination: corn cut off the cob, roasted and mixed with slow-cooked onions, pancetta or bacon, and sweet summer savory to finish it off.

Can't find savory in your farmers' market? You could substitute basil instead.

SERVES 6

4 medium ears very fresh sweet corn
2 tablespoons unsalted butter
2 tablespoons extra-virgin olive oil
Sea salt and freshly ground black pepper
2 to 3 ounces pancetta or bacon, diced
  (½ cup)
2 medium yellow onions, diced very small
1 tablespoon savory
About 1 pound (500 grams) shells, cavatappi,
  or similar small pasta
1 cup freshly grated parmigiano-reggiano

Shuck the ears of corn and, using a sharp knife, cut away the kernels and set them aside. Then, using a spoon, hold each cob over a bowl and scrape down along the cobs to extract all the remaining bits and the starchy juices.

Bring a large pot of water to a rolling boil.

While the pasta water is heating, combine the butter and oil in a large skillet and set over medium heat. When the butter has melted, add the corn kernels with a pinch of salt and cook, tossing and stirring, until the kernels start to roast and brown. Remove from the pan and set aside.

Turn the heat down to low and add the pancetta. Continue to cook until the pancetta starts to release its fat and to brown. Then stir in the onions and continue cooking while the onions soften. Finally, when the onions are soft, add the roasted corn kernels back in, along with the scraped juices from the bowl. Add plenty of pepper and the savory, stirring to mix well. Keep the corn mixture warm while you cook the pasta.

Add salt and the pasta to the boiling water and cook following the directions on page 33 until not quite al dente, 9 or 10 minutes. Drain the pasta and turn it into the corn mixture. Toss and mix over medium heat to let the pasta finish cooking in the sauce.

At the last minute before serving, stir ½ cup of the grated parmigiano into the pasta and toss again. Turn the pasta into a warm serving bowl and serve immediately, passing the remaining ½ cup cheese at the table.

Pasta Shells with Zucchini, Blossoms, Peas, and Mint

Another quick-and-easy pasta, with a sauce that can be turned out in the time it takes the water to boil and the pasta to cook. A rapid sauté of onions and garlic, then the addition of the vegetables, and finally a hit of fresh slivered mint—and that's it. Regular peas are usually long gone by the time summer squash comes around, but try this with either edible pod peas (snap peas) or Chinese snow peas (the ones that look too flat to hold a pea). Whichever you choose, sliver them diagonally to make a colorful addition. The blossoms could be from zucchini or summer squash. It doesn't make any difference. Just be sure they are fresh and pert looking.

SERVES 4 TO 6

3 tablespoons extra-virgin olive oil

1 spring onion, or ½ medium yellow onion, chopped fine

1 garlic clove, chopped fine

4 medium yellow zucchini, grated on the coarse holes of a box grater

Sea salt

½ pound edible podded peas (see headnote), slivered on the diagonal about ¼ inch thick

About 1 pound (500 grams) small pasta shells

12 fresh zucchini or summer squash blossoms

1 tablespoon unsalted butter

¼ cup slivered fresh mint leaves

Freshly grated parmigiano-reggiano

Bring a large pot of water to a rolling boil.

While the water is heating, make the pasta sauce: Combine the oil, onion, and garlic in a large skillet and set over medium-low heat. Cook rapidly, stirring, until the vegetables start to soften. Add the grated zucchini with a pinch of salt and toss to mix well. As the zucchini starts to soften, stir in the pea slivers and continue tossing. Cook until the vegetables are tender.

Meanwhile, when the water is boiling, add salt and the pasta and cook following the directions on page 33. Keep the sauce warm while the pasta cooks. Small shells should take about 10 minutes to reach the al dente stage.

Just before draining the pasta, add about ¼ cup of the pasta water to the skillet and stir in the blossoms, butter, and mint. Remove from the heat.

Drain the pasta, turn it into a warm serving bowl, and pour the sauce over it, tossing to mix everything together very well. Add a few tablespoons of the grated parmigiano and serve immediately, passing the rest of the cheese at the table.

Cooking Lobsters

For two 1½-pound lobsters, or three or four 1-pound lobsters, bring about 3 inches of water to a rolling boil in a pot large enough to hold the lobsters. When the water is boiling, add 2 or 3 large spoonsful of salt—in Maine we say the water should be as salty as the ocean itself—and as soon as the salt has dissolved, plunge the lobsters in headfirst. Cover the pot and boil vigorously for about 10 minutes, or until the lobsters are cooked. They will turn bright red when done. Another indication of doneness: Give a sharp tug to an antenna, and if it snaps off, the lobster is cooked through.

When the lobsters are done, use tongs to remove them from the pot. Set aside to cool, and as soon as you can handle them, crack the shells, remove the meat (see below), and set aside. For pasta recipes, return the shells and any unused interior material to the lobster steaming liquid. Add enough additional water to make about 6 quarts. Bring to a simmer and cook gently, covered, for 40 minutes, then strain through cheesecloth. This is the liquid in which to cook the pasta.

To shuck the lobsters: Set up a board close to the sink so that any liquid released will go down the drain. Turn the lobster belly side up and, using a sharp knife, cut right down through the body to the tail. Drain any liquid over the sink. Break off the big claws and crack them open using a nutcracker. Remove the meat all along the claw, covering each segment and using a lobster pick, or a walnut pick, where necessary. Break off the tails and, using a sharp knife, cut a deep slit down the inside of the tail. Separate the shells and remove the tail meat. Remove the dark vein that runs down the inside of the tail. For pasta dishes, chop all the meat into bite-size pieces.

Linguine all'Aragosta con Arance e Peperoncini

Lobster Linguine with Oranges and Chili Peppers

Like most lobster dishes, this will be best if you steam the lobsters yourself (see page 212 for instructions on cooking and shucking lobsters). Two 1½-pound or three 1-pound lobsters should give you about 1 pound of lobster meat.

SERVES 4 TO 6

Sea salt and freshly ground black pepper
¼ cup extra-virgin olive oil
2 fresh spring onions or shallots, finely chopped
2 garlic cloves, minced
2 oranges
Meat from three 1-pound lobsters (see headnote)
1 small dried red chili pepper, crumbled, or to taste
½ cup crème fraîche or mascarpone
¼ cup chopped flat-leaf parsley, plus a little more for garnish
1 tablespoon chopped thyme leaves
1 tablespoon chopped chives or cilantro, plus a little more for garnish
About 1 pound (500 grams) linguine

Start heating about 6 quarts lobster cooking water for pasta (see page 212) in a pot, adding a big spoonful of salt when it comes to a rolling boil.

While the pasta water is heating, combine the oil, onions, and garlic in a heavy skillet large enough to hold all the ingredients except the pasta, and set over medium-low heat. Add a pinch of salt and cook very gently, stirring, until the vegetables are thoroughly softened, melting into the oil.

While the vegetables cook, zest one of the oranges and set the zest aside. Then peel both oranges, cutting away all the white pith on the outsides to expose the flesh beneath. Chop the oranges coarsely in a bowl in order to retain as much of the juice as possible.

If the pasta water is ready at this point, plunge the pasta in. Cook, following the directions on page 33.

When the vegetables in the skillet are soft, stir in the oranges with their juice and the zest, the lobster meat, and chili. Raise the heat to medium and cook for 2 to 3 minutes, just to thicken the juice slightly, then stir in the crème fraîche and let come to a simmer. Remove from the heat and stir in the parsley, thyme, and chives. Taste and add salt and black pepper, if you wish.

When the pasta is done, drain and turn it into a warm serving bowl. Immediately pour the lobster sauce over and turn to mix well. Serve immediately, garnished with additional parsley and chives.

Spaghetti Congolese

Congolese Spaghetti with Lobster Sauce

Is this dish really from the Congo? No! Sara developed it at her East Village restaurant Porsena when a customer texted her requesting a recipe for pasta Congolese. She immediately imagined an outpost of Italian peacekeepers on assignment in the Congo, where, with limited ingredients, they like all Italians longed for a plate of home-cooked food. Perhaps, she thought, there might be some sort of spiny lobster available, and of course there would be olive oil and spaghetti—true Italians never travel with anything less. By the time she had fully formulated this imaginary dish cooked by imaginary Italians in a country she had never visited, the customer texted back, "Sorry, I meant pasta con le vongole," the classic pasta with clams, available at every seaside shanty in Italy!

Thus are great dishes created by spell-check.

When you boil the lobsters, save the water and cook the pasta in it; it will add even more briny lobster flavor to the dish (see page 212).

SERVES 4 TO 6

Meat from three 1-pound lobsters, prepared
  as on page 212
Sea salt
2 tablespoons extra-virgin olive oil
1 tablespoon unsalted butter
2 garlic cloves, minced
1 medium yellow onion, chopped
¼ cup finely chopped flat-leaf parsley
1 fresh red chili pepper, seeded and chopped
2 ripe fresh plum tomatoes, peeled, seeded,
  and chopped
½ cup heavy cream
2 tablespoons fresh tarragon leaves, chopped
Crushed red pepper flakes (optional)
About 1 pound (500 grams) spaghetti

Chop the lobster meat coarsely.

Bring 6 quarts of lobster cooking liquid or heavily salted water to a rolling boil.

While the liquid heats, combine the oil and butter in a large heavy skillet and set over medium-low heat. Add the garlic, onion, parsley, and red chili pepper and sauté, stirring frequently, until the vegetables are soft but not brown. Add 1 cup of the simmering lobster liquid or boiling water. Stir in the tomatoes and cook until very soft, about 10 minutes, then add the cream. Simmer gently for 15 minutes. Add the tarragon along with the lobster meat, and simmer for an additional 5 minutes. Taste the sauce and adjust the seasoning. If necessary, add a pinch or two of red pepper flakes.

Meanwhile, add the pasta to the boiling lobster liquid or water and cook following the directions on page 33.

When the pasta is al dente, drain and turn it into a warm serving bowl. Add about half the lobster sauce and mix with the pasta. Top the pasta with the remaining sauce and serve immediately.

Pasta alla Chitarra allo Scoglio

Guitar Pasta on the Rocks

"On the rocks" is the literal translation of *allo scoglio*, but in Italian it signifies any seafood preparation that depends on products from right along the coast, hence a summertime, vacation-at-the-seaside dish. Here we use fresh clams, mussels, shrimp, and squid, but you could use just clams, mussels, and chunks of swordfish, or clams, shrimp, and lobster. Traditionally it's a mixture of shellfish and finfish, but even that is not a rule cast in stone. Anywhere around the Mediterranean the shrimp would be added with their heads and shells intact, but North Americans probably would prefer to have the shrimp peeled and the black vein removed.

Pasta alla chitarra is a classic from the Abruzzi, handmade with durum flour and eggs and shaped using the curious "guitar" instrument from the region (see page 49 for instructions). Or use pasta secca—linguine or tonnarelli would be perfect.

Note: If you use all the fish in the ingredients list, it will be enough for eight generous servings. For a smaller quantity, either halve the recommended seafood ingredients, or simply omit one or more of them.

SERVES 8

4 garlic cloves, finely chopped
3 or 4 plump shallots, finely chopped
¼ cup extra-virgin olive oil, plus more for garnish
1 teaspoon fennel pollen or fennel seeds
Pinch saffron threads
2 bay leaves
2 or 3 thyme sprigs
½ pound small tomatoes (such as cherry or grape), halved
¼ cup passata di pomodoro (pureed tomatoes)
1 dried hot red chili pepper
¼ cup dry white wine
1 pound small Manila clams in their shells, cleaned (see page 14)
1 pound mussels in their shells, cleaned (see page 14)

Sea salt and freshly ground black pepper
12 medium shrimp
½ pound fresh squid, the smaller the better, sliced into rings
About 1 pound (500 grams) fresh pasta alla chitarra or dried linguine or tonnarellli
Slivered basil, for garnish

Combine half the garlic and all the shallots with the oil in a large deep skillet. Set over low heat and cook, stirring, until the vegetables are almost melting. Do not let them brown. Add the fennel pollen, saffron, bay leaves, and thyme. Stir together, then add the tomatoes and pureed tomatoes, along with the chili pepper.

Combine the wine and the remaining garlic in a separate saucepan and set over medium heat. As soon as the wine is simmering, add the clams and cook just until they open. Remove each clam as it opens and set aside. When all the clams are done, add the mussels to the same saucepan and again cook until they open, removing each one as it does so. (Any clams or mussels that do not open after 8 to 10 minutes should be discarded.)

Strain the juice left in the bottom of the pan through several layers of cheesecloth to get rid of the grit. Add the strained juice to the tomato sauce. Taste the sauce and add salt, if necessary, and plenty of freshly ground black pepper.

Bring a large pot of water to a rolling boil.

While the water is heating, add the shrimp and sliced squid to the tomato sauce and let simmer in the sauce just until cooked, 3 to 4 minutes. At the very end add the mussels and clams in their shells, simmering them just long enough to heat them up. If necessary, add a ladle of pasta water to the sauce.

Add salt and the pasta to the boiling water and cook following the directions on page 33. If you're using freshly made pasta alla chitarra, it will cook in about 3 minutes. Drain the pasta and transfer to a warm platter, then arrange the sauce over the pasta, piling up the different types of seafood. Garnish with a dribble of oil and some slivered basil.

Serve immediately.

COOK'S TIP *Restaurant kitchens, with access to very large skillets and cooking surfaces, often pull the pasta before it is completely cooked, drain it, and transfer it to the sauce right before adding the lobster, mussels, and clams, along with a ladleful of pasta water. The pasta finishes cooking in the sauce, absorbing all the flavors; then the lobster chunks, mussels, and clams are tossed in at the end. It's a great technique but, because of the quantities involved, a little awkward for most home cooks.*

Gnocchetti with Mussels and Saffron Potatoes

Gnochetti or cavatelli work well with this sauce, their curled insides trapping sauce and bits of potato. It seems strange to North Americans to pair potatoes and pasta, starch and starch, but it is a noble tradition from times of poverty.

This may be served as a soup, to be eaten with a spoon, or as a pasta to be eaten with a fork (but have hunks of country-style bread for sopping up the delicious juices).

SERVES 4 TO 6

5 pounds mussels (about 4 quarts)
3 celery stalks, diced (about ½ cup)
1 large shallot, diced (about ½ cup)
½ medium fennel bulb, diced (about ½ cup)
2 garlic cloves, crushed and chopped
½ cup extra-virgin olive oil
*½ cup flat-leaf parsley, minced, plus a little
    more for garnish*
1½ cups dry white wine
*1 pound waxy potatoes (fingerlings, yellow
    Finns, or similar), diced small*
Big pinch saffron threads
½ pound (250 grams) gnocchetti or cavatelli
*Pinch ground red chili pepper (piment
    d'Espelette or similar)*

Clean the mussels following the directions on page 14.

Combine the celery, shallot, fennel, and garlic in a pan large enough to hold all the mussels. Add ¼ cup of the oil and set over medium-low heat. Cook gently, stirring, until the vegetables are soft, then stir in ¼ cup of the parsley and the wine and bring to a simmer.

Tip in the cleaned mussels and cook, stirring, until they've opened, pulling each one out of the pan as it opens and setting it aside. If any refuse to open after about 10 minutes, discard them. Strain the mussel broth, discarding the vegetables and any sand or grit from the mussels. Return the mussel broth to a clean pan and keep just barely simmering while you finish the dish. Shuck the mussels and keep warm in a little broth.

In a separate skillet, combine the potatoes with the remaining ¼ cup oil and set over medium heat. Cook, stirring and tossing, until the potatoes start to brown along their edges, then toss them into the mussel broth, along with a big pinch of saffron, and simmer very gently.

While the potatoes are cooking, bring a large pot of water to a rolling boil. Add salt and the pasta and cook following the directions on page 33, checking the package recommendations for time. However, before it is fully done, drain the pasta and add it to the potatoes and mussel broth.

Taste the broth and add the ground chili pepper and remaining ¼ cup parsley. When the pasta is al dente, add the mussels in their small amount of broth and heat just to simmering. Serve immediately, either as a soup or as a pasta, sprinkling a little more parsley over the top.

Ditalini con Fagioli Freschi e Verdure

Ditalini with Fresh Shell Beans and Greens

The first shell beans show up in late July at farm stands and markets. They are a treat because their season is short and they are delicious, especially the vividly streaked red-and-white borlotti (aka tongues of fire). When shopping for shell beans, don't look for fresh green pods—that means the beans inside aren't quite mature enough to bother with. Unlike most produce, what you're looking for are pods that are slightly dry, slightly limp, not firm and fresh feeling. If you see plump beans inside each pod, that's all the better. Some other varieties to look for: cranberry beans (another name for borlotti), scarlet runner beans, flagrano (actually a French flageolet but grown to maturity as a shelling bean), and small white cannellini. In North American markets, there are dozens of different beans available, many of them heirlooms that are particular to a small region and not found elsewhere.

If using chard, strip the green leaves away from the center stems, reserving the stems for another purpose (chopped and added to a soup, for instance). Chop the greens coarsely to make about 4 cups raw greens.

This is a great summertime take on "pasta fazool."

SERVES 4 TO 6

2 pounds shelling beans in their pods (see headnote)
Sea salt and freshly ground black pepper
2 tablespoons extra-virgin olive oil, plus more for garnish
1 garlic clove, crushed with the flat blade of a knife and minced
1 small white onion, chopped fine (½ cup)
1 celery stalk, dark green if available, leaves included, chopped fine, to make ½ cup
¾ to 1 pound fresh chard or escarole, coarsely chopped, to make about 4 cups
1 medium or 2 small dried red chili peppers
Handful of basil leaves, torn
About 1 pound (500 grams) ditalini
¼ cup chopped pitted black olives, preferably Gaeta or similar
2 tablespoons coarsely grated parmigiano-reggiano or a young, soft pecorino

Shell the beans and add them to a saucepan with water to cover by 1 inch. Bring to a simmer over medium heat and add a pinch of salt. Cook the beans until tender, 15 to 20 minutes. Set aside in their cooking liquid.

Set another saucepan, one large enough to hold all the ingredients including the pasta, over medium heat. Add the oil, garlic, onion, and celery with a pinch of salt. Sauté gently, just until the vegetables start to soften, then add about 2 tablespoons water and continue to cook until the water has evaporated. Add the greens and about ½ cup water. Add the chili pepper and black pepper to taste. Bring to a simmer. Reduce the heat to medium-low and simmer gently, stirring occasionally, until the liquid thickens and reduces and the greens become wilted and tender, about 10 minutes. Add the beans, with any remaining liquid, and combine well with the greens. Cook another minute or two, then stir in the basil. Remove from the heat and taste, adding more salt and black pepper, if you wish.

Meanwhile, bring a large pot of water to a rolling boil. Add salt and the pasta and cook following the directions on page 33, until not quite al dente. Set aside about ½ cup of the pasta water.

Drain the pasta and combine in the saucepan with the beans and greens, tossing to blend well. Set over medium heat and finish cooking the pasta with the greens and beans, adding a little pasta water if it seems necessary. When the pasta is al dente, add the olives, then taste and adjust the seasoning, if necessary.

Transfer the pasta to a warm serving bowl. Sprinkle with the grated parmigiano and serve. (Note this is just a small amount of cheese. Don't overdo it—you want to taste the freshness of the beans.)

Fettuccine Pantesca

Fettuccine from Pantelleria

The island of Pantelleria sits out in the middle of the Mediterranean, between Sicily and Tunisia and a good deal closer to Tunisia than to any Italian point. Understandably, given its position, the cuisine of the island is simple, almost stark, yet full of delicious combinations of tastes, flavors, and ingredients. And it is famed for the quality of two products—sweet, fresh white wines, with hints of citrus, made from zibibbo grapes grown in low walled enclosures to protect the vines from the nearly constant wind; and salt-preserved capers, plump and savory and, many swear, the best in the world. Capers are actually the flower bud of a handsome low bush that also grows on walls throughout the Mediterranean. The buds are harvested before the delicate purple flowers appear, although if the buds are not harvested, caper berries, the fruit of the plant, naturally develop after the flowering. Whether capers or berries, however, the ones grown in Pantelleria's volcanic soil are of high quality, and islanders use them in just about every meal, one way or another.

This seafood pasta, enriched with tomatoes and capers, is a good example. We've used swordfish, but you could use a fine piece of hake or halibut, or any other kind of white-fleshed fish instead. Or you could use fresh shrimp, peeled, deveined, and cut into bite-size chunks.

If you can get Pantelleria capers packed in sea salt, they're the ones to use. Otherwise, any Mediterranean capers are fine, as long as they're salt-packed. The ones in brine or vinegar give an entirely different flavor, one that is almost unpleasantly acrid.

SERVES 4 TO 6

2 to 3 tablespoons capers, preferably salt-packed from Pantelleria

2 tablespoons coarsely chopped pitted black olives

⅓ cup freshly ground bread crumbs

¼ cup very finely chopped blanched almonds

4 tablespoons extra-virgin olive oil

About ¾ pound seafood (see headnote), cut into small bite-size pieces

Sea salt and freshly ground black pepper

Freshly grated zest of 1 lemon, preferably organic

2 tablespoons freshly squeezed lemon juice

About 1 pound (500 grams) fettuccine or linguine

3 tablespoons golden sultana raisins, soaked in hot water to plump, and drained

1 pound ripe fresh tomatoes (2 medium tomatoes), peeled and chopped

Rinse the capers thoroughly in a sieve to rid them of as much salt as possible. Dry with a kitchen towel and, if they are big and plump, chop them coarsely. Mix the capers with the olives.

Bring a large pot of water to a rolling boil.

While the water is heating, combine the bread crumbs and almonds with 2 tablespoons of the oil in a skillet over medium heat. Cook, stirring frequently, until the crumbs and almonds have crisped and turned golden. Remove from the heat and combine with the caper-olive mixture.

Pat the seafood dry on all sides with paper towels. Add the remaining 2 tablespoons oil to the skillet and set over medium heat. Add the seafood with a little salt, keeping in mind that the capers and olives will add salt to the dish. Cook the seafood, tossing and stirring, just until it changes color, then remove and set aside.

Add pepper, the lemon zest, lemon juice, and chopped tomatoes. Add the drained sultanas. Continue cooking and stirring until most of the tomato juice has boiled away. Return the seafood pieces to the skillet and keep warm while the pasta cooks.

When the pasta water is boiling, add salt and the pasta and cook following the directions on page 33.

Drain the pasta when it is al dente and turn it into a warm serving bowl. Toss with the sauce and garnish with the caper-olive–bread crumb mixture. Serve immediately.

Ravioli con Ricotta e Melanzane Bruciacchiate

Ravioli with Ricotta and Charred Eggplant

Charring eggplant gives it a deliciously smoky, burned flavor. Doing this is easy on a charcoal grill, but we have also successfully charred eggplants in a big old black iron skillet right on top of the stove. Turn the heat to high (and turn on the exhaust fan to avoid setting off smoke detectors) and add the eggplant to the unoiled skillet. Use tongs to turn periodically until the eggplants are blackened and charred all over.

Note the use of durum flour in the pasta dough (it's available from www.kingarthurflour .com). Durum flour is the result of milling hard durum wheat semolina a second time to make a softer, finer-textured flour that still maintains the high protein and the deliciously wheaten flavor of durum wheat. Sara makes pasta almost daily at her restaurant, often switching back and forth between all-purpose and durum and sometimes combining the two. In this case, using durum flour gives a stronger dough, to wrap around the loose eggplant filling.

Here's what she says about these ravioli: "I pride myself on a silky light ravioli dough, and as a result the ravioli don't have a lot of holding power. I make my filling the day before and then plan to roll out the dough and make the ravioli just an hour or so before I want to cook them. I rest the ravioli on a thick bed of semolina flour, slightly coarser than durum, which helps prevent them from sticking and then falls off in the water while cooking. I have the sauce warm and ready in the bowl or platter I plan to serve the ravioli in and then scoop them out with a large slotted spoon or strainer as they float on top of the water. Then I gently layer them with sauce and cheese rather than tossing them with the sauce."

For best results, make the filling the day before and let it drain overnight. Let the ricotta drain too, and you'll have fewer problems with an overly liquid filling for the ravioli.

MAKES 36 LARGE RAVIOLI, 6 SERVINGS AS A PRIMO, 4 AS A MAIN COURSE

FOR THE FILLING

2 large eggplants (about 2½ pounds)
Sea salt
1 pound ricotta, drained
½ cup freshly grated parmigiano-reggiano, or more to taste
¼ cup very finely chopped flat-leaf parsley
1 recipe Durum Flour Pasta Dough (page 45)
1 egg, whisked into ¼ cup water (egg wash)
Sea salt

2 cups tomato sauce (see pages 175–179)
½ to ¾ cup freshly grated parmigiano-reggiano

Prepare the filling: Begin the day before by charring the eggplants. Light a charcoal grill, if available, and when it is ready, set the whole eggplants on the grill. Turn them periodically to toast and char them evenly all over the outsides. This will take about 30 minutes in all.

If you don't have a charcoal grill, set a heavy black iron skillet over high heat, turn

on the exhaust fan, and add the eggplants to the skillet, again turning frequently, until they are blackened and charred on the outside and soft within. The eggplants will collapse slightly when the insides are soft.

Remove from the heat and peel the eggplants as soon as you can handle them but while they are still quite hot. Puree the eggplant flesh, putting it through a food mill or using a fork or a potato masher. You should have about 1½ cups of eggplant puree. Blend in 1 teaspoon salt and taste. There should be a good eggplant flavor with just a hint of saltiness.

Transfer the pureed eggplant to a fine-mesh sieve and set aside, covered with plastic wrap, to drain overnight.

Add the ricotta to another sieve and let drain overnight.

Next day, combine the eggplant and ricotta and stir in the grated parmigiano and parsley. Taste and add more cheese, if you wish.

Prepare the ravioli: Divide the pasta in two and roll out one half, keeping the other half under a damp cloth or kitchen towel. Roll the sheet of pasta to ⅟₁₆-inch thickness or less—*paper-thin* is the usual term for describing a perfect sheet of pasta. Using a pastry brush, brush half the dough with the egg wash. Pipe about 1 tablespoon of eggplant filling in regular rows about ½ inch apart. Fold the other half of the dough sheet over the fillings, pressing down around each little mound of filling to seal it carefully so no filling will escape while the ravioli are cooking. Using a round pasta stamp that is about 2½ inches in diameter, cut out the ravioli, each one with its eggplant filling.

Strew a thick layer of semolina over a separate board and set the filled ravioli to rest on the semolina. Proceed with the second half of the dough and the remainder of the filling.

Have the tomato sauce ready and simmering on the stove. Just before cooking the ravioli, spoon a ladleful of tomato sauce into a warm serving bowl.

Bring 4 to 6 quarts of water to a rolling boil in a large pot and add salt. Turn the heat down to simmering before adding the ravioli, a few at a time. The ravioli will bubble and float to the top. Let each one cook another minute or two after it floats to the top, then remove with a slotted spoon and set in the bowl. Dribble a spoonful of tomato sauce over the first layer and sprinkle with a spoonful of grated parmigiano.

Proceed with the rest of the ravioli, layering them with tomato sauce and cheese. When all the ravioli are done, serve immediately, passing any remaining tomato sauce and cheese.

Cuscussù Trapanese

Sicilian Couscous with Rich Shellfish Sauce

This is the way Pino Maggiore makes seafood *cuscus* (or couscous, or *cuscussù*) in Trapani, the fishing port on the far western end of Sicily, where his restaurant Cantina Siciliana is a must for anyone who loves good food. It seems obvious that cuscussù came to Trapani from North Africa, but no one knows when or under what circumstances. The technique for making it is very different from North African couscous and, we think, much simpler. In Trapani it is almost always a fish couscous, made with a selection of seafood from the great fish market next to the Trapani docks.

But is it really pasta? We think so, though some of our friends dispute the claim. But we believe that any food made from ground wheat (flour) mixed with water and dried, then reconstituted in moisture, whether boiling water as for spaghetti, or steam as for couscous, is pasta by definition.

You may make couscous grains from scratch, as Pino does at his restaurant, but you will have equally good results using a good commercially made couscous, which is what we suggest.

Note that you will need 8 cups of Fish Stock (page 10) to make 8 servings.

A couscoussiere is a special two-chambered pot, sort of like a double boiler, made for cooking couscous. The liquid goes in the bottom part and the couscous grains in the top. When the liquid boils, steam rises to cook the couscous. If you don't have such a thing, not to worry: You can improvise by setting a colander over a deep saucepan in which the colander will fit tightly with no gaps.

The seafood selection for Trapani couscous can vary enormously. You could use all monkfish, for instance, or all shrimp, but the dish is much more interesting if you vary the selection. You should have about 2½ pounds of seafood in all.

SERVES 8

About 1 pound (2½ cups) couscous, whole
   grain, if you prefer
½ cup very finely minced flat-leaf parsley
1 yellow onion, very finely minced (about
   1 cup)
¼ cup extra-virgin olive oil
Freshly ground black pepper
6 to 8 bay leaves, or more if necessary
2 lemons, preferably organic, each cut into
   8 pieces

About ½ cup unbleached all-purpose flour
8 cups Fish Stock (page 10)
1 pound monkfish tail, cubed
½ pound fresh shrimp, peeled and deveined
About 1 pound cooked lobster meat, cubed
Handful of basil leaves, slivered (about ½ cup),
   for garnish
½ cup chopped toasted almonds, for garnish

Spread the couscous grains out on a tray and sprinkle lightly with about ½ cup warm water. Rake the grains with your fingers to distribute the moisture evenly, then spread again on the tray and leave the grains to swell with moisture for about 20 minutes.

Combine the parsley and onion in a bowl, tossing to mix together well, then add the dampened couscous and dribble the oil over it. Grind plenty of pepper over the couscous and toss to mix well. Now take up a handful of couscous and rub it between your palms, then take up another handful. In this way, you'll incorporate all these ingredients together uniformly.

In the lower part of the couscoussiere add enough water to come within 2 inches, but no more, of the bottom of the top part. (The top part must never touch the water below; otherwise the couscous will get soggy.)

Add the bay leaves and lemon pieces to the water and bring to a simmer over medium heat.

While the water is heating, make a flour-and-water paste, simply mixing enough water into the flour to be able to roll it into a long snake. (You remember this from kindergarten, right?) With this you will seal the two elements of the couscoussiere.

Transfer the couscous to the top part of the couscoussiere and set it over the boiling water. Use the flour-and-water snake to make a seal between the top and the bottom, so that all the steam will go up into the couscous and none of it will escape into the air.

Let the couscous steam for about 30 minutes, then fluff gently with a fork so that the bottom grains come to the top and vice versa. Return to the heat to steam for another 30 minutes. Test the couscous at this point. It should be soft and tender. If not, return to the heat yet again for another 15 minutes.

Toward the end of the couscous cooking time, bring the fish stock to a simmer over medium-low heat and add the monkfish cubes. Let cook until the fish has turned opaque, then add the shrimp. Let simmer gently until the shrimp have turned pink, then add the lobster. Continue simmering just long enough to warm the cooked lobster through. Keep the fish stock warm until ready to serve the couscous.

When the couscous is tender, turn it out onto a tray or deep platter and spoon about 5 cups of the stock over the top of it, holding back the pieces of seafood. Toss the couscous with a fork as you dribble the stock liberally—so that all the grains of couscous come in contact with the stock. You may not need to use all the stock, but keep the rest warm to pass with the couscous when you serve it. Cover the couscous with kitchen towels and set aside in a warm place to absorb all the stock for at least 20 minutes before serving. Just before serving, garnish the top with the cooked seafood, plus the slivered basil and almonds.

COOK'S TIP *In Trapani couscous is often served with a garlic and almond mayonnaise, the mayonnaise made with 1 egg and up to ¾ cup oil. Garlic—4 or 5 crushed cloves—and ½ cup coarsely chopped toasted almonds are processed with the egg in the bowl of a food processor, then the oil is slowly added, just as you would with a mayonnaise, along with a little fresh lemon juice and of course sea salt and freshly ground black pepper.*

Fideuà

Catalan Pasta and Seafood Paella

An unusual take on traditional seafood paella, this Catalan classic is made with fideos, thin noodles about the size of spaghettini or capelli d'angelo, but cut in 1- to 2-inch lengths. And it has a history—the word *fideos* is said to come from medieval Arabic *fidawsh*, which describes very similar noodles, suggesting that the shape and the ingredient, if not the recipe itself, may have been brought to Spain by Arabs during their seven-hundred-year hegemony over much of the Iberian peninsula. The recipe is a modern invention, some say specifically an invention of cooks in Valencia in the early twentieth century, but the technique of toasting pasta noodles in oil before adding liquid is quite possibly ancient—and, incidentally, unknown in Italy. Moreover, cooking the pasta in its sauce until it is somewhat more than al dente is a process that, in our experience, one would never find in Italy. Both these techniques may well go back to an Arab original in the kitchens of Moorish Spain.

The garlicky, saffrony aioli (or in Catalan, *allioli*) is a plus to add at the end when the fideuà is served. Some cooks suggest using an earthenware cassola, but we follow Chef Maria José San Román, who makes fideuà in a wide paella pan and takes the whole pan to the table at her Alicante restaurant, Monastrell.

If this looks complicated, don't be daunted. A good plan of action is to start with the Fish Stock on page 10. You will need about 5 cups and you can make it days or even weeks in advance and refrigerate or freeze it until you're ready to use it. Make the sofrito and the salmorreta, two sauce bases that are typical of Catalan cuisine; bring the fish stock to a simmer; toast the noodles in olive oil; and you're good to go.

Ñora peppers are a Spanish dried chili variety, not very hot but with a nice spicy fragrance. You can find them at Spanish food suppliers such as La Tienda (www.latienda.com), or substitute a dried New Mexico or ancho chili. Spanish paprika (pimentón) is also not very spicy; don't confuse it with pimentón de la Vera, smoked paprika, unless you want a smoky flavor.

You could use the suggested seafood in any quantities, but the total should be about 1½ pounds of seafood, plus the clams and mussels. The seafood could be all shrimp, all squid (calamari), all firm-textured fish (swordfish and monkfish are ideal), or a mixture, depending on what's fresh at your fishmonger's.

**SERVES 8 AS A STARTER,
6 AS A MAIN COURSE**

1 red sweet pepper, finely chopped
½ medium yellow onion, finely chopped

About ¾ cup extra-virgin olive oil
3 plump garlic cloves, sliced
1 dried ñora chili pepper, rinsed and chopped,
  seeds discarded

1 large ripe fresh tomato, peeled, seeded, and
chopped
½ teaspoon sweet Spanish pimentón (see
headnote)
¼ cup chopped flat-leaf parsley
1 teaspoon aged sherry vinegar
Sea salt
5 to 6 cups Fish Stock (page 10)
Pinch saffron threads
About 1 pound (500 grams) long, thin pasta
(spaghettini or fedelini are ideal)
½ pound large shrimp, shells left on
½ pound cleaned squid, coarsely chopped
½ pound peeled shrimp, coarsely chopped
⅓ to ½ cup plain tomato sauce
12 or more cleaned mussels
12 or more cleaned Manila clams or cockles
1 cup Saffron-Orange Allioli (recipe follows),
for serving

Prepare the sofrito: Chop together half the
sweet pepper and all the onion to make a
fine mince. Add to a saucepan with 3 to 4
tablespoons of the oil. Set over very low
heat and leave to cook for 30 to 40 minutes,
stirring occasionally, until the vegetables
are thoroughly softened, melting in the oil
but not browned. If they start to burn, add
a very little boiling water to the pan. When
done, set aside.

Prepare the salmorreta: Combine the
garlic and 3 tablespoons of the oil in a
skillet and cook over medium-low heat,
until the garlic starts to take color. Remove
the garlic with a slotted spoon and transfer
to the bowl of a food processor. Add the
chili pepper and the remaining ½ cup sweet

pepper to the oil in the skillet. Return to
medium-low heat and continue cooking,
stirring occasionally, until the sweet pepper
is softened. Remove the peppers with a
slotted spoon and add to the garlic. Add
the tomato to the oil in the skillet and cook
over medium-low heat until the tomato has
released its juices and completely softened.
Remove the skillet from the heat and stir
in the pimentón and chopped parsley.
Scrape all this, including any remaining
oil, into the food processor bowl. Add the
sherry vinegar and process the salmorreta
in spurts until it forms a thick but not very
smooth paste. If the paste is too crumbly
and dry, add a little more vinegar. Taste and
add salt. If the paste is too thick, add a little
more oil—it should be tart but not sour, and
have a lumpy mayonnaise consistency.

Bring the fish stock to a simmer and let it
continue simmering very gently while you
prepare the rest of the recipe.

Add the saffron to ¼ cup very warm water
and set aside to steep for at least 1 hour.

Set the oven on 300°F.

Break the pasta into 1- to 2-inch lengths
and spread in a sheet pan with slightly
raised sides. Add 2 tablespoons of the oil
and toss the noodles, using your hands,
until they have absorbed the oil. Transfer to
the preheated oven and toast the noodles
for about 20 minutes, stirring once or twice,
until they are golden. Remove from the
oven and set aside.

To a paella pan or a similar wide skillet,
add about ⅓ cup of the oil, enough to
thoroughly coat the bottom of the pan.

Add the large shrimp in their shells to the pan and cook over medium heat, turning frequently, until the shrimp are thoroughly pink. Remove and set aside.

Add the squid to the oil in the pan and cook over medium heat, tossing, until the squid are opaque. Stir in the chopped *peeled* shrimp and continue cooking and tossing. Once the shrimp are pink, stir in the tomato sauce, salmorreta, and sofrito. Add the saffron water and stir to mix well. Add the toasted pasta noodles and stir again.

As soon as the noodles have absorbed all the liquid, add 4 to 5 cups of simmering fish stock—you should be able to see the liquid bubbling around the other ingredients, but the noodles should be immersed in the liquid. Tuck in the mussels and clams, along with the reserved large shrimp. Stir well and let simmer on top of the stove until the noodles are very soft and the dish is a little soupy. Add a little more simmering fish stock if at any point it seems necessary. Once the pasta is done, the whole pan is sometimes run under a preheated hot broiler to toast and crisp the topmost layer, but in most kitchens this is not feasible.

Remove from the heat and let rest and settle for 5 minutes or so. Then serve right in its cooking pan, with the saffron-orange allioli offered separately, as a garnish.

Saffron-Orange Allioli

MAKES 1½ TO 2 CUPS ALLIOLI

Pinch saffron threads
1 large egg
Sea salt
3 or 4 garlic cloves, crushed and chopped fine
1 to 1½ cups extra-virgin olive oil
1 or 2 teaspoons freshly squeezed orange juice
1 tablespoon freshly grated orange zest

First toast the saffron: Fold a sheet of ordinary white copy paper around the saffron to make a loose envelope. Set the envelope in a small skillet over medium heat and toast, turning the paper over with tongs, until the paper starts to brown and crisp along the edges. Remove and shake out the now stiffened saffron threads into a mortar. Grind lightly with a pestle.

Add the egg to the bowl of a food processor and buzz, then add a pinch of salt and the saffron and buzz again. Add the garlic and buzz once more.

Now start to add the oil. Have it ready in a measuring cup with a pourable spout. With the food processor going, slowly pour the oil, a few drops at a time, into the egg. As the mixture starts to come together and mount, increase the drops to a thin thread but be careful not to add too much at once. When ½ to ¾ cup of the oil has been added, add 1 teaspoon of the orange juice, then return to adding more oil. Continue adding oil slowly until you have added 1 cup. Stop the machine and taste the allioli. Add more salt and/or more orange juice, if necessary. Add the orange zest and buzz again. If the allioli is thick enough, remove it from the processor and put it in a small bowl to serve at the table. If it is not quite thick enough, continue adding more oil until you have reached the right consistency.

Autumn

Suddenly, just when it seems that summer might go on forever, we notice the days are growing perceptibly shorter, the nights are cooler, and it really does seem like time to bring in the last tomatoes from the garden, the ones that are still resolutely green. Perched on a sunny kitchen windowsill they might start to redden, but they will never have the explosive flavor of those from late August, now just a memory stored in jars in the pantry.

Fortunately, there are plenty of good things to take their place. Think of all the great Brassicas—from Brussels sprouts to Tuscan kale to broccoli and broccoli rabe (aka rapini). Crisp-textured members of the cabbage family, they come to us in autumn, their pungent bitterness often sweetened by an early frost; these are nutritional dynamos too, welcome correctives to summer's luxurious opulence.

Ripeness now means olives streaked green and purple as they fatten and mature, and wine grapes, weighing down their vines, cracking open under their own bulk and releasing their

Richness comes now from plainer tastes, from squashes and pumpkins, from leeks and root vegetables, turnips and potatoes, from braids of onions and garlic and garlands of dried chili peppers to spike winter beans and legumes.

intoxicating juice. The heady aromas of fermenting wine and newly pressed olive oil combine with the fragrance of wood smoke and the bosky scent of wild mushrooms to create a unique and seductive perfume. Bottle it, label it "Autumn," and you could become very rich.

Actually, *autumn* is a pretty fancy term for what we here in North America plainly call *fall*. Why? Falling leaves; acorns and chestnuts, quinces and apples, falling, dropping from the trees; the fall of the year itself, declining gently but inevitably into winter. The rest of the English-speaking world calls it *autumn*, a word, we are pleased to discover, that has its roots in ancient Etruscan; nevertheless, we like *fall*—it tells us what it is.

In Old English times, this three-month "fall" from summer to winter was called simply *harvest*, as it still is in German. And harvest is what it's all about—harvesting the last fruits of the garden, farmyard, and orchard; putting it all carefully by to sustain us in the depths of the cold that we know lies ahead. We harvest the gleanings of the forest, especially wild mushrooms and chestnuts, as well as the game that offers itself to the hunter's gun. We harvest the family pig in an annual ritual that turns it into hams, sausages, bacon, and pancetta, as well as lard to enrich the family pot.

Richness comes now from plainer tastes, from squashes and pumpkins, from leeks and root vegetables, turnips and potatoes, from braids of onions and garlic and garlands of dried chili peppers to spike winter beans and legumes. We turn away from summery basil in favor of more resinous flavors of sage and rosemary. This is also a major time for what we call comfort food. The all-American notion of comfort food abides in one significant dish—mac and cheese, a pasta confection that, perhaps surprisingly, goes all the back to the 1824 cookbook *The Virginia Housewife* (see page 275 for our version of the dish). Truly, there is nothing new under the autumnal sun.

We prowl autumn markets for wild mushrooms, even truffles if we're lucky, and if not for game then for satisfyingly fatty meats, pork and duck especially. We braise tough cuts of meat and tenderize them through long, slow cooking, taming their rude flavors with wine and olive oil. We look for pumpkins to carve for Halloween and another kind, less sweet, more tasty, to grate and brown with sharp garlic sausage in a pan. Autumn pasta dishes reflect available ingredients at the same time that they satisfy our innate appetites for richer, more warming food as daylight hours shorten and frost hovers in the night air. Leeks make an appearance, whether as stars on their own, sweated

Autumn, with its deep jewel tones of color, rust and ruddy amber, bronze and burgundy, brings intense fragrances and flavors to the table as well.

out with just a bit of prosciutto or bacon to toss with pasta, or for a bit part in a slow-simmered ragù, the kind of multiflavored, multilayered, multitextured fusion, fragrant with red wine and juniper, that seems so very right right now.

Autumn, with its deep jewel tones of color, rust and ruddy amber, bronze and burgundy, brings intense fragrances and flavors to the table as well. It's the time of year when we start to turn back in on ourselves, gearing up to return to school or focusing once more on an intense workload after the easy days of summer. And let's not forget that it is a time for gathering together, in the words of that old Thanksgiving hymn, to give thanks for the blessings of the harvest, to celebrate a full larder and a welcoming table, one where strangers, friends, and family assemble for the great feast of Thanksgiving, the quintessence of autumn and all it has to offer and command.

You can't say anything about autumn, says our poet friend Peggy, without quoting Keats. So here it goes: "Season of mists and mellow fruitfulness, / Close bosom-friend of the maturing sun; / Conspiring with him how to load and bless / . . . And fill all fruit with ripeness to the core. . . ." One of the most beautiful poems in the English language, written by a man who was barely twenty years old. Autumn celebrates his genius, just as he celebrated the magnificent gifts of this season.

Zuppa di Pasta e Ceci
Rich Chicken Soup with Pasta and Chickpeas

Pasta e Fagioli con Finocchio e Pomodoro
Pasta and Beans with Fresh Fennel and Tomatoes

Orecchiette alla Barese
Orecchiette with Spicy Broccoli Rabe

Pennette con Cavolfiore Romanesco al Forno
Pasta with Oven-Roasted Romanesco Cauliflower

Pennette with Brussels Sprouts
and Pancetta

Pumpkin and Pumpkin Seed Maccheroncini

Pasta with Crumbled Sausage, Sage,
and Winter Squash

Bavette with Fennel and
Spicy Bread Crumbs

Bucatini with Creamy Leeks and Bacon

Pappardelle con Patate al Rosmarino
*Pappardelle with Diced Potatoes
and Fragrant Rosemary*

Chestnut Agnolotti with Brown Butter,
Sage, and Fennel

Sweet Potato Gnocchi with Brown
Butter and Sage

Fedelini al Vino Rosso Piccante
*Skinny Pasta Cooked in Red Wine with
Lemon and Chili Pepper*

Elicoidali al Sole Siciliano
Pasta with a Sunny Sicilian Sauce

America's Favorite Pasta
Macaroni and Cheese

Tagliatelle with Gorgonzola
Cream and Fresh Walnuts

Orecchiette con Polpettine e Ricotta Salata
*Little Ears with Tiny Meatballs and
Shaved Ricotta Salata*

Paccheri with Black Olives, Escarole,
and Salt Cod

Tajarin ai Tartufi Bianchi
*Hand-Made Egg Tagliolini with
Shaved White Truffles*

Ragù alla Coda di Bue con Gnocchi di Patate
Mita's Oxtail Ragù to Serve with Potato Gnocchi

Mita's Potato Gnocchi

Pappardelle al Cinghiale o al Finto Cinghiale
*Ragù of Wild Boar or of Pork
with Boarish Pretentions*

Ragù al Coniglio con Vino Rosso,
Olive, e Capperi
*Braised Rabbit Ragù with Red Wine,
Olives and Capers*

Gemelli con Ragù d'Agnello
Pasta Twists with a Slow-Cooked Lamb Ragù

Pappardelle alla Boscaiola
(con Ragù di Porcini)
Pappardelle with a Woodsy Wild Mushroom Ragù

Lasagna con Funghi e Zucca Dolce
Mushroom Lasagna with Sweet Winter Squash

Palestinian Maftoul (Couscous)

Zuppa di Pasta e Ceci

Rich Chicken Soup with Pasta and Chickpeas

For this robust autumn recipe, you'll need a rich, flavorful chicken stock. We urge you to make stock in quantities—a good project for a rainy autumn Saturday or Sunday—and keep it in the freezer for soups, stews, risottos, and pasta sauces. You'll be glad you have it on hand.

Chickpeas (aka garbanzo beans or ceci) are another ingredient that are so much better when they come from a pot on the stove (see page 19), tastier, more flavorful, and with a finer, firmer texture than anything that comes from a can.

For greens, in this soup just about anything fresh and seasonal will do, including broccoli rabe (aka rapini), mustard greens, collards, lacinato (Tuscan) kale, turnip greens, chard, spinach—or a mixture. One or two bunches, weighing about a pound, should make enough for the soup when trimmed and slivered.

If you happen to have cooked chicken on hand (perhaps the chicken you used to make the stock), dice about one cup of meat to add to the soup.

SERVES 4 TO 6

6 cups Rich Chicken Stock (page 9)
1 or 2 bunches fresh greens (see headnote)
1 tablespoon extra-virgin olive oil
2 tablespoons finely diced pancetta or thick, country-style bacon
1 garlic clove, lightly smashed with the flat blade of a knife
Sea salt and freshly ground black pepper
1 cup cooked chickpeas, well drained (see page 19)
1 cup pasta (small shapes are best—miniature shells, cavatelli, mostaccioli, orzo, and the like)
1 red chili pepper, fresh or dried, if desired
Freshly grated parmigiano-reggiano, pecorino sardo, or other firm cheese

Bring the chicken stock slowly to a simmer over medium-low heat.

While the stock is heating, prepare the greens, stripping away the tough center stalks where necessary and slivering the leaves. You will have 7 to 8 cups trimmed and slivered greens.

Combine the oil and pancetta in a medium saucepan and set over medium-low heat. Cook until the pancetta fat starts to run and the little cubes begin to brown and crisp. Add the garlic and continue cooking, raising the heat slightly, until the garlic has browned on all sides. Remove the garlic and set aside. Add the greens to the pan with the water clinging to their leaves. (You may not be able to get all the greens in at once; let the early ones cook down a bit, then add another handful, and keep doing that until all the greens are in the pan.) You may wish to add about ½ inch of boiling water to the pan to keep the greens from scorching. Cook the greens until they are thoroughly limp, adding salt and pepper to taste.

By now the stock should be simmering. Add the greens and pancetta to the stock. You may add a tablespoon or so of liquid left in the bottom of the greens pan, but don't add a lot more because it may darken the clear, rich color of the stock. If you wish, chop the reserved garlic clove and add it to the stock. Stir in the chickpeas and pasta, along with as much or as little of the chili as you wish. (Add the diced cooked chicken, if available, at this point.) Let simmer until the pasta is done, 8 to 10 minutes.

Serve immediately, while the soup is hot. Pass the grated parmigiano at the table.

Pasta e Fagioli con Finocchio e Pomodoro

Pasta and Beans with Fresh Fennel and Tomatoes

Basically, this is pasta e fagioli (aka pasta fazool), a canonical dish all over Italy. But you're adding it to a fragrant tomato-fennel soup base and at the same time making a very nutritious dish. Sometimes this is served more brothy, sometimes thicker with pureed beans—you choose, whichever way you prefer.

Cook the cannellini beans according to the directions on page 19 (don't discard the cooking water); you will need about ½ pound (1 cup) dried beans to start with.

SERVES 4 TO 6

½ medium yellow onion, diced
2 garlic cloves, diced
1 large or 1½ small fennel bulbs, diced
¼ cup extra-virgin olive oil, plus
*   2 tablespoons for garnish*
Sea salt and freshly ground black pepper
1 tablespoon tomato extract or paste
1 tablespoon smoked Spanish paprika
*   (pimentón de la Vera)*
One 28-ounce can whole tomatoes (3 cups),
*   preferably San Marzano, with their juice*
1 small dried red chili pepper
1½ to 2 cups cooked cannellini beans with
*   their cooking liquid*
About 1 pound (500 grams) soup pasta (such
*   as ditalini or gnocchetti)*
Chopped fennel greens, for garnish

Combine the onion, garlic, fennel, ¼ cup of the oil, and a pinch of salt in a saucepan over medium heat. Cook gently until the vegetables are translucent. Add 1 cup water and the tomato extract, and let the liquid cook down until almost completely evaporated. Add the paprika and cook gently until the mixture is aromatic and colored. Add the tomatoes and chili pepper (or ½ chili pepper, if you prefer it less spicy) and cook until the tomatoes are falling apart into a sauce.

Transfer the mixture to a blender or food processor and add ¾ cup of the cooked, drained beans. Puree until smooth, then turn the whole puree back into the saucepan. (If you have an immersion blender, you could puree the mixture right in the saucepan. It will not be as smooth as using a stand blender or food processor, but a little roughness in the texture is not a bad idea.) Add the remaining whole beans to the puree. Taste and adjust the seasoning.

In a separate saucepan or large pot, bring 4 quarts of water to a rolling boil. Add salt and the pasta and cook following the directions on page 33. A few minutes before the pasta is al dente, drain and add to the bean and tomato puree. Simmer for a few more minutes, until the pasta is fully al dente, then serve, garnished with chopped fennel greens and a thread of oil.

Orecchiette alla Barese

Orecchiette with Spicy Broccoli Rabe

In the seaside town of Bari down in Puglia, the heel of Italy's boot, the orecchiette makers are out in force every morning, lining the stone-paved streets of vecchia Bari, the oldest part of this very old town. With quick, deft gestures, these ladies shape dabs of durum-and-water dough by hand into *orecchiette* (the name means "little ears"), small, thumbprint pasta shapes that are then set out to dry in the open air on big wooden trays. Shoppers passing by on their way home from the market make their selection, buying orecchiette by the kilo for the family lunch.

Alla barese, in the Bari style, always means this favorite preparation, made with the spicy greens called broccoli rabe or rapini in America, a little garlic, a pinch of dried chili pepper, and a few anchovies for the salt. Broccoli rabe is widely available in supermarket produce sections, but if by chance you can't find it, you may substitute another pungent autumnal green such as mustard greens, collards, or even Chinese broccoli. Patience Gray, who lived for many years in the Salentino, the tip end of the heel of the Italian boot, told us that cooks there sometimes made a similar dish using wild foraged arugula, but in that case they added a handful of pungent local cheese, grated on top.

Packaged orecchiette are easy to find, but you could substitute farfalle, conchiglie (small shells), or fusilli (corkscrews).

SERVES 6

2 bunches broccoli rabe (about 2 pounds)
Sea salt and freshly ground black pepper
2 garlic cloves, minced
3 tablespoons extra-virgin olive oil, plus more for garnish
6 anchovy fillets, chopped, or to taste
1 small dried hot red chili, crumbled, or hot crushed red pepper flakes to taste
About 1 pound (500 grams) orecchiette or similar pasta

Clean the broccoli rabe, discarding any wilted or yellowing leaves along with the tough part of the stems. Chop the broccoli rabe into pieces about 1 inch long. Rinse thoroughly and set aside.

Bring about 4 quarts of water to a rolling boil in a large pot.

While the water is heating, prepare the garlic-anchovy sauce: Add the chopped garlic to the oil in a small skillet and cook over gentle heat just until the garlic bits are soft. Stir in the anchovy pieces and use a fork to crush and mash them into the hot oil. Add the chili pepper and stir. Remove the skillet from the heat—but warm the

sauce again just to the sizzling point before pouring it over the pasta.

Add salt and the pasta to the rapidly boiling water, and cook following the directions on page 33. Orecchiette will take 12 to 15 minutes to become al dente.

Halfway through the pasta cooking time, add the broccoli rabe to the pasta and stir to mix well. Continue cooking until the pasta is done—the broccoli rabe should cook just 5 to 6 minutes, so time it according to the pasta package directions.

Reheat the garlic-anchovy-chili oil over medium-low heat.

When the pasta is done but still a bit al dente, drain the pasta and greens and turn immediately into a warm serving bowl. Stir to distribute the greens throughout the pasta, then pour the garlic-anchovy-chili oil over the top. Toss again, adding a little more oil, if you wish; add a generous amount of black pepper, and serve immediately.

Pennette con Cavolfiore Romanesco al Forno

Pasta with Oven-Roasted Romanesco Cauliflower

Sara has been making this dish for years. It's in constant rotation at her restaurant Porsena when romanesco is in season, early fall to winter at the farmers' market. If you can find this lovely lime-green cauliflower, do use it—its fractal design, spirals within spirals making little pyramids, and its delicious color make a spectacular presentation. It might be the most beautiful vegetable in the entire kingdom. Romanesco is a Brassica, a member of that big and super-nutritious family that includes white cauliflower, broccoli, and many similar vegetables that we associate with the cool months of the year. It's not always easy to find but it's a hardy vegetable that easily sustains long-distance travel, so if you can't find it, ask the produce manager of your supermarket if they can special order it for you. It's worth it for the handsome presentation.

And if you can't find it, the same dish will be just as delicious with common white cauliflower. Roasting brings out natural sweetness and also adds pleasing crispness to the final result. Discard any examples with loose florets or a proliferation of black spots, indicating something less than fresh. (The occasional small black spot can be cut out when you trim the vegetable for use.)

SERVES 4 TO 6

1 large or 2 small heads romanesco, weighing
    1½ to 2 pounds trimmed
½ cup extra-virgin olive oil
Sea salt and freshly ground black pepper
2 tablespoons unsalted butter
1 garlic clove, smashed with the flat blade of a
    knife and coarsely chopped
2 large salted or oil-packed anchovy fillets,
    coarsely chopped
1 small dried red chili pepper, or pinch
    crushed red pepper flakes
⅓ cup coarsely chopped pitted black olives,
    preferably Gaeta
2 tablespoons salt-packed capers, rinsed and
    drained

About 1 pound (500 grams) pennette or
    similar short, stubby pasta (lumache,
    garganelli, fusilli, and the like)
1 cup freshly grated grana padano or
    parmigiano-reggiano
⅓ cup chopped flat-leaf parsley
1 cup toasted bread crumbs

Set the oven on 400°F. Line a baking sheet with parchment.

Break the romanesco into small florets, each about 1 inch long. If they're very fat, cut them in half. Toss the florets in a bowl with 6 tablespoons of the oil and plenty of salt and pepper. Distribute the florets in an even layer over the parchment-lined baking sheet. Transfer to the hot oven and roast, stirring and turning every 10 to 15 minutes,

until the florets are tender but crisp and brown around the edges, 30 to 45 minutes. Remove from the oven and set aside.

Bring a large pot of water to a rolling boil.

In a heavy, deep pan large enough to hold the romanesco and the cooked pasta, heat the remaining 2 tablespoons oil with the butter over low heat until the butter has melted and foamed slightly. Add the garlic and cook very gently until the garlic is softened. Do not let the garlic brown. Add the anchovy fillets and continue cooking, crushing the anchovies into the oil with a fork. Break up the chili pepper, discarding some of the seeds (to reduce the heat), and add the chili pieces along with the olives and capers. Cook a little bit more, just to meld the flavors. Now stir in the roasted romanesco and toss to mix well. Keep warm until the pasta is ready.

When the pasta water boils, add salt and the pasta and cook following the directions on page 33.

When the pasta is almost done, add about ¼ cup of the pasta water to the romanesco mixture and set over gentle heat to come to a simmer. Drain the pasta before it is completely al dente and combine with the romanesco, tossing to mix. Let it cook together a few minutes longer until the pasta is thoroughly cooked. Turn it into a warm serving bowl.

Set aside a spoonful of grated cheese, a spoonful of parsley, and a spoonful of toasted bread crumbs to use as a garnish. Add the remaining cheese, parsley, and bread crumbs to the pasta and toss. Serve immediately, topped with the reserved cheese, parsley, and bread crumbs.

Pennette with Brussels Sprouts and Pancetta

Brussels sprouts have graduated from most hated item on the school lunch tray to the glory of the kitchen as smart chefs and adventurous cooks take this old-fashioned vegetable to new heights of flavor. Pulling the individual sprouts apart and separating the leaves gives them a touch of glamour that is accented by the crisp, salty pancetta dice and the resinous flavor of rosemary. Here's how to do it: Simply trim off the base of each sprout and pull off the leaves, then cut the base again and pull off the leaves; keep doing this until there's nothing left but a little nubbin of sprout that you can add to the leaves. The lightly browned and wilted whole leaves have a very pleasing effect, quite different from simply shredding the tight heads of the sprouts.

A wok is great for making this recipe, giving you plenty of room to toss and stir the sprouts with the pancetta.

SERVES 4 TO 6

1½ pounds Brussels sprouts
¼ to ½ cup dry unflavored bread crumbs,
    coarsely ground
3 tablespoons extra-virgin olive oil
¼ to ½ cup grated pecorino toscano or
    pecorino sardo
1 tablespoon unsalted butter
3 ounces pancetta, diced (½ cup)
1 tablespoon chopped fresh rosemary
Pinch red pepper flakes, preferably Aleppo
    pepper, or ground piment d'Espelette
Sea salt and freshly ground black pepper
About 1 pound (500 grams) pennette,
    maccheroncini, or other short stubby pasta

Prepare the Brussels sprouts, teasing the leaves apart, following the directions in the headnote. You should have 7 to 8 cups of sprout leaves in the end.

Combine the bread crumbs with 2 tablespoons of the oil in a small skillet and set over medium-high heat. Cook, stirring and watching carefully, until the crumbs have taken on a bit of color and crunch, then scrape into a small bowl. As soon as the crumbs have lost some of their heat, stir in the grated pecorino. Set aside.

Combine the butter and the remaining 1 tablespoon oil in a saucepan over medium-high heat. Let the butter melt and foam, then add the pancetta dice and cook, stirring, until the pancetta starts to change color and crisp. Add the sprout leaves in handfuls, stirring each handful in carefully and letting it start to wilt before you add another. If necessary, add a couple of tablespoons of boiling water to keep the sprouts from sticking to the pan—but the sprouts should brown and not simmer. Stir in the rosemary and a good pinch of red pepper flakes, along with a pinch of salt. Taste for seasoning, adding more salt if necessary along with several turns of black pepper. Then set aside in its pan.

Bring a large pot of water to a rolling boil. Add salt and the pasta and cook following the directions on page 33.

As soon as the pasta is al dente, drain and turn it into a warm serving bowl along with the warm sprouts and pancetta. Toss to mix well, then dress with the bread crumb–cheese mixture and serve immediately.

Pumpkin and Pumpkin Seed Maccheroncini

Pumpkin pasta with pumpkin seeds: What a great dish to serve for a Halloween supper! But the friendly golden color, like a fat harvest moon in the sky, makes it welcome on any chilly night in fall. Don't make the mistake, however, of using a leftover jack-o'-lantern for this dish. Those seasonal delights are bred especially for size and a one-night stand at October's end. They are not worth the effort to recycle them.

What you need here is an eating pumpkin or a hard winter squash. Some varieties to look for include a wonderful one called rouge vif d'Etampes (don't be misled by its exotic name, it's widely available in farmers' markets), cheese pumpkins (so-called because they look a little like big old-fashioned farmstead cheddar cheeses), dark orange kuri pumpkins, or hard winter squashes such as the ordinary and very accessible butternut, buttercup, acorn, and the big old-fashioned favorite Hubbard. We especially like kabocha, an Asian variety, for its deep, bright orange color that makes a stand-out dish on the autumn table. You'll need about 2½ pounds of peeled and trimmed squash—around 3 pounds of raw uncut squash to make 4 cups of grated squash.

Maccheroni are long hollow noodles, like what is often called macaroni in North America; maccheroncini are the same thing but shorter, about 2½ inches long.

Toast the pumpkin seeds by setting them on a dry baking sheet in a 350°F oven for about 10 minutes, or until they start to brown and turn crisp. Be careful not to let them burn. As soon as they are ready, turn them out onto a board. When cool, chop coarsely with a knife and set aside.

SERVES 4 TO 6

2½ pounds peeled and seeded pumpkin or
  winter squash
4 tablespoons extra-virgin olive oil
4 to 5 large sage leaves
2 garlic cloves, lightly smashed with the flat
  blade of a knife
Sea salt and freshly ground black pepper
½ cup pumpkin seeds, toasted and coarsely
  chopped (see headnote)
About 1 pound (500 grams) maccheroncini
½ cup freshly grated parmigiano-reggiano or
  grana padano, plus more to pass

Bring a large pot of water to a rolling boil.

While the water is heating, grate the squash on the largest holes of a box grater. You should have about 4 cups of grated squash.

Gently heat 3 tablespoons of the oil in a heavy-bottomed skillet large enough to hold the squash. Fry the sage leaves until crisp, about 2 minutes. Remove with a slotted spoon, drain on a paper towel, and reserve.

Add the garlic to the oil, raise the heat slightly, and cook, turning and flattening the cloves with a spatula, until the cloves are brown and have thoroughly impregnated the oil with garlic flavor.

Remove the browned cloves and discard.

Raise the heat to high and add a third to one-half of the shredded squash to the pan. Toss and stir the squash continuously, as if you were stir-frying, for 3 to 4 minutes, seasoning with salt as you toss. The squash bits will soften and give off moisture and some of them will brown and crisp in the hot oil. Don't wait for the squash to brown thoroughly—it should retain texture and not be cooked to a soft mush. Remove the batch of squash and set aside while you continue with the rest of it. When all the squash is done, combine it all in the skillet and stir in the pumpkin seeds. Turn the heat down to very low or set the squash in a very low (200°F) oven.

Add salt and the pasta to the rapidly boiling water and cook following directions on page 33.

Check the squash mixture at this point and if it seems a bit dry (some varieties are dryer than others), add a ladleful or two of the pasta water and mix it in over low heat to render the squash "sauce" creamy.

When the pasta is done, drain and turn it into a warm serving bowl. Mix the squash mixture into the pasta, adding the remaining 1 tablespoon oil and the grated parmigiano. Toss to mix well and crumble the sage leaves over the top, adding a liberal amount of freshly ground black pepper.

Serve immediately, passing more grated cheese at the table.

Pasta with Crumbled Sausage, Sage, and Winter Squash

We often use pennette when we make this dish, but any small shaped pasta will do—try orecchiette, creste di galli (cockscombs), Pastificio Faella's lumachine (small snails), Benedetto Cavalieri's ruote pazze (crazy wheels), or any similar quirky shape. This is a particularly good treatment for whole wheat pasta, with the flavors of sweet squash, spicy sausage, and nutty wheat all marrying nicely together.

For the squash, see our suggestions on page 257. Chop the trimmed squash coarsely and don't worry if the pieces are not equal. Part of the charm of the dish comes from some pieces disintegrating almost into a puree while others stay a little firm to the bite.

We use pure pork sausages with nothing but salt and aromatics added—whether sweet or hot is up to your taste. Consider adding a pinch of ground red chili peppers and some wild fennel pollen, if available, or crushed fennel seeds to emphasize the season.

SERVES 6

10 to 12 sage leaves
3 tablespoons extra-virgin olive oil
½ cup finely chopped red or yellow onion
2 garlic cloves, crushed and chopped
2 Italian-style sausages, sweet, fennel, or
  spicy (about ½ pound)
2 teaspoons fennel pollen or crushed fennel
  seeds (optional)
Pinch ground or flaked red chili pepper
  (optional)
Sea salt and freshly ground black pepper
4½ to 5 cups coarsely chopped firm orange-
  fleshed squash (see headnote)
About 1 pound (500 grams) pasta (see
  headnote)
⅓ cup parmigiano-reggiano, plus more to pass
½ cup chopped flat-leaf parsley

Set aside 4 or 5 of the largest sage leaves to crisp in oil and use for a garnish.

Chop the rest to make 1 or 2 tablespoons chopped sage.

In a large heavy-bottomed saucepan, heat 2 tablespoons of the oil over medium heat, then add the onion and garlic. Remove the sausage meat from its casings and as soon as the vegetables start to sizzle, crumble the ground sausage in. Let the sausage meat cook briefly, tossing and stirring it, until it has rendered out its fat. When it just stops being pink, stir in the chopped sage. If using fennel pollen and/or chili pepper, add them now.

Bring a large pot of abundantly salted water to a rolling boil.

Add the chopped squash to the sausage in the saucepan and turn up the heat to medium-high. Cook briskly until the squash is soft, cooked through, and some pieces are beginning to disintegrate. Keep the sauce just simmering over low heat while the pasta cooks.

Heat the remaining 1 tablespoon oil in a small saucepan over high heat and add the reserved whole sage leaves. Sauté, turning, until the leaves are crisp, then remove to a paper towel to drain.

When the pasta water is boiling vigorously, add the pasta and cook following the directions on page 33. When the pasta is al dente, stir a ladleful of pasta water into the sausage-squash sauce. Drain the pasta and turn it into a warm serving bowl. Add the sauce, along with the grated parmigiano, and toss. Garnish with chopped parsley and finally with the crisp-fried sage leaves. Serve immediately, passing more grated cheese at the table.

Bavette with Fennel and Spicy Bread Crumbs

Bavette are a curious sort of linguine, long, flat, thin noodles that are slightly convex in section. If you can't find bavette, use linguine or thin tagliatelle.

Bavette are a favorite pasta shape in Liguria, where they're often served with basil pesto. Here we've paired them simply with bits of fresh fennel, diced very small, and chopped fennel greens for a dish that's as pretty as it is tasty. The bread crumb topping, which takes the place of grated cheese, is spiced with garlic, parsley, and red chilies and garnished, if you wish, with grated bottarga.

Choose plump, dense fennel bulbs, with fresh green fronds attached. You will need 1½ to 2 pounds.

SERVES 6

1 large or 2 medium (1½ to 2 pounds) fennel
bulbs with long, green fronds attached
1 medium yellow onion, finely minced
1 garlic clove, minced
¼ cup extra-virgin olive oil
Sea salt
1 small dried red chili pepper
¾ cup dry white wine
About 1 pound (500 grams) bavette, linguine,
or other long, skinny pasta
¼ cup spicy fried bread crumbs (see page 13)
¼ cup freshly grated bottarga di muggine
(optional; see page 22)

Separate the green tops of the fennel from the bulbs. Chop the greens coarsely and set aside.

Cut the fennel bulbs into very small dice, not more than ¼ inch to a side. You should have between 3 and 4 cups diced fennel.

Combine the diced fennel, onion, and garlic with the oil in a skillet and set over medium-high heat. Add a pinch of salt and cook, stirring, until the fennel mix is softened and starting to brown along the edges. Toss in the chili, crumbling it as you add it to the pan. Add the chopped greens and wine and simmer until the wine has evaporated and the greens have wilted.

While the fennel is cooking, bring 6 quarts of water to a rolling boil in a large pot. Add salt and the pasta and cook following the directions on page 33.

When the pasta is al dente, drain and turn it into a warm serving bowl. Top with the hot fennel sauce and toss briefly. Garnish with spicy bread crumbs and, if you wish, with grated bottarga and serve immediately.

Bucatini with Creamy Leeks and Bacon

We often think all you need for a great pasta dish is a bit of cured pork—pancetta, guanciale, prosciutto fat, or even smoky bacon. Brown it and add to whatever seasonal vegetable is available, cook till done, and dress with either crunchy fried bread crumbs or grated cheese. Leeks and bacon are a classic combination, and the cream in this dish brings it all together. It is rich, however; and we advocate serving it Italian style, as a primo or first course, followed by a very plain grilled piece of fish or a simple gratin of autumn vegetables.

We recommend bucatini for this, but any long not-too-skinny pasta will do.

SERVES 4 TO 6

6 to 8 small leeks or 4 fat ones

4 slices thick-cut country-style bacon (about 4 ounces)

1 tablespoon unsalted butter

1 tablespoon extra-virgin olive oil

Sea salt and freshly ground black pepper

1 tablespoon chopped thyme

⅔ cup heavy cream

About 1 pound (500 grams) bucatini (see headnote)

1 cup freshly grated parmigiano-reggiano or grana padano

Trim the roots of the leeks, slice each one lengthwise, and cut into ¼-inch pieces on the bias. Swish the leek pieces in a bowl of water for a few minutes, then drain and repeat until they are clean and free of grit.

Slice the bacon into strips about ¼ inch wide and 1 to 2 inches long.

Bring a large pot of water to a rolling boil.

While the water is heating, melt the butter and oil in a heavy-bottomed skillet over medium heat. Add the bacon strips and cook, stirring occasionally, to render the fat and lightly brown the bacon. Add the drained leeks with a small pinch of salt and turn up the heat. Cook briskly until the leeks are wilted and browning on the edges. Stir in the thyme, then add the cream and ⅔ cup water and let reduce until the liquid is thickened and coats the leeks. Set aside but keep warm.

Add salt and the pasta to the boiling water and cook following the directions on page 33.

When it is al dente, drain and add to the pan with the leeks and bacon, turning the pasta and sauce together over very low heat until the pasta is well coated. Remove the pan from the heat and add ½ cup of the grated parmigiano and plenty of pepper, tossing once more. Taste and adjust the seasoning, if necessary. Serve immediately, passing the rest of the cheese at the table.

VARIATION *Although leeks are really fine cooked this way, the recipe can easily be adapted for a number of other vegetables. Try it with fresh mushrooms, or a combination of mushrooms and thinly sliced onions, or mushrooms and broccoli chopped into small florets.*

Pappardelle con Patate al Rosmarino

Pappardelle with Diced Potatoes and Fragrant Rosemary

Weird though this sounds, it's a delicious combination and a brilliant answer to the problem of "I'm hungry but there's nothing in the house to eat." Italians, with a long history of making do, have a repertoire of dishes such as this that are really just ways to jazz up very basic foodstuffs to create good flavors out of what seems like nothing at all. Here, that "nothing" is what we find in the pantry—some pasta, some potatoes, some olive oil, some garlic, a little rosemary from the bush growing outside the kitchen door, and a sprinkling of sheep's-milk pecorino or smoked provolone from a wedge of cheese in the back of the fridge.

And while looking for the cheese, maybe you found some leftover greens steamed for dinner last night—chop them up and add them in when you add the pasta water. Or a single small dark-green zucchini hiding in the vegetable drawer—dice it and add with the parsley and rosemary. Or just keep the simple purity of potatoes and rosemary. But treat these humble ingredients well and what you get is a very tasty dish.

We like to use Yukon gold potatoes with their creamy yellow flesh, but honestly just about any kind of potato will work well. For chilies, in this dish we used tiny dried Calabrian peperoncini (little red peppers). Dried New Mexico, de árbol, or Anaheim chilies would give the same sense of warmth and flavor without overwhelming heat.

SERVES 4 TO 6

1 tablespoon unsalted butter

2 tablespoons extra-virgin olive oil

2 small onions, diced

Sea salt and freshly cracked black pepper

1 garlic clove, minced

Leaves from 2 fresh rosemary sprigs, minced (2 tablespoons)

2 dried red chili peppers, (see headnote), crushed

3 cups diced Yukon gold or other yellow-fleshed potatoes (about 1½ pounds potatoes)

About ¾ pound (three-quarters of a 500-gram package) pappardelle or other long, flat noodles

About ¼ cup coarsely chopped flat-leaf parsley

½ cup freshly grated aged pecorino, preferably toscano or siciliano (as an alternative, smoked provola affumicata)

1 cup chopped cooked greens, or ¾ cup diced zucchini (optional)

Bring a large pot of water to a rolling boil.

While the water is heating, gently melt the butter with the oil in a cast-iron or heavy-bottomed pot. Add the onions and a pinch of salt and cook, stirring, until the onions are golden and just beginning to crisp and brown, about 6 minutes. Add the minced garlic and rosemary, along with the crushed chili peppers, and let cook another minute. Stir in the diced potatoes with another pinch of salt. Add ¼ cup water, reduce the heat, and stir steadily until the water is absorbed and almost gone. Keep stirring and adding water, ¼ cup at a time, until the potatoes are cooked through—this will take more or less 2 cups water. (At the end of this time, if you wish, add already-cooked chopped greens or diced zucchini and let cook just long enough to warm them through.)

When the water is boiling, add salt and the pasta and cook following the directions on page 33, starting to test the pasta 2 or 3 minutes before the package directions indicate it should be done. When it is al dente, drain immediately, turn into a warm serving bowl, and toss with the warm potatoes, adding the parsley, grated pecorino, and plenty of cracked pepper. Serve immediately.

Chestnut Agnolotti with Brown Butter, Sage, and Fennel

Agnolotti are ravioli as made in the Piemonte region of northwest Italy: small rectangles of dough folded over a meat or vegetable filling. Sara made chestnut agnolotti in Tuscany one year for Thanksgiving and they have become a staple for her winter menus ever since. They are rich and filling so they really work best in the Italian fashion, as a small primo before the main course.

Harvested in late October and early November and kept through the winter, chestnuts have been an important part of the Tuscan diet since Etruscan times. *L'albero del pane,* "the bread tree," is what they called the chestnut tree, and it's no wonder—poor people in the mountains often relied on chestnuts to get them through until spring. On cold winter nights chestnuts were roasted over the embers in the big fireplace that dominated the farmhouse. Hot from the fire, they were dropped into a pot of red wine to further loosen the tough outer peel, then cracked and consumed right out of the shell, with a glass of that wine to wash it all down.

You will need about a pound of steamed chestnuts for this recipe; if you wish to prepare them yourself, score a cross on the rounded side of each chestnut with a sharp knife, drop them into a pan of boiling water, and let them boil for 8 minutes. Turn off the heat and extract a few chestnuts at a time so the rest don't cool down. Pull off the outer shell and then the inner membrane that encases each nut. If the nuts become too difficult to work, return them to the boil once more. When all the chestnuts are done, put them through a food mill and continue with the recipe.

It's also possible to buy small bags (7.4 ounces in our experience) of already steamed and peeled whole chestnuts, and that's what we use.

SERVES 6

1 recipe Basic Pasta Fresca Dough (page 43), made from 3 cups unbleached all-purpose flour and 3 eggs

FOR THE FILLING

About 1 pound whole prepared chestnuts (two 7.4-ounce packages, vacuum packed or frozen)

1 tablespoon fennel pollen or crushed fennel seeds

Sea salt

1 pint (2 cups) heavy cream, plus water if needed

All-purpose flour, for dusting

1 large egg (to help seal the dough)

Semolina or fine cornmeal, for the tray

½ pound (2 sticks) unsalted butter

About ¼ cup fresh sage leaves

¼ cup coarsely grated parmigiano-reggiano, plus more to pass

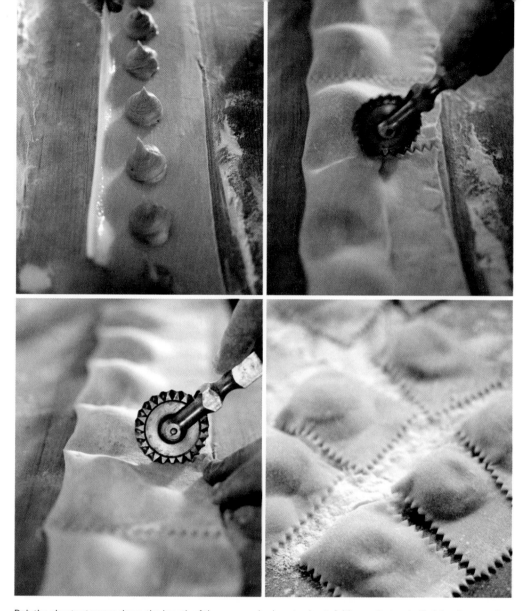

Dab the chestnut puree down the length of the egg-washed pasta sheet, fold over the top half of the sheet, and press down between the chestnut dabs with the side of your hand to seal the edges. Then cut between the ravioli, using a rotary pasta cutter. Set the finished ravioli on a tray with a layer of semolina or fine cornmeal to keep them from sticking.

Have ready the pasta dough, but do not roll it out until the filling has been prepared.

Prepare the filling: Transfer the whole chestnuts to a saucepan and add the fennel pollen, salt, and about three-quarters of the cream. Set over medium-low heat and bring to just below simmering. Turn off the heat and let the cream and chestnuts steep for 15 to 20 minutes.

At the end of this time, transfer the chestnuts and their cream to the bowl of a food processor and process to a thick cream. You're aiming for a mixture soft enough to pipe through a pastry bag but not so wet that it could leak through the dough envelopes. Add some of the remaining cream, a tablespoon at a time, until you have the right consistency. If you use up all the cream and still have a stiff mixture (it's hard to judge with chestnuts, which vary in consistency), add water, again a tablespoon at a time. But no more cream because the mixture is already quite rich. Taste and adjust the seasoning, adding more salt or fennel pollen, if necessary.

Working with half the pasta dough and keeping the other half covered with a cloth or an upside-down bowl, roll the dough through the pasta roller until you have a sheet that is 4 inches wide and about $\frac{1}{16}$ inch thick. Lay the sheet on a lightly floured board with the long side facing you. Combine the egg with about a couple tablespoons of water to make an egg wash, then use this to paint along the bottom of the pasta sheet.

Put the chestnut filling into a piping bag and pipe dabs of filling, about 1 tablespoon each and ½ inch apart, in a regular line down the length of the sheet. Don't put the dabs in the center of the sheet—rather, keep them toward the bottom so that you can fold the top half of the sheet over them. You should be able to get at least 18 dabs on the first sheet of pasta. Break the egg into a small bowl and beat in about ¼ cup water, then brush the mixture along the edges

and in between each of the dabs of filling. Fold the top half over all the way along and press down with the side of your hand all along the edges and in between each of the filling dabs to make a series of 18 little pillows, approximately 1½ by 2 inches, each one filled with chestnut puree. Use a rotary pasta cutter to cut between the pillows, making sure that each one is sealed well on all sides. Sprinkle a tray with a layer of semolina or fine cornmeal; pick up the pasta pillows and gently lay them on the tray without touching. If you're not going to cook them right away, cover them with a dry kitchen towel.

When all the pasta and filling has been used up, bring a large pot of water to a rolling boil and add a big spoonful of salt.

While the water is heating, melt the butter in a small skillet, and when it foams, add the sage. Let it cook gently as the butter browns and the sage leaves crisp, then keep warm until ready to serve.

Drop the agnolotti into the boiling water and cook for 3 to 4 minutes each. As they cook they will rise to the top. Let them cook another minute after rising, then remove them with a slotted spoon and pile them directly on individual warm serving plates, 6 agnolotti to a serving. When all the agnolotti are done, spoon sage butter over the top and scatter some of the grated parmigiano, passing more cheese at the table. Serve immediately.

Sweet Potato Gnocchi with Brown Butter and Sage

An alluring switch on the usual recipe for potato gnocchi (see page 290), this marries the jammy sweetness of the potatoes (sometimes called yams) with the spicy fragrance of fresh sage. Using durum flour, available from King Arthur Flour, lends strength to the mixture, and dropping the gnocchi into an ice-water bath after poaching also helps them retain their shape. For best results, these should be prepared just before you're ready to serve them. The potatoes *must* be worked with the flour while they're still quite hot.

SERVES 6

3 or 4 large sweet potatoes (3½ pounds)
1 to 1½ cups durum flour, plus a little more
 for the board
Sea salt and freshly cracked black pepper
8 tablespoons (1 stick or ½ cup) unsalted butter
½ cup extra-virgin olive oil
8 to 10 whole sage leaves
½ cup freshly grated parmigiano-reggiano

Set the oven on 425°F.

Prick the sweet potatoes all over with a fork. Place in the hot oven and bake until they are falling-apart tender, about 50 minutes. While the potatoes are still very hot, remove the peels and discard them. Mash the hot potatoes or put them through a food mill into a bowl. You should have about 4 cups pureed sweet potato. Stir in the flour and mix well, beating with a wooden spoon. Break off a small walnut-size piece of dough and roll it into a ball. It should hold together well, with a firm but malleable texture. If the dough seems too loose, add a little more flour, but be careful not to add too much, since it will make the gnocchi heavy.

Dust a clean work surface or a pasta board with a bit more flour and spread the potato mixture out. Knead it, adding a little more flour, if necessary, just until the dough comes together, then cover the mound of dough with a clean kitchen towel and leave it to rest for about 10 minutes.

Bring about 4 quarts of salted water to a rolling boil. On a counter next to the stove, fill a large bowl with ice cubes and water to be ready to receive the gnocchi once they are cooked.

While the water is heating, dust the work surface once more with a little flour. Break off a fistful of dough, leaving the rest under the towel. Using the palms of your hands, roll the dough into a rope, about 1 inch in diameter. Cut the rope into gnocchi, each piece about ⅓ inch long.

Holding your hand flat with the fingers together, briskly roll each gnocco on the board, back and forth under your fingers, to form a little dowel-shaped piece, then roll through a little flour to dust lightly. Transfer to a lightly floured baking sheet. Repeat with the remaining dough, until all the gnocchi are rolled.

Heat 4 tablespoons of the butter and

¼ cup of the oil in a small skillet, and as the butter begins to foam, add the sage leaves. Fry until the butter is nut-brown and the sage leaves are crisp. Set aside but keep warm.

Adjust the heat under the water so that the water boils gently but not fiercely. Gently drop the gnocchi, a few at a time, into the bubbling water. They will float to the surface when they are done. As they finish cooking, use a slotted spoon to skim them off and transfer to the ice-water bath, just dipping and then removing them before transferring them to a deep plate.

Have ready a warm serving bowl.

When all the gnocchi are poached, combine the remaining 4 tablespoons butter and ¼ cup oil in a large skillet and add the gnocchi, in batches. Toast them briefly, just long enough to heat them up once more. Add the first batch to the warm bowl.

Spoon a little of the sage and brown butter over the top, then a little of the grated parmigiano, and then continue, layer by layer, until all the gnocchi are cooked. Spoon the last sage and brown butter mixture over the top and dust with the remaining cheese. Add plenty of cracked pepper and serve immediately.

Fedelini al Vino Rosso Piccante

Skinny Pasta Cooked in Red Wine with Lemon and Chili Pepper

This became an instant hit in New York when Sara introduced it on the menu at 50 Carmine, a restaurant in the West Village where she was executive chef. In principle, the technique is more like risotto than pasta, cooking by shaking the pasta constantly and adding the wine little by little. The flavors are loud—big, strong, and complex. For people who avoid alcohol, be assured that all the alcohol burns off completely, leaving behind the rich flavors of the wine. We recommend a California cabernet sauvignon, full bodied and full flavored, for this.

Note that the quantity of wine is approximate—it gets added bit by bit and can be more or less depending on many variables, including the weather and relative humidity.

Fedelini are long, very thin noodles; capelli d'angelo (angel hair) could be substituted instead.

SERVES 4 TO 6

2 tablespoons extra-virgin olive oil

2 plump garlic cloves, lightly smashed with the flat blade of a knife

1 small dried red chili pepper

3 to 4 cups California full-bodied cabernet sauvignon

About 1 pound (500 grams) fedelini or capelli d'angelo

1 tablespoon unsalted butter

Sea salt and freshly ground black pepper

Freshly grated zest of ½ lemon, preferably organic

2 tablespoons finely minced flat-leaf parsley

In a large sauté pan wide enough to hold the pasta without breaking it, combine the oil and garlic and set over medium-low heat. Cook gently, turning the garlic, until it is starting to brown a little, then add the chili pepper—as much or as little as you wish. (If you want the flavor of the chili but not much heat, open the pod up and shake out the seeds before adding; that will reduce the overall heat by quite a bit.)

As soon as the chili starts to sizzle, add 1 cup of the wine, raise the heat to medium, and bring the wine to a boil.

Once the wine begins to boil, add all the pasta and shake the pan gently over medium heat until the pasta starts to soften. When the fedelini are soft enough to move, start stirring them and continue stirring until the wine has been almost completely absorbed. Add more wine, ½ cup at a time, letting each addition be absorbed before adding another. When the pasta is al dente, add the butter along with salt and pepper to taste, and shake or stir until the butter and seasoning have been fully absorbed.

Transfer the pasta to a warm serving bowl, or to individual pasta bowls, garnishing with the lemon zest and parsley. Serve immediately.

Elicoidali al Sole Siciliano

Pasta with a Sunny Sicilian Sauce

Elicoidali are similar to rigatoni, short tubes of pasta but possibly a bit narrower than classic rigatoni, with the striations along the sides curving like a corkscrew instead of straight up and down. Got it? Now try explaining why elicoidali are optimal for a Sicilian sauce of olives, capers, pine nuts, and raisins? Because that's the way Sicilians serve it, capturing all the warmth of sunshine—just what's needed on a chilly autumn day.

If you can't find elicoidali? Why, use rigatoni or any other short, stubby pasta shape instead!

SERVES 4 TO 6

¼ cup extra-virgin olive oil
¼ cup pine nuts
2 garlic cloves, minced
6 anchovy fillets, chopped
¼ cup plus 2 tablespoons finely minced flat-leaf parsley
12 large green olives, preferably Castelvetrano, pitted and chopped
¼ cup salted capers, preferably from Pantelleria, rinsed and chopped
⅓ cup golden sultana raisins, plumped in hot water and drained
½ cup finely slivered sun-dried tomatoes
Sea salt and freshly ground black pepper
About 1 pound (500 grams) elicoidali or rigatoni
2 to 3 tablespoons coarsely grated parmigiano-reggiano or aged pecorino

Bring about 6 quarts of water to a rolling boil in a large pot.

While the water is heating, make the sauce: Add the oil to a skillet large enough to hold the cooked pasta and set over medium-low heat. Add the pine nuts and cook just until they start to turn golden, being careful not to let them burn. Remove with a slotted spoon and set aside.

Add the garlic to the skillet and cook gently, stirring, until it is softened, but do not let it brown. Add the anchovies and cook briefly, crushing them into the oil with a fork. Add ¼ cup of the parsley and cook just long enough to soften, then stir in the olives, capers, and raisins. Stir all together well, then add the sun-dried tomatoes. Let the sauce sizzle while you cook the pasta.

Add salt and the pasta to the boiling water and cook following the directions on page 33. Remove the pasta before it is al dente. Drain and add it to the simmering sauce with a couple ladlesful of pasta water. Let the pasta finish cooking in the sauce. When done, turn it into a warm serving bowl and garnish with the reserved pine nuts, the remaining parsley, and the parmigiano. Add plenty of pepper on top and serve immediately.

America's Favorite Pasta (Macaroni and Cheese)

As iconically American as apple pie, macaroni and cheese has a long history on the American table. The first recipe we've found was written by Mary Randolph, a cousin of Thomas Jefferson's, back in 1824, and the recipe has changed very little since then. But, as with most traditional dishes, almost every household in America has its own way with mac and cheese. This one is ours, and if it differs from yours or your grandmother's, just keep doing what you're doing—we're certain your version will be fine. And if you've never made mac and cheese, if you've always relied on that stale-tasting, bland, highly processed stuff in a box, take the time now to make this—and enjoy!

Our recipe looks long at first glance, but it's not at all difficult and it will make a mac and cheese as suitable for a sophisticated dinner party as it is for a tailgate picnic. One key is a flavorful béchamel that lends such depth of flavor to the overall dish; once that's done, it's just a matter of assembling ingredients. And once baked, the pasta can be kept warm for several hours with no deterioration in flavor—though the aroma is so delicious we guarantee you'll have hungry diners clustering around the dish as soon as it comes out of the oven.

Elbow macaroni is traditional, but the high-quality pasta makers don't seem to produce this shape, so we use instead penne rigate, rigatoni, fusilli, farfalle, or any other short, stubby pasta shape. We also like a mixture of cheeses (it's a good way to use up those ends of cheese tucked away in the refrigerator drawer) and always include a bit of smoked cheese for the flavor. Don't feel you have to stick to traditional cheddar either—firm French and Italian cheeses can add surprising flavors. Think of various pecorino and caciocavallo cheeses, as well as reblochon, emmenthal, or a lightly smoked Spanish Idiazabal. Mozzarella goes on top to melt down in the oven heat. The best is imported Italian mozzarella, if you can find it. And always grated parmigiano-reggiano or another similar premium aged cheese for the final touch.

SERVES 4 TO 6

4 cups béchamel (page 11), prepared to the heavy cream stage

1 tablespoon Dijon mustard

4 cups mixed grated cheeses (see headnote)

Sea salt and freshly ground black pepper

2 tablespoons unsalted butter

1 tablespoon extra-virgin olive oil

Stale bread, crusts removed, cubed, to make 2½ cups

About 1 pound (500 grams) short, curly pasta (see headnote)

¼ pound fresh mozzarella, cubed

¼ cup freshly grated parmigiano-reggiano, grana padano, or other hard aged cheese

4 tablespoons minced flat-leaf parsley

When the béchamel sauce has reached the heavy cream stage, remove the pan from the heat and stir in the mustard and then the 4 cups grated cheeses. Taste and add a little salt and lots of pepper. Return the mixture to the heat, stirring just until the cheeses are melted. Set aside.

Bring a large pot of water to a rolling boil.

Set the oven on 350°F. Using 1 tablespoon of the butter, grease the bottom and sides of a 3-quart oven dish.

Melt the remaining 1 tablespoon butter and mix with the oil. In a bowl, toss the bread cubes with the mixture and set aside.

When the water is boiling, add the pasta (do not add salt because the cheese may be quite salty) and cook following the directions on page 33. Remove the pasta just short of al dente. Drain and immediately add to the béchamel cheese sauce. Taste the pasta again with the sauce and add more salt if it needs it.

Layer about half the pasta in the bottom of the greased oven dish. Sprinkle with half the mozzarella cubes and add the remaining pasta. Top with the buttery bread cubes and the remaining mozzarella cubes. Finish with the grated parmigiano, covering as much of the surface as you can manage.

Bake for 30 minutes, or until the top is golden and the sauce is bubbling around the edges. Sprinkle with the parsley before serving.

Tagliatelle with Gorgonzola Cream and Fresh Walnuts

This is one of a handful of recipes that we recommend serving with handmade pasta, rich with eggs (see page 43). The recipe itself is so simple that it deserves the very slight extra effort involved in making pasta by hand, but in a pinch you could use dried tagliatelle, linguine, or bavette instead. The sauce is lush with cheese and cream so it should be served in small amounts as a primo. A good choice for a main course could be a simple braised or roasted chicken, or a pan-grilled fillet of halibut or other white-flesh fish.

SERVES 4 TO 6

1 pound fresh handmade egg tagliatelle (see page 43)
1 cup walnut halves
1¼ cups heavy cream
¾ pound gorgonzola
½ cup grated parmigiano-reggiano or grana padano
Sea salt, if necessary, and freshly ground black pepper

If you're using fresh tagliatelle, which we highly recommend, have the pasta rolled out, sliced into tagliatelle, and ready to cook before you prepare the sauce.

Set the oven on 350°F.

Spread the walnuts on a sheet pan and roast in the oven for about 10 minutes, or until they are crisp and give off a delicious aroma. Remove and set aside to cool, then chop coarsely.

Bring about 6 quarts of water to a rolling boil in a large pot.

In a small saucepan over gentle heat, warm the cream and add the gorgonzola and parmigiano. Stir the cheese into the cream to melt into a sauce thick enough to coat the back of a spoon. Taste for seasoning (the cheese may add sufficient salt) and keep the sauce warm while the pasta is cooking.

Add salt and the pasta to the boiling water and cook following the directions on page 33. Freshly made tagliatelle will cook in just 2 or 3 minutes, boxed pasta secca will take 8 to 10 minutes. Drain the pasta and immediately turn it into a warm serving bowl, adding the sauce and about half the chopped walnuts. Mix together, top with the rest of the walnuts and plenty of pepper, and serve immediately.

Orecchiette con Polpettine e Ricotta Salata
Little Ears with Tiny Meatballs and Shaved Ricotta Salata

Orecchiette are little disks of pasta, each one no bigger than a thumbprint, that are the pride of a Pugliese cook. Handmade from local durum wheat flour, they are a miracle, but you can also buy them as pasta secca from first-rate pasta producers such as Benedetto Cavalieri or Rustichella d'Abruzzo.

Ricotta salata is a firm, somewhat aged ricotta, a southern cheese we think should be better known (see page 23). Pure white, it grates and shaves nicely and adds depth to anything on which it's served. If you can't find ricotta salata, use a young pecorino instead.

SERVES 4 TO 6

FOR THE MEATBALLS
1 garlic clove
1 teaspoon Sicilian or Greek oregano
2 tablespoons chopped flat-leaf parsley
Freshly grated zest of ½ lemon, preferably organic
Sea salt
½ teaspoon fennel pollen or crushed fennel seeds (optional)
6 ounces (170 grams) lean ground veal or young beef
6 ounces (170 grams) lean ground pork
1 large egg
¼ cup fine dry unflavored bread crumbs
¼ cup freshly grated parmigiano-reggiano
¼ cup extra-virgin olive oil

2 tablespoons extra-virgin olive oil
1 medium onion, finely minced
One 28-ounce can whole tomatoes, preferably San Marzano
Sea salt and freshly ground black pepper

About 1 pound (500 grams) orecchiette
¼ cup finely minced flat-leaf parsley
⅓ to ½ cup coarsely grated aged ricotta salata

Prepare the meatballs: Combine the garlic, oregano, parsley, and lemon zest with ½ teaspoon salt and mince together on a board to make a fine mixture, almost a paste. Add the fennel pollen, if you wish. Combine the ground veal and ground pork and thoroughly knead the herb paste into it, using your hands. Beat the egg lightly with a fork and add to the mixture, then knead in the bread crumbs and grated parmigiano. Shape into a large, round ball and refrigerate, covered with plastic wrap or aluminum foil, for at least 30 minutes. (You may also do this a day or more ahead.)

When you're ready to cook, shape the ground meat into tiny meatballs, about the size of your thumbnail. When all the balls are made, add the oil to a heavy-bottomed saucepan. Set over medium heat, and

when the oil is hot, quickly brown the meatballs in batches, not crowding them in the pan. As the meatballs finish browning, set them aside.

When all the meatballs are done, discard the oil in the pan and wipe out the pan with paper towels. (Don't worry about getting all the browned bits on the bottom. They will dissolve into the sauce.) Return to low heat and add the 2 tablespoons oil, the onion, and a pinch of salt. Cook the onion very slowly, stirring, until it is thoroughly softened and just browning a little. Add the tomatoes, with their juice, crushing the tomatoes in your hands as you add them. Raise the heat to medium and cook the tomatoes briskly, further crushing them with a fork or the side of a spoon. Cook until the sauce is thick.

Meanwhile, bring a large pot of water to a rolling boil. Add salt and the pasta and cook following the directions on page 33. At the same time, add the meatballs and the parsley to the simmering tomato sauce. Taste the sauce and add more salt, if necessary, and plenty of pepper.

When the pasta is done, drain and toss in the saucepan with the hot meatball sauce. Transfer to a warm serving bowl and garnish with the grated ricotta salata. Serve immediately, passing more grated ricotta salata, if you wish.

Paccheri with Black Olives, Escarole, and Salt Cod

An Italian pantry basic that has been in use probably since the Catholic Church invented meatless fasting days, salt cod, like most fasting foods, has a decidedly unglamorous reputation. Despite that, baccalà—to give salt cod its Italian name—has become chic in recent years and some of the finest chefs are discovering what great potential it has.

The salt cod that comes in cute little wooden boxes from Nova Scotia is not the best choice for this as the pieces are small and very dry, often with a tendency to be somewhat rancid. The best salt cod, in our opinion, comes from Iceland, where it is cured by a process called wet salting. (Fish markets in Portuguese, Italian, or Spanish neighborhoods are good places to find this.) It's not as dry and hard as traditional salt cod but still requires soaking for twenty-four to forty-eight hours, with frequent changes of water. Buy thick pieces of codfish fillet, rinse off the external salt, then soak the pieces in cool water to cover, changing every four or five hours, until they have just a touch of residual salt.

Once the fish has been soaked out, it's ready to be poached and then turned into a variety of dishes, from Provençal brandade de morue, to Neapolitan baccalà fritta with tomato sauce, to this terrific recipe that Sara developed at Porsena. Inspired by a southern Italian dish, she pairs the cod with wintertime escarole for a touch of green, and black olives for flavor sharpness. The poaching should be just enough to retain the firm texture of the fish, which stands up well to the treatment. Do use the poaching liquid as part of the water for cooking the pasta—all those flavors will add to the interest of the dish.

SERVES 6

1 pound salt cod, soaked for 24 to 48 hours
   (see headnote)

FOR THE POACHING LIQUID

1 celery stalk, including green leaves, cut into
   2-inch pieces
1 bay leaf
1 tablespoon whole black peppercorns
1 head garlic, cut in half
1 small onion, skin on, cut into quarters
1 leek
One 5-inch piece of orange zest

1 teaspoon fennel pollen or crushed fennel
   seeds

1 medium yellow onion, sliced thin
¼ cup extra-virgin olive oil
2 garlic cloves, crushed and chopped
½ cup pitted black olives, preferably Gaeta or
   Kalamata
1 large head escarole, cleaned and cut into
   3-inch-wide ribbons (6 cups)
1 tablespoon unsalted butter
1 tablespoon freshly grated lemon zest,
   preferably organic
1 teaspoon freshly squeezed lemon juice

Sea salt and freshly ground black pepper
About 1 pound (500 grams) paccheri or
*   rigatoni or similar*
¼ cup seasoned fresh bread crumbs (page 13)

Put the refreshed salt cod in the saucepan in which you will poach it and add water to just cover the fish. Remove the fish and add all the aromatics to the water in the pan: celery, bay leaf, peppercorns, garlic, onion, leek, orange zest, and fennel pollen. Cover, bring to a simmer, and cook for about 5 minutes to fix the flavors. Lower the heat to very low and add the fish, making sure the pieces are covered with liquid. Simmer very gently, covered, for 15 minutes, then remove from the heat. Using a slotted spoon or spatula, remove the fish from its poaching liquid and set aside. Strain the poaching liquid, discard the solids, and retain the liquid.

Break up the fish, using your fingers so you will be able to find and discard any bones. If you're not going to use the fish immediately, spoon a little of the poaching liquid over the top, cover with plastic wrap, and refrigerate. Also refrigerate the poaching liquid.

When you're ready to proceed with the recipe, warm up the poaching liquid.

Take a large deep skillet that will hold all the fish and the escarole greens and set it over medium-low heat. Add the sliced onion and oil, stir to blend, then cook for 15 minutes or so, until the onion slices are starting to brown. Stir in the garlic and black olives. Add about ½ cup of the warm poaching liquid and cook, simmering, until the liquid has reduced somewhat. Add the fish and escarole and cook down until the escarole is thoroughly wilted and the sauce is amalgamated. Stir in the butter, lemon zest, and lemon juice. (If the fish seems a little dry, by all means add more of the hot poaching liquid, ½ cup at a time, letting it cook down.)

Add the remaining poaching liquid to a large pot with enough water to bring it up to about 6 quarts. Bring to a rolling boil and add a small spoonful of salt–not too much as there may be plenty of salt in the fish. Add the pasta and cook following the directions on page 33.

When the pasta is al dente, drain and turn it immediately into a warm serving bowl. Add the fish and escarole sauce and toss to mix thoroughly. Sprinkle the top with spiced bread crumbs and serve immediately.

Tajarin ai Tartufi Bianchi

RICH EGG TAJARIN (TAGLIOLINI) WITH SHAVED WHITE TRUFFLES

Sara speaking: Years ago, when I was still a photographer and before I became a chef, I was sent to photograph the food at La Contea di Neive, a classic restaurant in the Langhe, one of the prominent wine-growing districts of Piemonte in northwestern Italy. It was October, already dark and foggy. Claudia, the chef/proprietor, met me at the little local train station. As I got into the car, the smell of the white truffles she had just picked up enveloped me. Seeing my nose twitch, she immediately suggested that I have some pasta and truffles when I got to the restaurant. I protested faintly that I would be fine eating something simpler. "What could be more simple than pasta and truffles?" She laughed, and I protested no more.

Whenever I am lucky enough to have a white truffle, this traditional Piemontese way to serve them is still my favorite. The pasta dough is interesting and rich; using no water and only the liquid of the egg yolk with soft white 00 flour results in a springy, not very sticky dough that works well for the finest cutter on the pasta roller. The fresh tajarin (*tagliolini* in Italian) cook in seconds. Dressed with abundant melted butter, they come to the table and the white truffle is shaved tableside over the pasta in front of you. The aroma of white truffle, rising from the warm pasta in its buttery sauce, is, as Italians say, *indimenticabile*. You should eat it immediately. And in seconds.

If you can get Italian 00 flour (called doppio zero, or double zero), it is ideal for this pasta. King Arthur Flour makes an Italian-style flour that is very similar, and Antimo Caputo's 00 flour is available on www.amazon.com. Otherwise, regular unbleached all-purpose flour may be substituted—but if you're going to all the trouble of getting a tartufo bianco, you might as well go an extra mile for the best flour too.

Once you've acquired a white truffle, usually at considerable expense, take good care of it. Wrap it loosely in paper towels and tuck it in a plastic or glass refrigerator container until you're ready to use it—which should be as soon as possible. Do not clean the truffle until you're ready to use it. The best cleaning should be as gentle as possible, using the kind of soft brush you use for cleaning mushrooms. (Note: Don't buy any truffles that are impacted with mud—you will be paying for the weight of the dirt, rather than the truffle itself.) Never rinse the truffle under running water. If necessary, dampen a bit of paper towel or a dishcloth and use that to get away stubborn bits of dirt. The point of a paring knife can also be used.

Note that this recipe makes 4 generous servings.

1¾ cups flour (see headnote), plus a little more for the board
Sea salt
14 to 16 egg yolks (a little more than 1 cup)
½ pound (2 sticks) unsalted butter (best quality you can buy)
1 fresh white truffle (50 to 60 grams; about 2 ounces)

This is one case where the pasta dough is easier to make, with better results, in the food processor than by hand. Place the flour and a pinch of salt in the bowl of the processor. Turn the machine on and, with the blade running, slowly pour in the egg yolks. Let the machine continue running until everything is well amalgamated.

Remove the dough from the food processor. Transfer to a very lightly floured board (just a shadow of flour to keep the pasta dough from sticking). Knead the pasta dough for a few minutes until you can feel it come together in a nice, supple ball, then wrap it tightly in plastic wrap and set aside to rest for at least 15 minutes. (You may also leave the wrapped dough resting for up to 3 hours, or even overnight refrigerated; if you refrigerate the dough, let it come back to room temperature before you continue.)

Break the dough into 7 or 8 even pieces. Working with one piece at a time and keeping the others covered with a cloth, roll the pasta out on a pasta machine, diminishing the openings until you reach number 5 on the small Atlas home pasta roller. Put the sheet through the tagliolini cutter. Dust with a little flour and curl the tagliolini into nests. Set each nest aside to dry for at least 30 minutes, but no more than 3 hours.

When you're ready to cook the pasta, bring a large pot of abundantly salted water to a rolling boil.

Melt the butter in a small saucepan and keep warm while you cook the pasta.

Add the pasta to the boiling water and give a gentle stir with a long-handled spoon. (Fresh egg pasta like this is a bit more fragile than pasta secca from a box.) The noodles are cooked when they float to the top—in 2 or 3 minutes.

Add half the butter to a warm serving bowl and roll it around to coat the sides. Scoop the noodles out with a sieve as they float to the top and transfer to the bowl. Add the remaining melted butter and toss; using a truffle cutter or a Japanese mandoline set to the thinnest setting, shave the white truffle over the top in very fine, scattered slices. Serve and eat immediately.

Ragù alla Coda di Bue con Gnocchi di Patate
Mita's Oxtail Ragù to Serve with Potato Gnocchi

There's a familiar saying that's good to keep in mind when thinking about ragù: The meat is always sweetest at the bone. As proof of that, we offer this traditional oxtail ragù. You can't get bonier than oxtail, and you can't get a sweeter, meatier flavor than marinating those bony cuts in red wine, then braising them at a low temperature for hours with tomatoes and aromatics. It's a long, slow process but makes a deliciously unctuous sauce.

To make the tomato puree called for, simply use an immersion blender to puree canned San Marzano tomatoes with their juice. A 14-ounce can will make more than you need for this recipe, but the remainder will keep well in the refrigerator or freezer, to be used any time you need a little plain tomato sauce.

Mita Antolini, our Tuscan neighbor, often made potato gnocchi for Sunday lunch, but if you don't have time for these plump dumplings (see page 290), serve the oxtail ragù with tagliatelle, spaghetti, or spaghettoni (big spaghetti) instead.

SERVES 6

FOR THE OXTAIL MARINADE
4½ pounds oxtail, cut into 1-inch lengths
2 celery stalks, cut into 2-inch lengths
2 carrots, roughly chopped
½ large yellow onion, roughly chopped
1 fresh rosemary sprig, 3 to 4 inches long
2 garlic cloves, crushed with the flat blade of a knife
1 tablespoon whole black peppercorns
3 cups robust red wine, preferably Chianti

FOR THE RAGÙ
Sea salt and freshly ground black pepper
¼ cup extra-virgin olive oil
2 carrots, roughly chopped
2 celery stalks, roughly chopped
½ large onion, roughly chopped
1 cup tomato puree (see headnote)

1 rosemary sprig, 3 to 4 inches long
1 bay leaf
¼ cup finely chopped flat-leaf parsley

Prepare the oxtail marinade: Rinse and dry the oxtail pieces and add to a bowl with the celery, carrots, onion, rosemary, and garlic. Coarsely crack the peppercorns in a mortar and add to the bowl. Toss the oxtail pieces with the aromatics, using your hands and slightly bruising the aromatics to release their flavors. Add the wine and stir to mix well. Cover the bowl and set aside to marinate overnight or up to 2 days, refrigerated.

When ready to make the ragù, remove the oxtail pieces and dry them on paper towels. Toss them with salt and pepper. Strain out and discard the aromatics but keep the wine.

Set the oven on 300°F.

Add the oil and oxtail pieces to a heavy saucepan or Dutch oven and set over medium-high heat. Brown the oxtail pieces well on all sides, transferring the pieces to a deep plate as they brown. (You may have to do this in batches.)

Lower the heat to medium-low and add the carrots, celery, and onion to the pan with a good pinch of salt. Cook, stirring, until the vegetables are wilting and just starting to brown. Using a slotted spoon, transfer the vegetables to the plate with the oxtail.

Remove all but about 1 tablespoon of the oil in the pan. Add the strained liquid from the marinade and deglaze the pan, scraping up any browned bits that cling to the bottom. Stir in the tomato puree and when it comes to a simmer, add the rosemary and bay leaf. Return the oxtail pieces and the vegetables to the pan. If necessary, add a bit of water to make enough liquid to just cover the meat. Bring to a slow simmer, cover the pan, and transfer to the oven. Bake for 2½ to 3½ hours, or until the meat is very tender.

Remove from the oven, and when the meat is cool enough to handle, pick the meat away from the bones. Discard the bones and shred the meat back into the sauce. Serve the sauce over gnocchi (recipe follows) or pasta, and garnish with the parsley.

Mita's Potato Gnocchi

Sara here: "Mita's gnocchi was the seminal dish of my Tuscan childhood. My brother and I both fell in love with the regular Sunday dish at our neighbor's house—her homemade eggless potato gnocchi with a meat ragù, often flavored with a few chicken livers from the freshly killed birds that were roasted in the wood-fired oven and consumed later in the meal. That bowl of gnocchi consisted of what seemed like endless layers of gnocchi, grated cheese, and ragù—but not too much ragù. It just coated the gnocchi, adding enough flavor to enhance the potatoes.

"After the first Sunday meal at Mita's table, when we unknowingly filled up on gnocchi only to be presented with three more abundant courses of food, we learned to stop at one serving of gnocchi if we had any hope of enjoying the rest of the meal. It's the dish I still eat when I visit and dine with Arnaldo, Mita's son, and his wife, Maura, who makes a spectacular gnocchi herself. My brother, Nico, was so in love with Mita's gnocchi that Mita began making them for him the minute he showed up in our village. But I still think I got the better part of the deal because she actually taught me how to make them. I love the rich oxtail ragù served with this even if it's not what I was fed as a child. But again, be sparing with the ragù if you want to make it authentically Italian."

Note well that the potatoes must be worked while they are still quite hot. And be prepared to cook, sauce, and serve the gnocchi as soon as they are made. Once made, they will not keep.

SERVES 6

2½ pounds large Yukon gold potatoes
8 ounces unbleached all-purpose flour (1¾ to
    2 cups), plus more for the board
Medium-coarse sea salt and freshly cracked
    black pepper
Grated parmigiano-reggiano or pecorino
    cheese, for garnish (optional)

Set the oven on 425°F.

Prick the potatoes all over with a fork and bake until tender, about 50 minutes.

While the potatoes are still quite hot, remove the skins and push the inside flesh through a ricer or a food mill into a large bowl or mound the flesh up on a clean, lightly floured board. Add 1¾ cups flour and mix it into the potatoes, then knead gently, just until the dough comes together. If necessary, add more flour, a tablespoon at a time, as you knead. The dough should be moist, but it should hold together if you roll a piece between your palms. Shape into a mound and cover with a clean kitchen towel. Set aside to rest for 10 minutes.

Bring about 4 quarts of water to a rolling boil in a large pot and add a large spoonful of salt.

Break off a fistful of dough, leaving the rest under the towel. Dust the board lightly with flour once more. Using the palms of your hands, roll the dough into a rope, about 1 inch in diameter, and cut it into pieces about ⅓ inch long.

Holding your hand flat with fingers together, briskly roll each gnocco back and forth on the board to form little dowel-shape pieces, then roll through a little flour to coat lightly. Transfer to a lightly floured baking sheet. Repeat with the remaining dough, until all the gnocchi are rolled. Keep them well floured and in a single layer or they will stick together.

Before adding the gnocchi to the boiling water, gently shake them in a wide sieve to remove the excess flour. Drop them into the boiling water, give them a gentle stir, and cook briskly for 3 to 5 minutes. The gnocchi are done when they rise to the surface. Remove with a slotted spoon and transfer to a warm serving bowl. Toss the gnocchi gently with the ragù (see page 287) and grated cheese, if using, then serve immediately

Pappardelle al Cinghiale o al Finto Cinghiale

Ragù of Wild Boar or of Pork with Boarish Pretentions

Wild boar ragù is a fall and winter classic in Tuscany, where the animals are stalked by passionate teams of huntsmen and their dogs through the oak and chestnut forests throughout the cold months of the year. We don't usually see the hunters, but we hear them all day—yapping dogs, Italian curses hurled into the chill air, and wild eruptions of shotgun fire—from dawn to just before sundown.

Wild boar has a darker flavor than domestic pork, and when the animal is truly feral, the meat is often musky and tough. Marinating in red wine is a traditional way to tenderize the meat and pull the funkiness out. The boar available in the United States is farm-raised and less wild-tasting, but we still like to marinate the meat to build the distinctive flavors of the ragù.

If you can find neither wild nor domestic boar, you may be just as happy making this with ordinary pork. Two pounds should be plenty to make 6 servings, but if the meat comes with bones attached (and they are a great flavor builder), count on 3 pounds. And if the butcher will include a piece of the skin or rind of the pork, called *cotiche* or *cotechino* in Italian, so much the better—it will add its own gelatinous richness to the stew (discard the rind before serving).

You'll note that this is different from the usual ragù in which vegetables are cooked, then meat added, to create softer, more delicate flavors. Here we sear the meat, then brown the vegetables in the residual fat to build up robust layers. This is not a quick dish to throw together just before dinner. Think of it as a three- or even four-day process, with a little bit of cooking each day and a lot of waiting in between. The ragù will be all the better for taking your time.

Traditionally this is served over freshly made pappardelle or tagliatelle, but you could also use sturdy rigatoni or penne rigate. You might also combine the ragù with partially cooked pasta, top it with grated cheese and bread crumbs, and bake it in a 350°F oven for 20 to 30 minutes (see Pasta al Forno con Ragù e Ricotta, page 88).

Much of the pork available in North America comes from animals raised in infamous CAFOs (Concentrated Animal Feeding Operations), with all that means in terms of animal and human health; be sure the pork you consume comes from animals raised only in a healthy, unconfined environment, preferably animals that are pasture-fed and unmedicated.

SERVES 6

FOR THE MARINADE

8 juniper berries

1 teaspoon whole coriander seeds

1 tablespoon whole black peppercorns

2 tablespoons extra-virgin olive oil

1 medium carrot, sliced thick

1 celery stalk (preferably dark green from the outside), cut into chunks

3 garlic cloves, crushed with the flat blade of a knife and chopped

1 medium yellow onion, cut into chunks

1 medium shallot, cut into chunks

2 fresh rosemary sprigs

2 bay leaves

2½ cups robust dry red wine

FOR THE RAGÚ

2 pounds wild boar shoulder, cut into large chunks; or about 3 pounds wild boar with the bone

4 tablespoons extra-virgin olive oil

1 tablespoon tomato paste, preferably double concentrate (doppio concentrato), imported from Italy

1 carrot, chopped

1 celery stalk, sliced thin

1 fat garlic clove, crushed with the flat blade of a knife and chopped

1 medium onion, chopped

Sea salt

Leaves from 1 rosemary sprig, chopped (1 teaspoon)

One 14-ounce can whole tomatoes, preferably San Marzano, with their juice

First, prepare the marinade: Combine the juniper berries, coriander, and peppercorns in a mortar and pound gently to crack the seeds and release their flavors. Add to a saucepan with the oil and set over medium heat. As the aromatics warm up, add the carrot, celery, garlic, onion, shallot, rosemary, and bay leaves, stirring all the while. When the vegetables start to sizzle slightly, add the wine and bring to a simmer. Let simmer very gently for about 5 minutes, then remove the pan from the heat and set aside to cool to room temperature or a little warmer.

Trim the pork pieces, if necessary, but don't cut off any bones. Slice any rind or skin off the meat, but keep it to add separately to the marinade. Put all the wild boar pieces, including the rinds, in a bowl, and when the marinade is cool, pour it over the meat. Cover the bowl and set aside in a cool place to marinate for at least 24 hours or up to 48 hours, turning the meat periodically in the marinade.

When you're ready to start cooking the ragù, remove the meat from the marinade and dry it well on paper towels. Add 2 tablespoons of the oil to a heavy saucepan and set over medium-high heat. Brown all the pieces of meat, including any rind, in the pan, turning frequently to brown well on all sides. Don't try to do all this at once—if the pan is too crowded, the meat will steam instead of browning. As the pieces brown, remove them from the pan and set aside.

While the meat is browning, strain the marinade and discard the vegetables and aromatics. Set the marinade in a small saucepan over medium-low heat to warm. As it warms, stir in the tomato paste.

Chop together the carrot, celery, garlic, and onion.

When all the meat is nicely browned, you may find you have a lot of burned fat in the pan. In that case, tip the burned fat out and add a tablespoon or two of fresh oil. Lower the heat to medium-low. Add the chopped vegetables and about 1 teaspoon salt and cook, stirring to scrape up any browned bits, until the vegetables start to soften. Then return the meat to the pan and stir all together.

Measure the reserved marinade and add water if necessary to bring it to 2 cups. Pour the liquid into the pan with the meat and vegetables. Bring to a simmer, cover, and cook at a very low simmer for about 2 hours. Remove from the heat and set aside to cool and let the fat rise to the top. (Pork shoulder may release a lot of fat; a little fat is good for you, but too much can spoil the dish.) Remove as much of the fat as you can and discard it. Also discard the pork rind or skin if you have used it, along with any bones—they should pull away from the meat easily.

Return the stew to medium-low heat and add the tomatoes, breaking them up in your hands or using the side of a spoon. Cover once more and cook again for another hour. If you have time, let the stew cool, then gently break apart the meat chunks, shredding them into the rich thick sauce to make a real old-fashioned country-style ragù. It is now ready to serve, but it may be kept, refrigerated, for several days before using.

Ragù al Coniglio con Vino Rosso, Olive, e Capperi

Braised Rabbit Ragù with Red Wine, Olives, and Capers

We can't say it often enough: Rabbit belongs on American tables. It is lean and tasty, high in protein, low in fat and calories, and often raised in a more healthful environment than ordinary chicken, beef, or pork. If you're at all hesitant, try it in this delicious ragù with tomatoes and red wine. We recommend a hearty Italian or Provençale red—nero d'Avola from Sicily, Tuscan Chianti, or a robust Côtes du Rhône from southern France.

Rabbit ragù is an excellent choice to serve with pappardelle or any other type of wide, flat noodles—southern Italian lasagnette would be another good choice. But it also works well with short, chunky pasta shapes, such as garganelle, cavatappi, or rigatoni.

SERVES 4 TO 6

One 3-pound fresh rabbit, cut into 8 pieces
Sea salt and freshly ground black pepper
1 large carrot, diced
1 garlic clove, crushed with the flat blade of a
   knife and chopped
1 small yellow onion, chopped
1 celery stalk, chopped
1 tablespoon chopped flat-leaf parsley, plus
   more for garnish
2 tablespoons tomato concentrate or paste
1 cup robust dry red wine (see headnote)
About ½ cup extra-virgin olive oil
One 28-ounce can whole tomatoes, preferably
   San Marzano, with their juice
1 rosemary sprig
1 small dried red chili pepper
½ cup coarsely chopped pitted black olives,
   preferably Gaeta
¼ cup salt-cured capers, carefully rinsed and
   dried
About 1 pound (500 grams) pappardelle,
   tagliatelle, or similar

Freshly grated grana padano or parmigiano-
   reggiano, for garnish

Pat the rabbit pieces dry with paper towels and season them generously with salt and pepper.

Combine the carrot, garlic, onion, celery, and parsley, and chop together to make a battuto, a finely chopped mixture.

Whisk the tomato concentrate into the wine to mix well.

Set a heavy-bottomed pot, large enough to hold all the rabbit pieces in one layer, over medium heat. As soon as it is hot, add ¼ cup of the oil and the seasoned rabbit. Brown the rabbit pieces on all sides, being careful not to crowd the pan. As the pieces brown, remove them and set aside. When all the rabbit has been browned, strain the fat out of the pot and discard.

Lower the heat to medium-low and set the pot back with the remaining ¼ cup oil and the chopped vegetables. Cook gently, scraping up any browned bits, until the

vegetables are starting to wilt in the heat of the pan. Then add the wine mixture, raising the heat to boil the wine and burn off the alcohol. Turn the heat down to low once more and add the tomatoes with all their juice. Break up the tomatoes using the side of a long-handled spoon. Return the rabbit to the pan, along with a big pinch of salt, the rosemary, and chili pepper. Cover and cook at the lowest possible simmer for about 1 hour, or until the rabbit meat is so tender that it's falling off the bone.

Remove the rabbit pieces, reserving the cooking liquid. Pull the rabbit meat off the bones and discard the bones. Also remove and discard the rosemary sprig and chili pepper.

Puree the cooked vegetables with the cooking liquid—do this with a handheld immersion blender for a rough texture or in a food processor for a smoother mix. Combine with the rabbit meat. When ready to use the ragù, gently reheat, adding the olives and capers.

Bring 6 quarts of water to a rolling boil in a large pot. Add salt and the pasta and cook following the directions on page 33.

When the pasta is al dente, drain and turn it into a warm serving bowl. Add a ladleful of rabbit ragù and mix with the pasta, then spoon the remaining ragù over the top. Garnish with grated cheese and parsley, and pass more cheese at the table.

Gemelli con Ragù d'Agnello

Pasta Twists with a Slow-Cooked Lamb Ragù

Ragù d'agnello is a great example of a dish that uses lesser parts of the animal, cooked very slowly to tenderize the meat and bring together all the gelatinous bits to create a rich sauce. At Porsena, Sara makes this with lamb neck, a particularly savory part of the creature but one that is not always easy to find. If you can't find necks, use lamb shanks instead to get the same meaty, gelatinous, rich flavor and texture. In keeping with its origins, the ragù will be best with a robust Pugliese primitivo or negroamaro red wine. In Puglia the mushrooms would be local cardoncelli: They look like oyster mushrooms and grow prolifically across the Murge, the rolling hills of central Puglia. Use any kind of tasty dried mushrooms in their place—or do as Sara sometimes does and leave them out altogether.

Ideally this is a two-day procedure; the ragù will develop even greater flavor if it sits for a day or two after the initial cooking.

Note that, like most of the ragùs described in this book, ragù d'agnello would also work well in lasagna (see master recipe, page 46) or pasta al forno (see page 88).

SERVES 4 TO 6

About 6 tablespoons extra-virgin olive oil
2 lamb shanks (about 2 pounds)
1 large yellow onion, coarsely chopped (about 1 cup)
2 garlic cloves, coarsely chopped
1 medium carrot, coarsely chopped (about ¾ cup)
2 celery stalks, coarsely chopped (about ⅓ cup)
2 tablespoons finely chopped flat-leaf parsley
2 bay leaves
1 frosemary sprig
1 small dried red chili pepper, seeds removed
1 cup dry red wine
One 28-ounce can whole tomatoes, preferably San Marzano, with their juice
Sea salt and freshly ground black pepper
4 cloves

½ teaspoon fennel pollen, if available
One 2-inch cinnamon stick
1 ounce dried porcini (about ⅓ cup)
About 1 pound (500 grams) fusilli, strozzapreti, gemelli, or similar pasta shape
½ to ¾ cup freshly grated parmigiano-reggiano, grana padano, or aged pecorino

Dry the lamb shanks. Add 2 tablespoons of the oil to a heavy skillet and set over medium heat. Add the lamb and brown quickly on all sides, turning frequently, then remove and transfer to a 4-quart covered baking dish, preferably terra-cotta.

Combine the onion, garlic, carrot, celery, and parsley and chop to a fine mince, or process in a food processor.

Set the oven on 300°F.

Tip the burned oil out of the skillet and use paper towels to wipe it clean. Add another 3 or 4 tablespoons oil, along with the minced vegetables. Set over medium-low heat and cook, stirring occasionally, until the vegetables are softened and starting to caramelize, but do not let them get thoroughly brown. (If the vegetables start to brown before they are soft, add a tablespoon or two of water to the pan.)

When the vegetables are softened, add to the lamb in the baking dish, along with the bay leaves, rosemary, and chili pepper.

Add the wine to the skillet and deglaze, boiling down the wine slightly and scraping up any browned bits in the pan. Add the tomatoes, breaking them up with the side of a spoon. Bring to a simmer, then add to the lamb in the baking dish. Set the dish over low heat (use a flame tamer if the dish is terra-cotta or ceramic), bring the juices to a simmer, and if the mixture appears too dry, add a small amount of boiling water. As the sauce starts to simmer, add salt and black pepper, along with the cloves, fennel pollen, and cinnamon. Cover the baking dish, transfer to the hot oven, and leave to cook for 1½ hours.

While the ragù is baking, set the dried mushrooms in a bowl of very warm water and let them soften, following the directions on page 30.

After 1½ hours, remove the ragù from the oven. Turn the lamb shanks over and add the chopped mushrooms, along with the strained mushroom liquid, stirring them into the sauce surrounding the lamb. Cover the pan again, and return it to the oven for another 1½ hours.

When the sauce is done, the meat on the shanks will be very soft and falling off the bone. Remove the pan from the oven and take the shanks out. Remove the meat from the bones and shred it into fairly big pieces.

Set the sauce in a cold room or refrigerate to let the fat rise and congeal. Once solidified on top, the fat is easy to remove and discard. Also remove and discard the cloves, cinnamon stick, and bay leaves.

Return the defatted sauce to the stove top, add the shredded meat, and cook once more, just long enough to warm everything through very thoroughly.

While the sauce is warming, bring a large pot of water to a rolling boil. Add salt and the pasta and cook following the directions on page 33.

Add a big spoonful (about ½ cup) of ragù to the bottom of a warm serving bowl.

When the pasta is al dente (8 to 12 minutes), drain and immediately turn it into the serving bowl. Add a few more spoonsful of ragù and start to turn the pasta in the sauce, being careful not to break it up until it is coated with the ragù. Then add the remaining ragù to the top of the pasta and sprinkle with several spoonsful of grated parmigiano. Serve immediately, passing more grated cheese at the table.

Pappardelle alla Boscaiola (con Ragù di Porcini)

Pappardelle with a Woodsy Wild Mushroom Ragù

Not all ragùs are made with meat. This one is vegetarian, calling for meaty porcini mushrooms or cèpes (*Boletus edulis*), available in early autumn in weekly markets all over Italy and France—and all over woodlands too for those lucky enough to find them. In Tuscany we delight in postdawn hikes, tramping through steep oak and chestnut forests, searching for porcini and dodging wild boars and hedgehogs. There are other mushrooms too, but darkly tawny porcini are the prize, so much so that when our neighbors talk about funghi, we know it's specifically porcini to which they refer. When there are too many of these treasured mushrooms to consume at one go, the rest are cleaned, sliced thickly, and dried outdoors for days in the clean mountain air and sunshine, in order to have a supply of *funghi secchi*, dried mushrooms, for winter. Though she kept her hiding places secret, our neighbor Mita Antolini was a true champion of funghi foraging, and she always had dried funghi stored in an old pillow case in her dispensa, ready to reconstitute and add to wintertime ragùs and sauces.

Porcini are found in North America too, in New England, Colorado, and the Pacific Northwest. You will often find them in farmers' markets in those regions. If you don't have porcini (or can't find any in the woods nearby), chanterelles, black trumpets, indeed any edible mushrooms you find on your foraging expeditions can be used in this ragù—but be sure of what you find. Some mushrooms can be toxic and a few are fatal. A local mycological society or your county Cooperative Extension Service should be able to educate you on mushroom safety.

If no wild mushrooms at all are available, use the cultivated mushrooms available in supermarket produce sections. You should easily find shiitake, but even button mushrooms and cremini will be okay in this. Just add a few reconstituted dried porcini (see page 30) to boost the flavor of the sauce.

Wide, flat pappardelle are good with this, although in a pinch tagliatelle or similar long, flat noodles would be just fine. If you don't have crème fraîche, you could use Greek-style thickened yogurt. Just don't let the mushroom juices come to a full boil once the yogurt has been added, as it may curdle.

SERVES 4 TO 6

1 pound fresh wild or cultivated mushrooms, preferably porcini

1 medium yellow onion, finely chopped

1 celery stalk, preferably dark green (from the outside), chopped

½ cup finely minced flat-leaf parsley

2 tablespoons unsalted butter

3 tablespoons extra-virgin olive oil

1 garlic clove, lightly smashed with the flat blade of a knife

Sea salt and freshly ground black pepper

½ tablespoon minced thyme (or other herbs such as marjoram, chives, or lovage, herbs that will make a spicy counterpoint to the musky, meaty flavor of the mushrooms)

½ cup dry white wine

3 tablespoons crème fraîche

1 pound (500 grams) pappardelle or similar wide, flat, ribbon noodles

½ cup freshly grated parmigiano-reggiano or grana padano

Clean and trim the mushrooms (see Mushrooms, Dried and Fresh, page 30). If using porcini, separate the stems from the caps and cut into fine dice. Slice the caps about ¼ inch thick. If using shiitake, discard the tough woody stems and slice the caps. Chop the onion, celery, and parsley to a fine mince, by hand or in a food processor.

Start heating 6 quarts of water in a large pot over high heat.

Set a large skillet over gentle heat and add 1 tablespoon of the butter and 2 tablespoons of the oil. When the butter has melted in the oil, add the garlic and toast it gently and slowly until soft and golden. Remove the garlic and reserve.

Turn up the heat a little and add the diced mushroom stems. Cook briskly until they start to brown, then add the onion, celery, parsley, and a pinch of salt and let the vegetables simmer in the oil a minute or two, just enough to start softening. Now add the sliced mushroom caps and sauté over medium heat until the slices soften and give up some of their liquid.

Add the thyme and wine and let the whole cook down until the mushrooms are very tender, almost falling apart, and the liquid has reduced by half. Just before taking the mushrooms off the heat, stir in the crème fraîche.

Have ready a warm serving bowl.

Add a big spoonful of salt to the rapidly boiling water and toss in the pasta. Cook, following the directions on page 33.

When the pasta is al dente, drain and turn it into the warm bowl. Immediately add the mushrooms, along with the remaining 1 tablespoon oil and 1 tablespoon butter, tossing to mix well. Add a generous amount of pepper and stir in the parmigiano in handfuls, tossing after each addition. Taste and adjust the seasoning. Serve immediately.

Lasagna con Funghi e Zucca Dolce

Mushroom Lasagna with Sweet Winter Squash

If vegetarian dishes sometimes strike meat eaters as unacceptably austere, this lasagna may change their minds. The richness of the cheese-flavored béchamel (white sauce) and parmigiano-reggiano interleaved with the mushrooms and grated squash make a sumptuous dish that could be the centerpiece of a dinner party as easily as a family supper. It's a bit time-consuming to prepare, but most of the ingredients can be made well ahead of time—even a day ahead—and the lasagna itself can be baked hours before serving and kept warm or gently reheated when it's time to send it to the table.

We use a combination of wild and cultivated mushrooms, adding dried porcini to boost the flavor, but you could use only fresh wild mushrooms if they're available, in which case we suggest 2 pounds rather than the 1½ pounds called for in the recipe. Porcini (aka cèpes or boletes) are ideal for the recipe, but a mixture of different mushrooms would also be enticing—chanterelles, black trumpets, hen of the woods, and the like. If you have only button, cremini, or portobello mushrooms, almost always available in supermarket produce sections, use 1½ pounds fresh, plus the dried mushrooms as described below.

We like to make lasagna with fresh pasta—if properly made, rolled so thin you can read a newspaper through it (but don't, please, literally roll it out on newsprint), it's a great addition to the dish, lending silky texture as well as richness of flavor (see page 43). But if you don't have time, use the best-quality packaged lasagna sheets you can find, preferably from an artisanal producer. You will need at least 12 ounces (¾ pound) of dried lasagna.

SERVES 8 TO 10

1 recipe Basic Pasta Fresca Dough, using
   3 cups unbleached all-purpose flour and
   3 to 4 eggs (page 43), or ¾ pound dried
   lasagna sheets

1½ ounces dried porcini mushrooms

3 pounds fresh mushrooms, including wild, if
   available

½ cup extra-virgin olive oil

1 tablespoon unsalted butter, plus a little
   more for the baking dish and to dot the top
   of the lasagna

1 pound spring onions, including tender green
   tops, or 1 medium yellow onion, chopped
   very fine

1 garlic clove, crushed with the flat side of a
   blade and minced

½ cup finely minced flat-leaf parsley

1 tablespoon minced thyme

Sea salt and freshly ground black pepper

5 cups Béchamel (page 11)

4 cups winter squash, shredded on the large
   holes of a box grater

¼ to ⅓ cup grated parmigiano-reggiano or
   grana padano cheese

First, if using fresh pasta, make the dough following the directions on page 43. If using dried mushrooms, reconstitute them as described on page 30; save the strained soaking liquid to add later, if necessary.

Pick over the fresh mushrooms, trimming away any grit or damaged areas. Separate the caps from the stems. Slice the caps and dice the stems. (If using shiitake, or any similar mushrooms with tough stems, discard the stems.)

Add ¼ cup of the oil to a skillet and set over medium-high heat. Add the onions and garlic and cook rapidly, stirring, until the onions have just begun to crisp and brown. Stir in the diced mushroom stems and the chopped reconstituted dried mushrooms. Add ¼ cup of the parsley and the minced thyme. Cook the mushrooms for 10 to 15 minutes, or until they are cooked through; season with salt and pepper, and stir the contents of the pan into the béchamel.

In a separate skillet, combine the sliced mushroom caps with the remaining ¼ cup parsley, 1 tablespoon of the oil, and the 1 tablespoon butter and cook gently over medium-low heat until the mushrooms are just cooked through, 7 or 8 minutes. Add plenty of salt and pepper to taste. Set aside.

Roll the pasta out as thin as you can, as described in the lasagna directions on page 46.

Bring a large pot of salted water to a rolling boil and have ready a bowl of ice water. Add the pasta to the boiling water and cook as described in the directions on page 46, laying the cooked sheets of pasta out on clean kitchen towels. (If you are using dried packaged pasta, simply follow the directions on the box.)

Set the oven on 350°F.

Lightly butter the bottom and sides of an 8 x 12-inch rectangular baking dish that is at least 2 inches deep.

Spread a few tablespoons of the béchamel on the bottom of the baking dish, then add a layer of pasta sheets. Spoon about one-quarter of the béchamel in a layer over the pasta, then about one-third of the sautéed mushroom caps and one-third of the grated squash. Sprinkle a couple of tablespoons of parmigiano over this layer. Repeat these layers—pasta, béchamel, mushroom caps, grated squash, and cheese—until the pan is full and the filling is used up. For the top layer, use the last of the béchamel, spreading it a little thicker and smearing it out to the edges of the pan to seal the pasta inside. Dot butter here and there on the top.

Bake for about 30 minutes, then increase the heat to 400°F. Bake for another 10 minutes, or until the lasagna is bubbling and the top is golden brown.

Remove the lasagna from the oven and set it aside for at least 10 to 15 minutes, or up to an hour, in a warm place before serving. This allows the lasagna to settle and makes it easier to cut and serve.

Palestinian Maftoul (Couscous)

Couscous, we used to think, was a strictly Maghrebi (North African) preparation, an iconographic dish from the Berbers of Morocco and Algeria. But we were wrong. It turns out that couscous is ubiquitous all over the Islamic part of the Mediterranean, including Anatolian Turkey, Lebanon, and Palestine, and even beyond, in Sicily, Sardinia, and Greece. (Of course, couscous is now a favorite dish in southern France and Israel too, but in these cases it was either brought in by North African immigrants or adopted from the indigenous population, hence not truly a national tradition.) The couscous made in the Middle East is often a little different from the tiny, delicate grains produced by the most adept Moroccan cooks. Palestinian couscous, called *maftoul*, is the most untypical of all since it is made from durum wheat bulgur, or *burghul*, the staple processed wheat—cooked, sun-dried, and cracked—of the Levant. Because it is entirely hand-made, maftoul has a delightfully erratic construction, a mixture of small grains and larger ones, which means that in the cooking, some grains are thoroughly cooked, even overcooked, while others retain the al dente texture that Italians demand from their pasta.

The following is a simplified adaptation of Palestinian maftoul, which you can find, made by hand and sun-dried, at www.canaanfairtrade.com. You may be surprised to find cinnamon, allspice, and star anise among the spices, but these are quite typical of certain areas of the Middle East.

Please don't use canned chickpeas in this. It's so easy to cook and freeze chickpeas that we wonder why people don't do it. A cup of dried chickpeas, simmered with a few bay leaves in boiling water to cover for 30 to 50 minutes, will make 3 cups cooked. Use what you need in the maftoul recipe and freeze the rest. You'll be glad you have them next time you make a hearty winter soup.

SERVES 6 TO 8

One small fresh chicken (2½ to 3 pounds),
 preferably free-range, cut into 8 pieces
Sea salt and freshly ground black pepper
½ teaspoon ground cardamom
½ cup extra-virgin olive oil
1 medium yellow onion, unpeeled
4 allspice berries
One 2-inch cinnamon stick
2 bay leaves
2 star anise

Pinch ground turmeric
½ teaspoon whole cumin seeds
1½ cups cooked chickpeas (see headnote)
1 red sweet pepper, trimmed and sliced thin
½ medium red onion, sliced into moons
 (longitudinally)
2 cups maftoul
¼ cup coarsely chopped toasted almonds
3 picked sprigs cilantro, for garnish

Rub the chicken pieces all over with salt, pepper, and the cardamom. Heat ¼ cup of

the oil in a heavy- bottomed stockpot over medium heat. Add the chicken and brown thoroughly on all sides. Remove the chicken pieces and set aside. Remove the pot from the heat and when the oil is cool, tip it out and wipe out the pot with paper towels to remove all traces of burned oil.

Return the pot to medium-low heat and add the chicken back along with 8 to 10 cups of water, enough barely to cover the chicken. Do not peel the onion, but rub off any loose papery peel, then cut the onion in half and add to the pot along with the allspice, cinnamon stick, bay leaves, star anise, turmeric, and cumin. Cover the pot and bring to a simmer. Cook at a bare simmer for 1 hour, at which point the chicken should be done and very tender.

Remove the chicken from the broth and set aside. When it is cool enough to handle, set the pieces in an oven dish, preferably one with a lid.

Strain the bits of spices and bay leaves from the broth and discard. Once the broth has cooled down a bit, transfer it to a cool place or the refrigerator to let the fat rise and congeal. When the fat is solid on the top, skim it off with a slotted spoon and discard. (The recipe can be made ahead of time up to this point, even a day or two ahead of time, but the broth and the chicken should be refrigerated.)

When ready to proceed, set the oven on low, 200° to 250°F.

Return the defatted broth in the stockpot to medium heat and bring to a simmer. Simmer, uncovered, until the broth has reduced by half, that is, to about 4 cups.

Remove 1 cup of the broth and pour it over the chicken pieces in the oven dish. Cover the chicken with a lid or a sheet of aluminum foil and transfer to the oven to warm while you make the maftoul.

Warm up the cooked chickpeas, if necessary, adding a few tablespoons of broth or plain water. Bring to a simmer over low heat, just enough to warm them through. Keep warm while you finish the maftoul.

In a small skillet, combine the sweet pepper and onion slices with the remaining ¼ cup oil and gently sauté until the slices start to soften. Add the maftoul and cook, stirring, for about 3 minutes just to lightly toast the maftoul grains and bring out their wheaten flavor. Bring the broth back to a simmer, if necessary, and add the maftoul and vegetables. Simmer, uncovered, for 15 minutes, or until the grains of maftoul are tender.

Arrange the maftoul on a platter, then set the chicken pieces on top, spooning any residual broth over the maftoul. Finally, spoon the chickpeas over the top and garnish with the toasted almonds and cilantro.

Serve immediately.

Index